TEACHING
IN THE BLOCK
STRATEGIES FOR ENGAGING
ACTIVE LEARNERS

Edited by

Robert Lynn Canady
University of Virginia

Michael D. Rettig
James Madison University

EYE ON EDUCATION

6 Depot Way West, Suite 106
Larchmont, N.Y. 10538
(914) 833-0551 (phone)
(914) 833-0761 (fax)

Library of Congress Cataloging-in-Publication Data

```
Teaching in the block : strategies for engaging active learners /
  edited by Robert Lynn Canady, Michael D. Rettig.
      p.   cm.
  Includes bibliographical references.
  ISBN 1-883001-23-4
    1. Schedules, School--United States.  2. School year--United
States.  3. Teachers--United States.   I. Canady, Robert Lynn.
II. Rettig, Michael D., 1950-   .
LB3032.T43  1996
371.2'42'0973--dc20                                    96-12419
                                                          CIP
```

10 9

Editorial and production services provided by Richard H. Adin Freelance Editorial
Services, 9 Orchard Drive, Gardiner, NY 12525 (914-883-5884)

Published by Eye On Education:

Block Scheduling: A Catalyst for Change in High Schools
by Robert Lynn Canady and Michael D. Rettig

Teaching in the Block: Strategies for Engaging Active Learners
edited by Robert Lynn Canady and Michael D. Rettig

Educational Technology: Best Practices from America's Schools
by William C. Bozeman and Donna J. Baumbach

The Educator's Brief Guide to Computers in the Schools
by Eugene F. Provenzano

Handbook of Educational Terms and Applications
by Arthur K. Ellis and Jeffrey T. Fouts

Research on Educational Innovations
by Arthur K. Ellis and Jeffrey T. Fouts

Research on School Restructuring
by Arthur K. Ellis and Jeffrey T. Fouts

Hands-on Leadership Tools for Principals
by Ray Calabrese, Gary Short, and Sally Zepeda

The Principal's Edge
by Jack McCall

The Administrator's Guide to School-Community Relations
by George E. Pawlas

Leadership: A Relevant and Practical Role for Principals
by Gary M. Crow, L. Joseph Matthews, and Lloyd E. McCleary

**Organizational Oversight:
Planning and Scheduling for Effectiveness**
by David A. Erlandson, Peggy L. Stark, and Sharon M. Ward

Motivating Others: Creating the Conditions
by David P. Thompson

**The School Portfolio:
A Comprehensive Framework for School Improvement**
by Victoria L. Bernhardt

School-to-Work
by Arnold H. Packer and Marion W. Pines

Innovations in Parent and Family Involvement
by William Rioux and Nancy Berla

The Performance Assessment Handbook
Volume 1: Portfolios and Socratic Seminars
by Bil Johnson

The Performance Assessment Handbook
Volume 2: Performances and Exhibitions
by Bil Johnson

Bringing the NCTM Standards to Life
by Lisa B. Owen and Charles E. Lamb

Mathematics the Write Way
by Marilyn S. Neil

Transforming Education Through Total Quality
Management: A Practitioner's Guide
by Franklin P. Schargel

Quality and Education: Critical Linkages
by Betty L. McCormick

The Educator's Guide to Implementing Outcomes
by William J. Smith

Schools for All Learners: Beyond the Bell Curve
by Renfro C. Manning

DEDICATION

We dedicate this book to our first teachers, our parents: Iris and Richard Rettig of Commack, NY, and James Clinton and Mary A. Hunter Canady, Hickman and Dickson Counties, Tennessee. Thank you for teaching us to play with blocks!

ACKNOWLEDGMENTS

First, we thank our authors for their patience and dedication as they suffered through many drafts, phone calls, and faxes. Thank you for sharing your practical expertise.

We also wish to thank our many colleagues at both the University of Virginia in Charlottesville and James Madison University in Harrisonburg for their support and inspiration. We would especially like to thank Paula Price at the University of Virginia for her secretarial assistance and graduate assistant Kathleen McDougald at James Madison University for her proofreading and reference checking efforts.

In addition, we wish to thank the following educators who provided valuable feedback regarding many of the chapters: Christine N. Garrison, assistant principal of Charlottesville High School in Charlottesville, VA; Hinda R. Bornstein, assistant executive director of the Delaware County Intermediate Unit in Media, PA; Mary Lou Kuhns of Conestoga High School in Berwyn, PA; Marie Slobojan, director of instructional and staff development at the Tredyffrin/ Eastown School District in Berwyn, PA; and Barry Chlebnikow, doctoral student, University of Virginia.

We also thank our developmental editor, Celia Bohannon of Saxton's River, VT, for her expert and timely editorial advice and revisions. As before, we thank our publisher, Robert Sickles, for his support and encouragement.

Finally, we thank our wives, Marjorie and Sally, and our children—Carol, Donna, Robert, and Sarah Canady; and Danny, Anne, and Alison Rettig—mostly for their patience.

TABLE OF CONTENTS

ABOUT THE AUTHORS

Wanda H. Ball, a native of Grundy, Virginia, is in her 18th year of teaching. She has taught in Virginia, Maryland, and North Carolina in grades 5–12. During the past 7 years she has focused on team teaching literature and history using the Paideia seminar approach at Person High School in Roxboro, North Carolina. Mrs. Ball received her initial training at the National Paideia Center at the University of North Carolina, Chapel Hill. She credits the seminar approach for revitalizing her teaching career and for putting the joy back into teaching. In 1992, she was the recipient of the Stovall Excellence in Education Award for Innovative Teaching. Mrs. Ball is married and has a son in middle school. She is a 1976 Berea College graduate with a B.A. degree in English Education. She may be contacted at Person High School, 1010 Ridge Road, Roxboro, NC 27573.

A North Carolina native, **Pam Brewer** is a 14-year veteran high school teacher of English, journalism, and drama. For the past 5 years, Pam has served as assistant principal for instruction at Person High School, in Roxboro, North Carolina. She has trained district staff in implementing the effective schools process, learning styles research, Paideia Seminar Teaching, as well as leading the school's successful restructuring movement to a 4/4 block schedule. A former North Carolina Teacher of the Year, Pam has presented many workshops on the topics of school reform, high school block scheduling, successful strategies for teaching in the 90-minute block, and Socratic questioning through seminars—the single best strategy she knows for active, student-owned learning. She can be contacted at Person High School, 1010 Ridge Road, Roxboro, NC 27573.

Robert Lynn Canady is professor and former chair of the Department of Educational Leadership and Policy Studies at the University of Virginia. His major publications have been related to restructuring schools through block scheduling, implementing fair and effective grading practices, and designing programs for at-risk students. He has taught in grades 4 through 12 and has served as principal of elementary, middle, and junior high schools in Tennessee and Kentucky, serving also at the central office level in both Chattanooga and Oak Ridge, Tennessee.

Professor Canady has worked extensively with school districts in 32 states and Germany. He also has served as a Fellow in the National Center for Effective Schools. He has received the Phi Delta Kappan Distinguished Service Award, been named the Outstanding Professor in the Curry School of Education of the University of Virginia, and has received two university-wide awards for distinguished teaching and service. He may be contacted at the Curry School of Education, University of Virginia, Charlottesville, VA 22903.

Jean Friend Condrey, a doctoral student in the field of educational technology at the University of Virginia, has nearly 20 years of teaching and supervisory experience in mathematics and science education, including teaching experience in the alternate-day block schedule. She strongly supports the use of technological tools in instruction for active student participation in the learning process. Jean is a member of Kappa Delta Pi International Honor Society in Education, the American Association of Physics Teachers (AAPT), the National Science Teachers Association (NSTA), and the Association for Educational Communications and Technology (AECT). Currently, she is serving on the instructional Media Committee and acts as a Physics Teaching Resource Agent (PTRA+) for AAPT. She may be contacted at 10305 Cardigan Circle, Glen Allen, VA 23060.

Laurie Nelson-Gill's public school experience was as a reading specialist. As a university professor she focused on training preservice and in-service teachers to work with academically at risk students. At present she is an educational consultant, working closely with teachers on thematic literacy instruction. She may be contacted at 405 Marlboro Rd., Kennett Square, PA 19348.

Tom Gill is an associate professor in the Department of Childhood Studies and Reading at West Chester University, West Chester, Pennsylvania. After teaching middle and high school, he received advanced degrees in Reading Education at the University of Virginia. For 9 years he directed UVA's TEMPO Reading program, a field-based and televised outreach program for teachers throughout the state. His present interests include close work with preservice teachers in urban settings and his continuing efforts with in-service teachers in literacy across the language arts and content area curricula. He may be contacted at 405 Marlboro Rd., Kennett Square, PA 19348.

Pamela Ridge Moran has served as a biology teacher, middle school teacher, middle school associate principal, and as a coordinator of K-12 science, gifted, and division staff development programs.

Currently, she is an elementary school principal in Albemarle County, Virginia, and is completing a doctoral program in Educational Leadership and Policy Studies at the University of Virginia. For more than 15 years, Pam has developed and implemented parallel block schedules with emphasis on facilitating and training teachers to use various teaching models, including critical and creative thinking strategies, cooperative learning structures, seminar approaches, 4–MAT learning styles, and classroom workshop settings. As a middle school science teacher, she found the use of learning centers and stations critical to the creation of a differentiated instructional program where all students were engaged actively in learning for extended instructional time blocks. She may be contacted at Stony Point Elementary School, Route 2, Box 604, Keswick, VA 22947.

Elizabeth D. Morie, associate professor in the School of Education at James Madison University in Harrisonburg, Virginia, has served as superintendent of schools in Lexington, Virginia, and as a teacher, assistant principal, and principal in elementary, middle, and secondary schools in Virginia. Currently she conducts undergraduate practicum seminars for secondary education students and teaches graduate courses in educational administration. She uses simulations in her own teaching and conducts workshops for middle and secondary teachers on using this instructional technique in the block schedule. She may be contacted at the School of Education, James Madison University, Harrisonburg, VA 22807.

Deborah D. Pettit has worked with students at all grade levels from elementary to college. A former teacher, central office administrator, and elementary principal, Dr. Pettit currently is the principal of Louisa County Middle School, Virginia, and serves as an adjunct professor for University of Virginia, teaching the course "Models of Instruction". She may be contacted at Louisa County Middle School, P.O. Box 448, Mineral, VA 23117–0361.

Michael D. Rettig, assistant professor at James Madison University in Virginia, served as a classroom teacher and school administrator in New York and Virginia for 16 years. He currently is an assistant professor in the School of Education at James Madison University in Harrisonburg, VA. During the past 5 years he has written extensively and presented at over 30 national and state conferences on the topic of school scheduling. In addition, he has served as a consultant on school scheduling issues in 24 states with over 200 school districts nationally. He also has conducted workshops on the topics of teaching in the block, cooperative learning, models of teaching, and school improvement. He may be contacted at the School of Education, James Madison University, Harrisonburg, VA 22807.

John D. Strebe is a math teacher at Mt. Hebron High School in Howard County, Maryland. John has demonstrated successful teaching with both high academic classes, such as calculus, and with lower, ninth grade Algebra I classes. He contributes much of his teaching success to being able to use cooperative learning structures appropriately in his classes. In addition to his public school teaching experience, for the past decade he has served as an adjunct instructor for cooperative learning classes, University of Virginia. John also is highly sought after to conduct teacher workshops throughout the southeastern United States relative to his effective use of classroom cooperative learning structures. He may be contacted at 5412 Huckleberry Lane, Sykesville, MD 21784.

Brenda M. Tanner currently is Assistant Superintendent for Instruction for the Louisa Public County Schools in Virginia. She has experience as a teacher, staff developer, and director of instruction. Brenda is coauthor with Robert L. Canady and Michael D. Rettig of "Scheduling Time to Maximize Staff Development Opportunities," which appeared in the Fall, 1995, issue of *The Journal of Staff Development*. Brenda is scheduled to receive her doctoral degree from the University of Virginia in May, 1996. She may be contacted at the Louisa County Public Schools, PO Box 7, Mineral, VA 23117.

David V. Vawter was a public high school social studies teacher for nine years in the Charlotte-Mecklenburg Public Schools in North Carolina. Currently, in addition to his doctoral studies at the University of Virginia, David conducts workshops throughout the southeast on such topics as block scheduling, cooperative learning, motivating students, and instructional strategies. He was named Most Innovative and Most Inspirational Teacher by the faculty of West Mecklenburg High School in 1993. He may be contacted at 441-D South Linden Avenue, Waynesboro, VA 22890.

Readers may be interested in a video entitled HIGH SCHOOL ALTERNATIVE SCHEDULING, presented by Robert Lynn Canady, available from The Video Journal of Education, 549 West 3560 South, Salt Lake City, Utah 84115–4225. Phone (800) 572–1153.

PREFACE

As we stated in the preface of our 1995 book on high school scheduling, within the school schedule resides *power:* the power to address problems, the power to facilitate the successful implementation of programs, and the power to make possible the institutionalization of effective instructional practices. With the publication of this book we now add the power to help teachers become more creative and exciting and students to become more engaged in their learning.

We remain convinced that during the past 90 years too little thought and action have been given to the educational and emotional impact of a school schedule on the lives of students and teachers. After working in 36 states with thousands of middle and high school students, teachers, administrators, and parents, we are excited about what is happening in schools throughout the U.S. Block scheduling has become a catalyst for instructional change in secondary schools across the country; it has encouraged teachers and administrators to reflect upon curriculum and methods of instruction and to begin to implement improvements. A change in the school schedule has become a major part of many reform efforts, including School-to-Work programs, dropout reduction efforts, and accelerated opportunities for selected students.

We understand, however, that the implementation of a new school schedule is not an end in itself. Just mechanically changing a school's schedule will not meet the expectations the public has for our schools. What teachers do with students in their classrooms is still the most critical component of any change effort. We find that most teachers will learn to manage blocks of time and change teaching strategies so that students become more active learners, even with very little training. We remain convinced, however, that to fully achieve the potential of block schedules schools must provide staff development opportunities which prepare teachers to utilize strategies which engage our active learners.

The block scheduling movement has opened a rare window of opportunity; teachers are searching for ways to first "survive" and then "thrive" in the block. For those professionals dedicated to improving their teaching, we have prepared this book. In most cases, we began by identifying authors who as teachers had demonstrated success in the block and who had developed expertise with a particular teaching strategy. We worked closely with these fine practitioners as they committed their practices to paper. And while we know it is difficult to learn active teaching strategies from a book, we hope this book can serve as a practical beginning point, arousing the interest of readers sufficiently to encourage them to learn more about each strategy from other readings and hands-on workshops. Emphasis on long-term, sustained staff development is needed in most school districts across the U.S. May this book be a catalyst for those changes and may our students be the benefactors as they become more engaged, active learners.

Lynn and Mike
Charlottesville and Harrisonburg, VA
March, 1996

BLOCK SCHEDULING: WHAT IS IT? WHY DO IT? HOW DO WE HARNESS ITS POTENTIAL TO IMPROVE TEACHING AND LEARNING?[1]

During the past 10 years, secondary schools across the country have changed from the traditional six-, seven-, or eight-period school schedule to "block schedules," in which students meet only three or four classes of longer duration daily. The pace of growth of schools implementing block scheduling has been dramatic. Based on Cawelti's (1994) national survey and Rettig's (1995) work in Virginia, we estimate that over 50% of high schools in the United States currently either are operating or are studying some form of block scheduling. The purpose of this book is to help teachers design lessons that will maximize the potential of the block schedule and provide students with engaging learning

---

[1] This chapter was written byRobert Lynn Canady, Professor, Department of Educational Leadership and Policy Studies, Curry School of Education, University of Virginia, and Michael D. Rettig, Assistant Professor, School of Education, James Madison University.

activities. In this chapter, we begin by discussing the rationale that motivates the block scheduling movement. Second, we introduce the reader to the basic models of block scheduling and their various curricular and instructional implications. Third, we outline a practical format for planning lessons for longer classes. Finally, we introduce our authors and highlight the importance of their contributions to this book.[2]

WHY ARE SCHOOLS CHANGING TO BLOCK SCHEDULING?

The following criticisms of traditional school schedules have motivated middle and high schools across the United States to implement changes in the organization and use of time.

♦ **Instruction is fragmented for students attending schools having single period schedules.**

The problem of fragmented instruction caused by short periods is not new.

> In case the school is much larger . . . , and the classes necessarily so numerous as to make the time allowed to each study very short, then the principle of alternation may be introduced; that is, some studies may be recited Mondays, Wednesdays, and Fridays,—and some other studies, with other classes, take their places on the alternate days. It is decidedly better for the teacher to meet a class, in arithmetic for instance, especially of older pupils, but twice or three times a week, having time enough at each meeting to make thorough work, than to meet them daily, but for a time so short as to accomplish but little. The same remark may be applied to reading, and indeed almost any other branch. The idea is a mischievous one, that every class in reading, or in any other branch, must be called out four times a day, or even twice a day—except in the case of very young children. It may be compared to nibbling at a cracker as many times in a day, without once taking a hearty meal—a process which

---

[2] Parts of this chapter are adapted from Canady & Rettig (1995a) and Rettig & Cannizzaro (1996).

would emaciate any child in the course of three months. These scanty nibblings at the table of knowledge, so often and so tenaciously practised [*sic*], may perhaps account for the mental emaciation so often discoverable in many of our schools (Page, 1855, pp. 228–229).[3]

Single-period schedules not only fragment the school day for both students and teachers, but they also affect the manner in which curriculum is organized and delivered. Students traveling through a six-, seven-, or eight-period day often are exposed to six, seven, or eight pieces of unconnected curriculum each day. They rarely, if ever, have time to study anything in depth. To each teacher in his or her discipline, the work may make sense; but to students who receive a fragmented, piecemeal education, the relevance of their efforts is sometimes lost (Canady and Rettig, 1995a; National Association of Secondary School Principals, 1996).

♦   **An impersonal, factory-like environment is created by the assembly-line, single-period schedule.**

In traditional schedules, students generally attend six, seven, or eight different classes daily and teachers teach five or six different classes. Each day, teachers are asked to address the intellectual and emotional needs of 100–180 adolescents. The task is equally challenging for students, who are expected to adjust to the differing academic standards, behavior codes, teaching styles, homework requirements, and tests of six, seven, or eight different teachers daily. It has been suggested for several years that if schools are ever to improve, teachers must work with fewer students and students must work with fewer teachers (Sizer, 1992, 1984; National Association of Secondary School Principals, 1996).

♦   **Discipline problems are exacerbated by the single-period schedule.**

Releasing thousands of adolescents into narrow hallways six, seven, or eight times each school day for 4 or 5 minutes to go to the bathroom, to their lockers, or to "get a date," creates noise, stress and, in many schools, bedlam. We often wonder how and why such a practice has continued for so long in America's schools, especially when we know a preponderance of a school's disciplinary referrals

---

[3] We wish to thank Dr. David Massey, Associate Superintendent for Instruction and Assessment, Hall County Public Schools, Gainesville, Georgia, for providing us with this quote, from David Page, the late principal of the State Normal School in Albany, New York, published in 1855.

emanate from these transitions. School discipline also is affected negatively by teachers' large student loads and short periods. Teachers who are responsible for 100–180 students find it difficult to develop the close relationships necessary to avoid "in your face" challenges.

◆ **Instructional possibilities are limited in short periods.**

One of the major revelations of the 1990s has been that when "boiled down," the actual amount of instructional time available in a traditionally scheduled school day is alarmingly brief (National Education Commission on Time and Learning, 1994). Because of the time lost to class openings, closings, interruptions, and various noninstructional activities, the actual class time available for instruction is far less than the allotted period. Consequently, teachers faced with limited time often feel pressed, at the very least, to **EXPOSE** children to curriculum. This exposure is most often accomplished by lecturing, which may be one of the least effective teaching methods used in schools today, especially for students who are not highly motivated.

In place of the lecture we can recommend many teaching strategies. Yet, how many steps of the writing process can be addressed in a single-period English class? How much library research is possible in a social science class in such a limited amount of time? How much physical activity do students get in a 50-minute physical education class after dressing, showering, and redressing? How can science teachers complete comprehensive lab work in 45–55 minutes?

Short instructional periods not only make laboratory-type activities difficult to provide, but they also make it difficult to implement creative models of teaching such as Socratic seminars, simulations, learning centers, and cooperative learning structures. Other teaching models that promote active student learning, such as concept development, concept attainment, synectics, and inquiry, must have time for reflection and discussion to be effective.

◆ **Traditional scheduling models do not provide varying learning time for students.**

Perhaps one of the most critical issues facing schools regarding the allocation of time is the indisputable fact that some students need more time to learn than others. In secondary schools, reliance on the Carnegie Unit as a seat-time measure of credit has made all students "Prisoners of Time":

> High-ability students are forced to spend more time than they need on a curriculum developed for students of moderate ability. . . . Struggling students are forced to move with the class and receive less time than they need to master the material. . . . (Average) students get caught in the time trap as well. Conscientious teachers discover that the effort to motivate the most capable and help those in difficulty robs them of time for the rest of the class. (National Education Commission on Time and Learning, 1994, p. 15.)

Since the advent of the Carnegie Unit, credit for high school courses has been allocated based primarily upon seat time. All teachers, however, know that some students take longer to learn a specified amount of content than do others, and that some students need less time to learn the same content.

In traditionally scheduled middle and high schools, the only means of accommodating students who need extended learning time has been to assign them a grade of "F" and then require them to repeat the course either in summer school or during the next academic year. This practice is a punitive system for students who simply need more time to master the required material (Juarez, 1996); it also is an ineffective system for students whose problem is motivation!

Similarly, the possibilities for acceleration in American schools are very limited. In most districts, there is, however, one celebrated occasion for possible advancement. At the end of grade 7 in middle and junior high schools throughout the nation, a decision must be made as to whether a student should enroll in algebra during grade 8. This decision determines if it will be possible for a student to be accelerated in mathematics and possibly take calculus in the senior year. If a student takes algebra in 8th grade, the calculus option remains open; if not, calculus is ruled out for many high school students. We argue that this is an unreasonably inflexible system, which forces instructors to decide prematurely as to a student's potential in mathematics. If the school schedule were not as rigid, perhaps the decision to accelerate could be made at different and more appropriate times for students.

To address these and other problems prevalent in middle and high schools across the country, educators have designed new schedules which attempt to accomplish some or all of the following goals:

- Reduce the number of classes students must attend and prepare for each day and/or each term.
- Allow students variable amounts of time for learning, without lowering standards, and without punishing those who need more or less time to learn (see Chapter 5; Canady & Rettig, 1995a and 1995b).
- Increase opportunities for some students to be accelerated.
- Reduce the number of students teachers must prepare for and interact with each day and/or each term.
- Reduce the number of courses for which teachers must prepare each day and/or term.
- Reduce the fragmentation inherent in single-period schedules, a criticism that is especially pertinent to classes requiring extensive practice and/or laboratory work.
- Provide teachers with blocks of teaching time that allow and encourage the use of active teaching strategies and greater student involvement.
- Reduce the number of class changes.

The following section serves as introduction to the basic models of block scheduling. For a more detailed discussion of each model, see Canady and Rettig (1995a).

MODELS OF BLOCK SCHEDULING

The following four basic models of block schedules have been implemented by schools around the country: the alternate-day schedule; the 4/4 semester plan or accelerated schedule; trimester plans; and various reorganizations of the 180–day school year, such as the 75–75–30 plan. After introducing each plan, benefits and concerns are addressed.

ALTERNATE DAY SCHEDULES

Rather than meeting classes daily, in alternate-day schedules students and teachers meet their classes every other day for extended time "blocks." Alternate-day schedules also are referred to as "A/B," "Odd/Even," "Day 1/Day 2," and "Week 1/Week 2" schedules.

Figure 1.1 illustrates an alternate-day, seven-course schedule. Students and teachers meet three of their classes in double periods one day and another three the next day, with one single period (period 5) meeting daily all year.

FIG. 1.1. ALTERNATE DAY BLOCK SCHEDULE BUILT FOR 7 COURSES (2 LUNCH PERIODS)[4]

	Blocks and Times	M Day 1 A	T Day 2 B	M Day 1 A	T Day 2 B
		½ of School Follows This Schedule		½ of School Follows This Schedule	
P	Block I & HR 8:00–9:49 am	1	2	1	2
		1	2	1	2
E	Block II 9:55–11:37 pm	3	4	3	4
		3	4	3	4
R	Lunch and Period 5 11:43–1:12 pm	Lunch 11:43–12:07 pm		Period 5 11:43–12:42 pm	
I					
O		Period 5 12:13–1:12 pm		Lunch 12:48–1:12 pm	
D	Block III 1:18–3:00 pm	7	6	7	6
		7	6	7	6

[4] Reproduced by permission from Canady, R.L., and Rettig, M.D. (1995). *Block Scheduling: A Catalyst for Change in High Schools*. Princeton, NJ: Eye On Education, p. 55.

In a 7-hour school day (420 minutes), a six-course alternate-day schedule usually includes blocks of approximately 120 minutes; eight-course models have blocks of approximately 90 minutes; and seven-course schools typically have three alternating blocks of 100–105 minutes, with one class that meets every day for 45–55 minutes.

The following advantages are offered for alternate-day schedules:

♦ **Teachers benefit from increased usable instructional time.** Because there are fewer transitions and less time is lost with class openings and closings, usable or actual instructional time is increased.

♦ **Teachers are able to plan lessons for extended periods of time.** Classes of 90 minutes or longer make it possible to engage students in a lengthy simulation or seminar, to do significant research in the library, or to view an entire movie-length video on a historical topic. With longer class periods, teachers have opportunities to provide a variety of instructional activities other than lecture. Teachers are motivated to employ a variety of instructional strategies, such as models of teaching, centers, cooperative learning structures, and Socratic seminars.

♦ **The number of class changes is reduced.** Fewer transitions result in a less stressful and cleaner school environment, an automatic reduction in the number of tardies, and fewer disciplinary referrals.

♦ **Because one or more days lapse between classes, when discipline problems occur, both teacher and student have time to "cool down" before facing each other in the next class.**

♦ **Compared to single-period, daily schedule models, students in an alternate-day schedule have fewer classes, quizzes, tests, and homework assignments on any one day.** Students are given some leeway in planning their work; for example, if a ball game is scheduled on one night, extra work can be completed on the nongame evening.

At least five instructional concerns arise with the alternate day schedule. They are related to maintaining students' attention over the block, balancing teachers' planning time and students' workload, adjusting the schedule for unplanned school closings, and dealing with the concern, expressed by many teachers, that an inordinate amount of review may be necessary when classes meet Thursday and not again until Monday.

+ **Maintaining students' attention.** Before implementing a block schedule, teachers often express concern regarding students' abilities to maintain attention for 90 or 100 minutes. We have found, however, that attention depends more upon the variety of active learning strategies utilized than on the length of the class period. This book has been written to assist teachers in designing such activities.

+ **Providing balanced teacher planning time.** Care must be taken in assigning teacher planning periods in alternate-day schedules. In schools where teachers teach five out of six blocks, in the alternate-day schedule, teachers must have a double-length planning period every other day, with no break the next day except lunch. Some schools operating such schedules have scheduled a longer duty-free lunch for teachers on the day they have no planning period.

    In the seven-period, alternate-day schedule, if teachers teach five of the seven periods, approximately 20% of the teachers must be willing to have one single period of planning time on one of the alternate days, with a three-period planning block on the other day. We recommend that teachers be permitted to volunteer for the alternate day of one planning period (usually period 5) and the other day with a triple planning period. We have found that there are many teachers, especially those working in interdisciplinary studies, who will welcome the opportunity to have a triple-period planning block every other day!

    Obviously, in those schools with an eight-period, alternate-day schedule, in which teachers instruct six of the eight periods, it is relatively easy to assign all teachers equally two planning periods each of the two days. Again, some teachers may prefer to have one day with four classes and another with two, so they and their team members can have a four-period planning block every other day. For additional ideas on providing extended planning time for teachers, see Canady & Rettig (1995a, Chapter 7) or Tanner, et al. (1995).

+ **Providing daily balanced schedules for students.** Many of the benefits of block schedules for students will be lost if students are not scheduled classes with a balanced work load on both Days 1 and 2. This need becomes even more critical for students in the 4/4 schedule. Some classes in both middle and high schools simply require more homework, notebooks and tests than other classes! For example, it is unwise to schedule a student with three advanced placement classes on Day 1 and three electives on Day 2. One way to provide a balanced schedule for students would be to ask a school committee of teachers (possibly also include parents, students and administrators) to classify classes according to high and low homework requirements; then code the computer to schedule each student some of both types of classes on each of the days in the alternate-day schedule and during each term in the 4/4 schedule.

♦ **Providing a predictable calendar for planning school activities.** When school is canceled for a day or more because of inclement weather, should the school stick to the calendar schedule or slide the schedule based on the number of days missed? Most schools have opted to stick to the calendar schedule; sliding causes problems with scheduled field trips and planned school activities, such as guest speakers. If by following the calendar schedule an imbalance of Day 1 and Day 2 classes occurs, we recommend that teachers be asked not to schedule any advanced activities specific to a particular class during the last 10 days of a semester; during that time, the number of classes can be equalized.

♦ **Requiring additional review time.** In the alternate-day schedule, teachers often express concern that they will need to spend more time reviewing material taught, especially in a class that meets Thursday and not again until Monday. While some teachers in alternate-day schools report an increased need for review, they never report doubling of review time. Many teachers also design lessons that naturally review previous concepts and/or skills as part of the introduction of the new lesson.

While the alternate-day block schedule offers many advantages over daily, single-period schedules, a number of issues remain unaddressed. For example:

♦   Students continue to be responsible for six to eight subjects all year long.

♦   Students failing a course typically must remain in the course for an entire year; they usually have no opportunity to retake the failed course until summer or the following school year.

♦   Students have limited opportunities for acceleration.

♦   The number of course choices for students remains unchanged.

♦   Teachers still must work with 100–180 students during the semester/term/year.

♦   Teachers may be responsible for as many as six different preparations and must keep records for 100–180 students all year in schools.

THE 4/4 SEMESTER PLAN

The 4/4 semester plan (Fig. 1.2), or "accelerated" schedule, as it is called in Texas and a few other states because a few students may be allowed to graduate in 3 years, begins to deal with some of the issues not addressed in the alternate-day schedule. In the 4/4 schedule, students enroll in four courses which meet for approximately 90 minutes every day for 90 days. Teachers teach three courses each semester. Most "year-long" courses are completed in one "semester." Students enroll in four courses (teachers teach three) for each semester.

The 4/4 semester plan offers the following additional advantages not inherent in the alternate-day block schedule:

♦   **Teachers work with fewer students during any one semester.** In the 4/4 plan, more personalized instruction can be facilitated because teachers work with only 60–90 students during any one semester.

♦   **Teachers prepare for fewer courses each semester.** Teachers instruct three classes daily. Because semester plans require a reorganization of the curriculum and a redesign of traditional lesson format, it is recommended that only two different preps be assigned for any single semester and, hopefully, no more than a total of three preps for the total school year.

FIG. 1.2. 4/4 SEMESTER BLOCK SCHEDULE (4 BLOCKS DAILY; 8 COURSES ANNUALLY; 2 LUNCH/STUDY PERIODS; 420 MINUTES)[5]	
8:00–9:30 am	Block I
9:34–11:00 am	Block II
11:04–11:30 am	Lunch A Study/Activity B
11:34–12:00 pm	Study/Activity A Lunch B
12:04–1:30 pm	Block III
1:34–3:00 pm	Block IV

- **Teachers generally have longer and more useful planning time.** A 90-minute daily planning period usually is provided.
- **Teachers and students have two "fresh starts" each year.**
- **Teachers must keep records and grades for only 60–90 students per semester.**
- **Students concentrate on only four courses per semester.**
- **Students may retake failed courses in the second semester.**
- **Students have greater opportunities for acceleration.** A student who takes algebra during the first semester of ninth grade and excels can move on to geometry second semester, thereby "catching-up" to the calculus track.
- **Eight credits can be earned without the stress of taking eight courses at the same time.**

---

[5] Reproduced by permission from Canady, R.L., and Rettig, M.D. (1995). *Block Scheduling: A Catalyst for Change in High Schools*. Princeton, NJ: Eye On Education, p. 77.

♦ **Fewer textbooks are required.** Because half the students scheduled to take English 9 do so in the Fall, those students scheduled for the course in the Spring may use the same sets of books.

A number of concerns arise, however, when contemplating implementation of the 4/4 semester plan.

♦ **Will retention of learning decrease?** Because in the 4/4 schedule it is possible for students to have longer periods of time between courses, many teachers and parents express concern that an unreasonable need for review will be created by the 4/4 plan. The concern is exacerbated for those classes considered to be sequential, such as foreign languages and mathematics. The experience of schools using the 4/4 plan, and research on this issue (often referred to as the forgetting curve), may assuage such concerns. Experienced teachers from schools in the 4/4 plan report that they can discern very little difference between the retention of students who recently completed a prerequisite and other students with greater time lapses between courses (Sessoms, 1995). By the second Fall semester, the summer lapse from school appears to equalize the students who, for example, completed Algebra I during the previous fall or spring semesters.

The major issue of retention appears to be related to "depth of learning;" in other words, how well did the students ever learn the material? If the focus remains on surface learning and low-level recall, then the recency of exposure is critical!

In addition, research in cognitive psychology may be applied to this issue. One study discovered that students retained 85% of major concepts they originally had learned after 4 months, and 80% after 11 months (Semb, Ellis, & Araujo, 1993, p. 309). This slight additional decline in retention may be worth other benefits of the 4/4 semester plan.

♦ **Will we be able to cover the same curriculum?** An important phase of the planning process for the 4/4 plan is the development of course-pacing guides, which prescribe a timetable for the completion of course objectives. Teachers' reactions to teaching in the 4/4 schedule are nearly always positive; however, some report that, "I covered less, but they learned it better," while others report "I never taught so much in my life."

Critics of block scheduling, particularly the 4/4 plan, argue that curriculum is being "dumbed down" because less time is being spent per course. Less time per class is provided when a change is made from a six- or seven-period schedule in which courses last for 180 days of 50-minute periods to a schedule where courses receive 90 days of 90-minute blocks. This issue usually does not arise when eight period schools switch to the 4/4; time per course generally increases.

Opponents of block scheduling have difficulty accepting the idea of "less is more"; less material or concepts covered well may result in more meaningful learning. Several Canadian studies which compared students' science and math achievement suggest that students learn somewhat less in semesterized courses (Bateson, 1990; Raphael, Wahlstrom, & McClean, 1986). Other research has suggested no significant differences between students' achievement in intensive block schedules and year-long courses (Carroll, 1994; Lockwood, 1995; Averett, 1994). Continuing study and scholarly debate is necessary to answer this important question.

In studying this issue, it is important to remember that students in most schools have opportunities to take four or more additional courses in high school compared to the six-period daily schedule. Suppose the math class covers one less chapter, but the students complete another semester math class; or one less novel is included in the traditional English class, but the students complete an additional semester in a speech or writing class? It may be important to require that some of the additional credits available to students in the 4/4 plan be allocated to "core" subjects to maintain an appropriate balance between time spent in core and elective courses.

In an attempt to address the retention issue, a few high schools across the country have adapted the 4/4 plan by dividing the school day into five 70-minute blocks and dividing the school year into trimesters (Stumpf, 1995). Most core academic courses span two trimesters; however, advanced placement (AP) courses and musical performing groups extend throughout the year. Each trimester course earns half a unit, for an annual total of 7.5 credits. While this plan lessens the gap to one trimester, it is difficult to ensure that students will be instructed by the same teacher for both halves of these core courses.

♦ **How will we handle year-long AP courses such as U.S. history or government?** Instructors, parents, and students are concerned about the 4/4 schedule's potential effect on AP testing success. Some schools provide review sessions in the Spring in preparation for the exam for students who have completed AP courses in the Fall. Instead of scheduling these classes for either Fall or Spring, other schools have scheduled AP courses for 27 weeks for 1.5 credits, with a 9-week 0.5-credit course to follow. Other AP classes, especially lab classes such as chemistry and biology, are scheduled for both semesters and allocated 2 credits. In schools where students enroll in more than one AP course, two courses can be paired in one block. These matched courses, for example, AP English and AP U.S. government and economics, can meet either in single periods daily or in double periods on alternate days all year long. The best solution for this problem may be for AP exams to be administered at least twice annually (January and June).

♦ **How will students participate in programs such as band, choir, and orchestra, which must meet both semesters?** Accommodating music programs in a sensible fashion continues to be one of the most important details to address when implementing the 4/4 plan. Previously, we have outlined several possibilities: (1) require students to enroll in music both semesters and allocate 2 credits; (2) require enrollment one semester, and make a second semester of participation elective; and (3) pair music classes with other courses and embed this minischedule into one or more blocks which meet either every day as single-period classes, or, preferably, every other day as blocks. (These options are addressed in great detail in Chapter 3 of Canady &

Rettig, 1995a.) We add to these suggestions the solution arrived upon at Angola High School in Angola, Indiana. All band students participate in marching band during the first 9 weeks of the school year, meeting for 90 minutes daily. At the conclusion of the football season, the remaining 27 weeks of the school year are divided into two single-period classes, which meet daily. Students are able to enroll in concert band for one period and jazz band in the other of these periods, or take another course in either slot.

A variety of other school-wide issues are important to address when considering the implementation of the 4/4 semester plan. (For a thorough discussion, see Chapter 3, Canady & Rettig, 1995a).

Despite the many advantages of the 4/4 semester plan for both teachers and students, several scheduling issues are left unaddressed. For example, students in the 4/4 semester plan still must fail before they can gain extended learning time, because time is still held constant for all students.

TRIMESTER PLANS

Several additional scheduling models that have been implemented around the country offer shorter, more intense courses of instruction. Some schools, for example, are operating trimester plans, in which students take two or three core courses every 60 days to earn 6 to 9 credits per year. One school in Broward County, Florida, for example, has modified this plan by adding three year-long classes to six trimester classes; this accommodates courses such as musical performing groups and AP subjects, which either need or prefer to extend classes all year long. The benefits and concerns regarding these plans are very similar to those discussed regarding the 4/4 semester plan.

A modification to the typical trimester schedule is illustrated in Figure 1.3. As shown, each trimester students take two, two-hour classes; in addition, two 60-minute extended learning periods are provided for students who need more time to learn the designated course material. At the beginning of each trimester, some students may be scheduled for both sessions of the two courses. These 60-minute periods also are used to provide year-long rehearsal time for performing groups. Thus in this schedule variable amounts of learning time are provided for students to complete course requirements without having to wait in a "failing class" for an entire semester or year before intervention or assistance occurs. Because of the high failure rate of students in grade 9, we believe this type of schedule has merit for a school considering a special schedule and program for grade 9 students. For example, students who fail to master content in an English 9 or Algebra I class the first trimester could be given an incomplete grade and scheduled for extended learning time during the second or even third trimesters. Other students take electives during those periods. This schedule also offers possibilities for addressing several current middle school issues.

RECONFIGURING THE 180–DAY SCHOOL YEAR

Some districts across the nation are reconfiguring the 180-day school year into a combination of long terms and short terms for the purpose of providing instructional time for remediation and enrichment for students. W. Marshall Sellman School in the Madeira School District in Cincinnati, Ohio, implemented a 180–day school schedule called the 75–75–30 plan for the 1994–95 school year (Canady & Rettig, 1993, 1995b). For the first 150 days of the year, this middle school operated a team block schedule, with 12 short periods blocked together to provide four periods of language arts, two periods of mathematics, two periods of social studies and science, three periods of physical education, exploratories and common time, and one period for lunch. During the 30-day term, students enrolled in short courses, with the same proportion of their day being spent in the core areas. These specialized courses were created and designed by teachers to provide additional learning time for students who had yet to master grade level objectives, as well as to offer academically enriching activities for all students. Course titles included "Principles of Mathematics," "Team Accelerated Instruction," "Shopping Spree," "MARS," "Water Science," "Inventioneering," "Mock Trial," "Writing Process," "Fun with Poetry," "Goldrush," and "Cincinnati." Teachers, students, and parents report that the program was a great success. According to the principal, teachers took more risks in teaching their 30-day classes; one teacher commented, "I should do more of this kind of teaching during the 'regular' school year."

Fig. 1.3. Trimester Plan with Extended Learning Time (ELT)[6]			
	60 Days	60 Days	60 Days
Block I 8:00–10:00	Course 1	Course 3	Course 5
10:00–10:05	Break		
Block II 10:05–12:05	Course 2	Course 4	Course 6
12:10–12:40 (Rotated)	Lunch		
Block II ELT 12:40–1:40	Course 2 ELT	Course 4 ELT	Course 6 ELT
Block I ELT 1:45–2:45	Course 1 ELT	Course 3 ELT	Course 5 ELT
2:45–3:30	Professional Planning and Student Activities		

A school district in Pennsylvania is in the planning stages for another variation of the 75–75–30 plan (Fig. 1.4). In the 1996–97 school year, their students are scheduled to enroll in four classes each 75–day term. During the 30–day term, students will participate in two 15–day interdisciplinary courses. Tentative plans have been made for three teachers to work together with 45 students for 14 days; the 15th day of each short course will be spent in public demonstrations of students' work.

A third reconfiguration of the 180–day school year has been implemented by two high schools in California. In the 75–30–75 plan, students attend six courses daily for the first 75 days of the school year, have a 30–day intersession, and then return to their Fall courses for a 75–day spring term.

---

[6] Adapted by permission from Canady, R.L., and Rettig, M.D. (1995). *Block Scheduling: A Catalyst for Change in High Schools*. Princeton, NJ: Eye On Education, p. 126.

FIGURE 1.4. 75–75–30 BLOCK SCHEDULE (10 COURSES) INTERDISCIPLINARY SPRING TERM[7]				

		Fall Term 75 Days	Winter Term 75 Days	Spring Term 30 Days	
				14+1 Course 9	14+1 Course 10
P **E** **R** **I** **O** **D** **S**	1	Course 1	Course 5	**Interdisciplinary Term**	
	2			♦ Special Interdisciplinary Courses	
	3	Course 2	Course 6	♦ Extended Trips	
	4			♦ Community Service	
	5	Course 3	Course 7	♦ Remediation	
	6			♦ Demonstration Projects	
	7	Course 4	Course 8		
	8			♦ Etc.	

In Figure 1.5 we show a seven-course, alternate-day format of the 75–30–75 plan. Course five meets every day, year-long, and is designed for band and other subjects that may need to bridge the intersession. The Winter term is used for remediation and enrichment activities, as well as for extended field trips, community service, and the preparation of senior graduation projects. Because the Winter term can be utilized to reinforce and practice the concepts learned in courses students are taking in the Fall term, it becomes another means of providing some students extended learning time. The intersession also offers advanced students enrichment activities.

Any of these scheduling models requires significant rethinking

---

[7] Reproduced by permission from Rettig, M.D., and Cannizzaro, J. (1996). *Block Scheduling: Social Studies Educator's Handbook.* Upper Saddle River, NJ: Prentice-Hall, p. 10.

of curriculum organization and instructional planning. In the next section we begin to address these issues.

	Fall Term 75 Days A/B Schedule		Winter Term 30 Days	Spring Term 75 Days A/B Schedule	
FIGURE 1.5. 75–30–75 PLAN TWO 75–DAY TERMS WITH A/B SCHEDULE[8]					
	Day 1	Day 2		Day 1	Day 2
Block I HR, Per. 1 & 2 110 minutes	Course 1	Course 2	Enrichment, Elective, Community Service, Remedial Work, etc.	Course 1	Course 2
Block II Per. 3 & 4 105 minutes	Course 3	Course 4		Course 3	Course 4
Period 5/L 50 minutes + 30 for lunch	Course 5 & Lunch	Course 5 & Lunch	**Course 5 Lunch**	Course 5 & Lunch	Course 5 & Lunch
Block III Per. 6 & 7 105 minutes	Course 7	Course 6	**Enrichment, Elective, Comm. Serv., etc.**	Course 7	Course 6

[8] Reproduced by permission from Rettig, M.D., and Cannizzaro, J. (1996). *Block Scheduling: Social Studies Educator's Handbook.* Upper Saddle River, NJ: Prentice-Hall, p. 11.

CURRICULUM PLANNING AND INSTRUCTIONAL DESIGN FOR THE BLOCK SCHEDULE

Of greatest concern to teachers implementing block schedules are issues of curriculum and instruction, specifically: "How do I reorganize my curriculum to fit the new schedule?" and "What do I do with students for 100 minutes?"

CURRICULUM REORGANIZATION

Obviously, restructuring a school schedule from a single-period model to an alternate-day plan requires far less curriculum reorganization than a change to any version of the 75–75–30 plan; however, it is both wise and necessary to create a curriculum-pacing guide for all courses regardless of the scheduling model used. This long-term planning tool maps out tentative completion dates for the instruction of various concepts in the course. It prevents teachers, especially those new to block scheduling, from succumbing to the "I have plenty of time" fallacy. For example, several teachers from 4/4 schools have reported that during the first semester of their program, a sense of panic arose when the Thanksgiving holiday arrived, and with it the realization that the "year" was more than half over!

It also is true that teachers will be ineffective in the block if two formerly 45-minute long lessons are simply stacked on top of each other to form one 90-minute lesson. Concepts and activities must be reorganized within the new time frame.

INSTRUCTIONAL DESIGN IN THE BLOCK SCHEDULE[9]

One means of successfully planning instruction for a block schedule is to divide the lesson into three parts: explanation, application, and synthesis.

EXPLANATION

One-quarter to one-third (25–35 minutes) of a block class is spent

---

[9] This section is adapted from Chapter 8 of Canady, R.L., and Rettig, M.D. (1995). *Block Scheduling: A Catalyst for Change in High Schools*. Princeton, NJ: Eye On Education.

with teachers doing what they have done for years. A minilecture is given; previous lessons are reviewed through questioning; students are shown how to do math problems on the overhead or chalkboard; students view a short videoclip or a science demonstration, or a selection is read to the class. Teachers focus on what is to be learned; they identify objectives and specify tasks to be completed.

APPLICATION

Following explanation, teachers, move into a phase called application, which extends for approximately one-third to one-half of the block (40–60 minutes). Active learning strategies are utilized; students apply what the teacher has explained. Examples include the following:

♦ The teacher conducts a Socratic questioning seminar after students have read a selection dealing with a civil rights encounter. The teacher might ask the following opening question: "Today are we ever justified in not following rules, regulations and laws?" After the seminar, students might be assigned position papers to prepare either individually, in pairs, or in teams.

♦ Students are allowed to experience how a historian goes about the task of locating, discovering, identifying, classifying, and writing history by becoming a historian for a period of time in their community.

♦ Students engage in mapmaking at one of the several centers established in the classroom.

♦ Students, in pairs or small teams, work with a set of data in a math class in preparation for writing their own research projects.

♦ Students browse the Internet to locate climate and weather information, summaries of recent Supreme Court decisions, international news briefs, or a host of other topics.

♦ Students engage in a simulation (peace talks between the Bosnians, Bosnian-Serbs, and Croats, for example, or sessions of Congress or the U.N.).

♦ Students travel through a series of learning centers devoted to the study of different aspects of a country's culture.

Providing "hands-on" active learning strategies during the application stage may be the most important determinant of the success or failure of teaching in the block.

SYNTHESIS

Lessons end with "synthesis," which consumes between 15 and 30 minutes, depending on the content of the lesson and the length of the block. The teacher assists the students in connecting the explanation part of the lesson with the application phase. Students reflect and review; the teacher assesses students' learning through questioning, observations, or paper-pencil means; the teacher may reteach and give meaning to the lesson.

Obviously there are many ways to teach successfully in a block schedule, and teachers should not feel limited to the somewhat artificial division of time described above.

Occasionally, it may be necessary to say to a class: "I have a great deal of introductory material to share with you today and I need to lecture; tomorrow, we will begin a 3-day simulation, but today I lecture."

Another model proposed by Hotchkiss (personal communication, Summer 1995) for designing a lesson for a block of teaching time is the following: (1) review homework, (2) present new material for the day's lesson, (3) follow with an appropriate activity, (4) offer guided practice, (5) if problems are noted during guided practice, reteach, and (6) provide closure to the lesson. Figure 1.6 illustrates an adaptation of this model and offers sources for the various strategies suggested.

These steps are supported by Rosenshine's (1995) and Madeline Hunter's views of direct instruction (Hunter, 1972, 1982). During homework review, the teacher may be "center stage" by simply providing feedback to the students, or the teacher may involve the students in various types of activities that not only give students the necessary feedback on their work but also contribute to team-building and class-building skills. Some examples of appropriate activities for active, student-involved homework review might include various forms of roundtable, pairs check, and inside-outside circles (Kagan, 1990; Canady & Rettig, 1995a).

Following review of homework, the teacher could move into a presentation of the day's lesson. That presentation might follow the format of direct instruction (Chapter 9)[10], but may include the use of technology (Chapter 7), or follow the steps of another model of teaching such as concept attainment (Chapter 4) or inquiry. A Socratic seminar also might be in order (Chapter 3). More student-centered activities

---

[10] All references such as this, "(Chapter 9)," are to this book.

FIGURE 1.6. DESIGNING LESSONS FOR THE BLOCK SCHEDULE WITH ACTIVE LEARNING STRATEGIES[11]

Homework Review (10–15 Minutes)

Inside-Outside Circles (Kagan, 1990)
Pairs-Check (Kagan, 1990)
Team Interview (Kagan, 1990)
Graffiti (Kagan, 1990)

Roundtable (Ch. 2)
Think-Pair-Share (Ch. 2)
Mix-Freeze-Group (Kagan, 1990)
Send a Problem (Ch. 9)

Presentation (20–25 Minutes)

Interactive Lecture (Ch. 2)
CD Rom (Ch. 7)
Video Disc (Ch. 7)

Videotape (Ch. 7)
Socratic Seminars (Ch. 3)
Inquiry (Gunter, et al., 1995)
Direct Instruction (Ch. 9)

Demonstration
Inductive Thinking (Ch. 4)
Directed Reading/Thinking
    Activity (Ch. 8)
Concept Attainment (Ch. 4)
Concept Formation (Ch. 4)
Synectics (Ch. 4)
Memory Model (Ch. 4)

Activity (30–35) Minutes

Role Play (Gunter, et al., 1995)
Simulation (Ch. 5)
Synectics (Ch. 4)
Science Laboratory
Computer Reinforcement
Mix-Freeze-Group (Kagan, 1990)
Inside-Outside Circle (Kagan, 1990)
Writing Lab (Ch. 8)
Teams Games Tournaments (TGT)
    (Slavin, 1986)
Student Teams Achievement Divisions
    (STAD) (Slavin, 1986; Ch. 2)

Team Review
Graffiti (Kagan, 1990)
Roundtable (Ch. 2)
Pair-Share (Ch. 2)
Learning Centers (Ch. 6)
Send a Problem (Ch. 9)
Pairs-Check (Kagan, 1990)
Jigsaw (Slavin, 1986)

Guided Practice (10–15 Minutes)

Reteach (10–15 Minutes)

Closure (5–10 Minutes)

---

[11] Adapted from Phyllis R. Hotchkiss, Hotchkiss Educational Consulting Services, Richmond, Virginia.

also may be part of the presentation of new material; the teacher may lead the class in a simulation (Chapter 5), accompany the students to the computer lab (Chapter 7) for writing lab or reinforcement of math skills, engage students in a "5-minute pause that refreshes the memory and increases the odds for retention" (Canady & Rettig, 1995a, p. 238), involve students in a Directed Reading Thinking Activity (DRTA) (Chapter 8), or follow one of several cooperative learning structures such as Listen/Think/Pair/Share (Chapter 2) or Send-a-Problem (Chapter 9).

Following the teacher's presentation, which we hope most days includes a high degree of student engagement, the teacher may allow 10 or 15 minutes of time for guided practice. Guided practice, done correctly, means the teacher is actively monitoring both individual and group learning in the classroom, not grading papers as students complete "homework." During guided practice, the teacher may observe that several or all students are experiencing difficulty with some part of the assignment. When this occurs, it is desirable for the teacher to intervene and **reteach** the material, concept, or skill that is a problem for the student or students.

To complete our adaptation of Hunter's model of direct instruction, the teacher spends the final 5 or 10 minutes of class bringing **closure** to the lesson. During this time, the teacher may briefly review or summarize the key points of the lesson, indicate critical concepts to be retained, and then suggest how the next lesson will build on today's lesson. One useful means for having students complete this review is the Circle of Knowledge (Chapter 2). Questions about upcoming homework or papers to be turned in also might be considered to be part of closure.

STRATEGIES TO ENGAGE ACTIVE LEARNERS

Through our work in schools across the country, we have been privileged to become acquainted with many talented and dedicated educators who are committed to the improvement of instruction in our middle and high schools. The authors of the remaining chapters of this book were invited to prepare manuscripts because they had demonstrated successful teaching and also because they had established professional reputations for their expertise with a particular teaching strategy.

Pamela F. Brewer, assistant principal, and Wanda H. Ball, English teacher, at Person County High School, a 4/4 school in Roxboro, North Carolina, draw from their considerable experience as classroom teachers and workshop leaders to share the inner workings of "Socratic Seminars" in Chapter 2. This model of teaching, also known as the "Paideia Seminar" (Adler & Van Doren, 1984) moves far beyond the traditional classroom discussion to engage students in deep reflection and reaction to important readings.

In Chapter 3, "The Collaborative Classroom," John D. Strebe, a math teacher at Mt. Hebron High School in Howard County, Maryland, and a trainer of thousands of teachers in the mid-Atlantic and southeastern states, describes the successful implementation of cooperative learning strategies in the block-scheduled classroom. He demonstrates how this versatile model of teaching can be utilized to engage and instruct all learners, from the least motivated to the most gifted.

In Chapter 4, "Four Models of Teaching," Deborah D. Pettit, principal of Louisa County Middle School, and Brenda M. Tanner, assistant superintendent of Louisa County, Virginia, detail a step-by-step process for the practical use of concept development, concept attainment, and synectics—three creative strategies for developing deeper understanding of important concepts. They conclude by outlining the use of the memory model, which links new content meaningfully to previously acquired content and is appropriate for use in any discipline when students are asked to memorize information.

Elizabeth D. Morie, associate professor in the School of Education at James Madison University, Harrisonburg, Virginia, adds Chapter 5, "Using Simulations in the Block." Through her thorough research and workshop presentations, she has developed significant assistance for teachers who wish to provide students with lifelike problem-solving experiences.

In Chapter 6, "Learning Centers," Pamela Ridge Moran, a public school teacher and administrator for the past 20 years, demonstrates how learning centers can be a practical and beneficial means of engaging students in the learning process.

Jean Friend Condrey, a former high school physics teacher and current doctoral student in instructional technology, takes the reader beyond computer-assisted instruction to describe how computer and video equipment can blend into the teaching and learning process, in Chapter 7, "Integrated Technology."

Chapter 8, "Reading and Writing Strategies," offers teachers of all disciplines a vision of appropriate and practical literacy development for middle and high school students. Tom Gill, an associate professor at West Chester University in Pennsylvania, and Laurie Nelson-Gill, an educational consultant, bring their many years of teaching experience, workshop presentations, and research in K–12 and postsecondary education to this important task.

Finally, David H. Vawter, a former high school social studies teacher, current doctoral student, and frequent workshop presenter, reminds us that an engaging lecture still can be an effective part of lessons taught in block classes. In Chapter 9, "Direct Teaching and Lecturing," he offers tips for improving and utilizing the lecture and updates the direct instruction model for use in the block schedule.

We believe even more strongly now, that "Regardless of a school's time schedule, what happens between individual teachers and students in classrooms is still most important, **and simply altering the manner in which we schedule schools will not ensure better instruction by teachers or increased learning by students**" (Canady & Rettig, 1995a, p. 240). Consequently, the success or failure of any block schedule will be determined largely by the ability of teachers to harness the potential of the block and improve instruction. **THIS IS OUR CHALLENGE!**

REFERENCES

Adler, M. & Van Doren, C. (1984). The conduct of seminars. In M. Adler (ed.), *The Paideia program: An educational syllabus* (pp. 15–31). New York: Macmillian.

Averett, C.P. (1994). *Block scheduling in North Carolina high schools.* Raleigh, NC: North Carolina Department of Public Instruction.

Bateson, D.J. (1990). Science Achievement in semester and all-year courses. *Journal of Research in Science Teaching* 27(3), 233–240.

Canady, R.L. & Rettig, M.D. (December 1993). Unlocking the lockstep high school schedule. *Phi Delta Kappan*, 310–314.

Canady, R.L. & Rettig, M.D. (1995a). *Block scheduling: A catalyst for change in high schools.* Princeton, NJ: Eye On Education.

Canady, R.L. & Rettig, M.D. (November 1995b). The power of innovative scheduling. *Educational Leadership*, 4–10.

Carroll, J.M. (1994). *The Copernican plan evaluated: The evolution of a revolution.* Topsfield, MA: Copernican Associates.

Cawelti, G. (1994). *High school restructuring: A national study.* Arlington, VA: Educational Research Service.

Gunter, M.A., Estes, T., & Schwab, J. (1995). *Instruction: A models approach.* 2nd ed. Boston: Allyn and Bacon.

Hunter, M.C. (1976). *Improved instruction.* El Segundo, CA: TIP Publications.

Hunter, M.C. (1982). *Mastery teaching.* El Segundo, CA: TIP Publications.

Joyce, B. (1992). *Models of teaching.* Boston: Allyn and Bacon.

Juarez, T. (1996, January). Why any grades at all, father? *Phi Delta Kappan*, 374–377.

Kagan, S. (1990). *Cooperative learning: Resources for teachers*. San Juan Capistrano, CA: Resources for Teachers, Inc.

Lockwood, S.L. (1995). *Semesterizing the high school schedule: The impact on student achievement in algebra and geometry in Dothan City Schools*. Unpublished doctoral dissertation. Tuscaloosa, AL: University of Alabama.

National Association of Secondary School Principals (1196). Breaking ranks: Changing an American institution. Reston, VA: National Association of Secondary School Principals.

National Education Commission on Time and Learning (1994). *Prisoners of time: Report of the National Education Commission on Time and Learning*. Washington, DC: U.S. Government Printing Office.

Page, D.P. (1855). *Theory and practice of teaching or the motives and methods of good school-keeping*. New York: A.S. Barnes & Co.

Raphael, D., Wahlstrom, M., & McLean, L.D. (1986). Debunking the semesterizing myth. *Canadian Journal of Education*, 11(1), 36–52.

Rettig, M.D. (1995). *Directory of high school scheduling models in Virginia: 1995–96 school year. A report of the "Study of innovative high school scheduling in Virginia."* Harrisonburg, VA: James Madison University.

Rettig, M.D. & Cannizzaro, J. (1996). *Block scheduling: Social studies educator's handbook*. Upper Saddle River, NJ: Prentice-Hall.

Rosenshine, B. (1995). Advances in research on instruction. *The Journal of Educational Research, 88(5)*, 262–268.

Semb, G.B., Ellis, J.A., & Araujo, J. (1993). Long-term memory for knowledge learned in school. *Journal of Educational Psychology, 85,* 305–316.

Sessoms, J.C. (1995). Teachers' perceptions of three models of high school block scheduling. Unpublished doctoral dissertation, University of Virginia.

Sizer, T. (1992, 1984). *Horace's compromise: The dilemma of the American high school*. Boston: Houghton Mifflin.

Slavin, R.E. (1986). *Using student team learning*. 3rd ed. Baltimore, MD: The Johns Hopkins Team Learning Project, Johns Hopkins University.

Stumpf, T. (November 1995). A Colorado school's un-rocky road to trimesters. *Educational Leadership*, 20–22.

Tanner, B., Canady, R.L. & Rettig, M.D. (1995). Scheduling time to maximize staff development opportunities. *Journal of Staff Development, 16(4)*, 14–19.

2

SOCRATIC SEMINARS[1]

SOCRATIC QUESTIONING: THEN AND NOW

Innovative and ancient, the Socratic seminar is an exciting and effective strategy, K–12, for provoking student thought, dialogue, and ownership for learning. It is a unique alternative to traditional class discussions because in seminar students speak 97% of class time.

In this model, participants sit in a circle, and, prompted by their teacher's open-ended, provocative questions, engage each other in thoughtful dialogue. Their subject is a shared reading, identified for its richness of ideas and issues. Students are responsible for talking with each other, not with the teacher, who facilitates and clarifies through questioning, but who never contributes to the discussion. Often, 55 minutes isn't enough time when students own the discussion; therefore, the strategy lends itself well to school schedules built for longer blocks of time.

The great philosopher and moral teacher, Socrates, had no bell schedule when he walked and talked with the young men of Athens 2400 years ago, but he inspired awe and ire with his unconventional teaching practices. His approach was to take a subject, an idea, statement, or argument of his day and then raise thoughtful questions, without proposing to have any wise answers himself. This deliberate and repeated probing of his students' thought, would lead, he hoped, to their self-knowledge and understanding, as well as to the establishment of truth.

More recently, in 1982, Mortimer Adler returned to Socratic questioning in *The Paideia Proposal*, one of three "columns" for learn-

---

[1] This chapter was written by Wanda H. Ball, English Teacher, and Pam F. Brewer, Assistant Principal, Person High School, Roxboro, NC.

ing. He suggested that didactic instruction, coaching, and exercises are appropriate methodology for the goals of gaining specific content (the facts) and skill building (the practice). But he highlighted Socratic questioning in a class seminar for reaching the third goal, exploring and understanding the ideas and issues surrounding content (the enlarged understanding).

In secondary school, the seminar strategy may be applied frequently, as much as once or twice a week for English and social studies, where literature or primary documents are the text for seminar. The strategy works beautifully for humanities courses that link these two subjects. A 4/4 (semester/semester) block schedule with a double humanities block allows for up to a 3-hour seminar. In most other disciplines, namely science, mathematics, foreign languages, and vocational courses, Socratic seminars offer an occasional strategy for teachers to use in making the content relevant and expandable. Math students may read Euclid's "Geometry" or Asimov's "The Feeling of Power." Biology students may explore Rachel Carson's environmental treatise *Silent Spring* or an essay on genetic engineering. These readings are not used to "teach" mathematic equations or the DNA molecule, but to generate thinking about the ideas and usefulness of math and the awesome capabilities and responsibilities of science.

Such meaning making, placing the curriculum into context, and establishing emotional connection to content are all documented methods for locking in new learning. These are the catalysts for linking new learning with old, thus entering the new learning into the system. Socratic seminars tap this meaning-making frame in a powerful way and help motivate all types of students.

Socratic seminars likewise return ownership for learning to students as they explore a reading, back up their opinions with textual evidence, challenge each other's views, and, most importantly, find, articulate, and develop their "voice." Just as Eudora Welty writes in *One Writer's Beginnings* of the importance of an author finding his voice, young people gain confidence as they direct the discussion, listen to their peers, and hear their own intelligent thoughts. They find a voice. Sometimes they and their teachers are surprised by the insights that emerge and the learning that gets anchored.

High retention rates are linked with strategies that have students speaking with each other about content. In discussion or cooperative learning groups, pairs, or Socratic class seminars, teachers get off the stage and out of the way. These active strategies prove highly effective as long as there are rules of engagement for student interchanges that have individual accountability.

Why does increased retention dovetail with instructional strategies that require students to talk with each other? First, let's accept that community, connection, communication and control are core human needs. Then let's add that young people tuning in to their peers almost exclusively is developmentally appropriate. Does it not then make sense that greater learning takes place in structures that acknowledge their humanity and harness the academic power of their strongest influence, their peers?

School people must create supportive environments that encourage students to risk sharing their thoughts about academic matters with each other. Students remember what their buddies say around the lunch table about a rap group, about a boyfriend, about last night's "Melrose Place." And through a seminar, they also remember what their buddies say about "I Have a Dream," *Cry, The Beloved Country,* or even an essay on quantum physics! As they hear each other's voices, they refine their own; they tend to stay focused, and they grow to appreciate each other's differences.

Unfortunately, much of high school methodology, namely lecture, teacher-led Q&A, and individual pencil/paper/book tasks, inhibits this important need for community, limits student communication about academic matters to monosyllables, and maintains tight teacher control that translates into silence. Many troubled kids just drop out. Gangs, not schools, massage their human and developmental needs. Other students accept that survival in the high school depends on complacency, conformity, and, above all, studied silence. One thing is certain. A high school block schedule that traps students for longer than 55-minute classes invites and exacerbates both extremes in the absence of strategies, such as Socratic seminars, that get teachers off the stage and students to center stage!

PREPARING FOR A SOCRATIC SEMINAR

ROOM ARRANGEMENT

Some rearrangement of classroom seating is necessary when one uses the seminar as a teaching strategy. Students must be seated in a circle so that there is eye contact among them. Because they talk to each other, not just to the teacher, both students and the seminar leader/facilitator should be seated on the same level within the circle. In most classrooms, a class of 25 to 30 students can be seated comfortably using individual student desks arranged as one circle. Not only does this arrangement help to maintain eye contact, but it also "equalizes" students; no student is thrust into a prominent position at the front of the room, nor is a student able to hide away in a corner. The circle invites all to be a part of the seminar process.

Not all teachers are fortunate enough to have a large classroom or to have an average-sized class. Small rooms or very large classes may create overcrowding when the room is set up for seminar in a single circle. To alleviate the crowding, teachers may elect to use an inner/outer circle arrangement. Those students seated in the inner circle are participants while those on the outer circle are observers who have a task to complete. Outer circle members are not entirely excluded from the seminar. The inner/outer circle concept includes "hot seats," which are two or more empty chairs that are placed strategically, within easy access, within the inner circle. Outer circle members are free to leave their assigned seats to enter the hot seats. Once a student enters a hot seat, he technically becomes a member of the inner circle and can be recognized as a fully functioning participant. After he has been recognized and has spoken, the student immediately vacates the hot seat and returns to his original seat in the outer circle, thereby making the hot seat available for the next student who desires to use it.

The inner/outer circle seating arrangement facilitates combining classes for team-teaching experiences or grouping students within a single classroom. For instance, bringing American literature and United States history students together is a logical teaching approach that can prevent repetition of the curriculum; however, many teachers fail to do so because they have no method of combining 50 or more students in an organized, orderly manner. When teachers use the inner/outer circle to combine classes for integrated English and history seminars, there is controlled movement and structured activity. Under these circumstances, the joining of classes is not only feasible but also desirable.

All teachers need to group students within a classroom for cooperative lessons, special activities, or seminars. This grouping is made somewhat easier by use of the inner/outer arrangement. For example, though reading readiness is highly emphasized in the preparation for seminar, unfortunately not all students will come to class prepared. Many teachers find it necessary to have students qualify for the seminar by taking an objective reading quiz or other preseminar evaluation of reading readiness. Those students who do not meet the teacher's standards of readiness automatically are placed in the seminar's outer circle. While this placement process may at first appear purely punitive, it actually is a teaching strategy that enables students to use the portion of reading they have completed by going to the hot seat. Additionally, students on the outer circle have a different focus from the inner circle. Instead of concentrating on speaking in seminar, students shift their attention to skills such as note-taking or listening. Outer circle participants must not only complete the seminar reading satisfactorily, but they also must write their ideas down. The weaker reader's understanding of the selection, however, has been enlarged by having heard peers discuss the material in seminar; consequently, the student's writing should reflect the richness of the seminar process.

TEACHER PREPARATION

The teacher has four primary responsibilities in preparing for seminar. First is the selection of seminar readings, which come from any discipline, including science, literature, art, history, mathematics, vocational, and philosophy. Because most schools have a clearly defined curriculum and specific objectives, teachers must select works that already are embedded in the curriculum and lend themselves to the seminar strategy. Several guidelines should be observed in determining whether a text is suitable for an effective seminar. Is the selection filled with issues and ideas worthy of discussion? Will the text sustain discussion and allow for exploration of concepts? Does the text include complexities, ambiguities, contradictions, or mysteries which offer several possible interpretations of issues? A text that does not meet these requirements probably should be taught didactically, not as a seminar.

It is also very important to remember the purpose of the seminar. It is not used to teach facts or to coach skills. The seminar text, therefore, is not pure science, but the ethics of science; not mathematical computation, but the theory and the usefulness of math; not the chapter on the six causes of the Civil War, but a soldier's diary and the Gettysburg address. The text may be taken from a variety of sources; possible genres include plays, poems, sermons, stories, essays, novels, films, and music.

Once the text has been identified, the teacher should define objectives and outcomes. In other words, what should students learn and apply from the text? What aspects of the lesson need to be taught didactically and what concepts need to be explored in seminar? Can the teacher give students the freedom to uncover information and to interpret it without thrusting "the teacher's viewpoint" into the discussion? Can the teacher allow a slight misunderstanding of facts and wait for another student to correct that factual inaccuracy before the teacher jumps into the discussion? Using the seminar approach requires mental flexibility, for the teacher is trusting students to learn from each other through reading, exploration, and analysis of the text. Students' interpretations may differ from the teacher's; however, if they can logically document their opinions with evidence from the text, then they are entitled to their views. The seminar is never used just to teach facts; instead, it concentrates on understanding, discovery, and application. Within the framework of the teacher's objectives and expectations, an environment must exist where students can uncover what "they know" instead of passively waiting for the teacher to say: "This is what you should know."

Another before-seminar preparation is the designing of preseminar and postseminar tasks. The preseminar tasks get students ready for the seminar; the postseminar tasks assess or extend student learning. While the actual design and content of these tasks will vary according to specific objectives, the teacher uses the task design to draw the students' attention to concepts in the reading that warrant exploration. For example, if the leader does not ask the seminar's closing question (which may happen because of time constraints), this question may provide the basis of the postseminar assignment. Often the teacher prepares several preseminar and postseminar tasks and gives students the freedom to choose the task that most interests them. For the teacher, however, defining the task is not enough; rubrics should accompany the task so that students know what is expected of them in the assessment process. A rubric is an assessment instrument that states exemplary behaviors or expectations of students. We discuss the application of rubrics to the assessment of students' participation in the Socratic seminar later in this chapter.

Perhaps the most challenging responsibility for the teacher (seminar leader/facilitator) is the writing of seminar questions. Frequently, the questions that are asked determine the overall success or failure of the entire seminar. The leader is responsible for asking three types of questions: opening, core, and closing (Fig. 2.1). While a fourth type of question is also used, the follow-up or clarification questions are not planned in advance.

The first and most crucial question is the opening one that directs students into the reading. It needs to be a broad question that allows for a wide berth of responses. For example, the question "what is Antigone about?" will evoke varied responses such as "it's about loyalty to family" or "it's a story about stubbornness." The opening question cannot have a simple answer. If it does, the question is too narrow and too focused on specific content. The question should spring from content, but should spur thought because it has many possible responses. The desired outcome of the opening question is to get students directly into the exploration and analysis of the text. Ideally, an effective opening question should sustain discussion for at least 15 to 20 minutes.

FIGURE 2.1. TYPES OF SEMINAR QUESTIONS

OPENING QUESTION (1 question)

♦ Is general and directs students into the text for an answer

♦ Introduces and explores topics, ideas, themes
  - Are schooling and educating the same thing in this piece?
  - Why is this titled "Mother to Son"?
  - Finish the statement, "This is really a story about . . . (theme)." Tell students to reflect and write their responses down. Do a round robin to list all themes. Then say, "Let's start with Bill's. How is Antigone about greed?"

CORE QUESTIONS (2–5 questions)

♦ Are content-specific

♦ Examine central points

♦ Interpret a passage, explore a quotation

♦ Are often "how" or "why" questions
  - What is meant by "of the people, by the people, and for the people?"
  - Why does the author call it a "crystal stair"?
  - Who is the "savage" here?

CLOSING QUESTION (1 question)

♦   Establishes relevance

♦   Connects with real world

♦   Applies to self
   • How have we answered Chief Seattle's prophesy?
   • Is your school more in the business of schooling or educating?
   • What would Socrates think of your classroom?
   • Are you more a city or country mouse?

The second type of question, the core question, serves an entirely different purpose. These questions narrow down the discussion to specific lines, themes, or issues in the text. Though interpretations may vary, still the question should be supportable by textual evidence. Normally, the teacher prepares three to five core questions before beginning the seminar. A core question could be any of the following: "In line 28, what does the author mean when he says . . . ?" "Why did Antony repeat 'and surely they are all honorable men'?" "How is *The Scarlet Letter* a novel about redemption for sin?" Core questions zero in on responses to the opening question. For instance, in a seminar on *The Scarlet Letter*, the opening question could ask students for Hawthorne's purpose in writing the novel. This question would most likely lead to a listing of the themes, such as sin, guilt, and redemption. Having anticipated these responses, the leader would zero in on these three themes in the core questions: "What in the text tells you that the novel is about redemption?" The core questions cause students to concentrate on one issue until it has been discussed in depth. The quality of the leader's questions directly determines how much and how deeply the text is explored and to what extent the teacher's lesson objectives are covered in seminar.

The final type of question is the closing question, which is somewhat similar to the broad opening. Unlike the opening question, which directs students into the text, the closing question encourages students to relate what they have learned to their own lives. Appreciation and understanding of the text is deepened when relevance has been established. For instance, students discussing *The Scarlet Letter* will come to a clearer understanding of human nature and of the consequences of human behavior, including their own. As Reverend Dimmesdale flogs himself for his sins, students will think about the whipping post or about other unique forms of punishment such as caning. Drawing connections between the text and modern society locks in meaning, and *The Scarlet Letter* has purpose beyond something students have to read.

Question development is critical to the success of the seminar. Before the seminar begins, the teacher must carefully process the information in the text, anticipate students' reactions, and write thoughtful, structured questions that will ensure that goals are achieved. See Figure 2.2 for guidelines for writing appropriate seminar questions.

FIGURE 2.2. GENERAL GUIDELINES FOR SOCRATIC QUESTIONING

♦ FOCUS ON THE GOAL
   The goal of the seminar is to enlarge understanding by exploring ideas and issues of text, not to establish facts.

♦ USE OPEN-ENDED QUESTIONS
   Avoid yes/no questions without follow-ups. Ask no fact questions.

♦ KEEP QUESTIONS VALUE-FREE
   Participants make judgments, connections; you remain neutral.

♦ USE QUESTIONS WITH MEAT
   Can the group explore this for 15–20 minutes? Does it prompt thinking beyond the obvious? It shouldn't be answerable without reading the text. Question arises from experiences, events, and language that are common to all.

♦ FOLLOW THE ORDER OF QUESTION TYPES
   Use an opening question first, then two to five core questions, and a closing question.

♦ FOLLOW-UP QUESTIONS
   Follow-up questions are not planned ahead, but are asked of individual speakers to clarify and probe. Examples include:
   "Are you saying that. . . ?"
   "Where in the text do you find support for that?"
   "What do you mean by. . . ?"
   "Would someone take issue with. . . ?"
   "What is your point?"

   These questions push the student to defend or clarify a view with proof and prompt others to challenge a view.

STUDENT PREPARATION

Seminar preparation involves several components: reading the text, marking the text or taking notes, reflective thinking, and completing preseminar tasks. Obviously, the reading of the text is the most crucial stage of preparation; however, simply reading the text without engaging in the other preparation activities is insufficient. To become competent in the seminar process, students need to master all steps of the preparation process.

Reading the text prior to the seminar is critical, for no student can discuss and document opinions with evidence from a text they have not read. Reading for seminar requires reading for total understanding of both facts and concepts. A cursory reading to glean facts for a multiple-choice or true-or-false test is not adequate preparation for seminar. Students must acquire the facts and probe deeply into key concepts, issues, and implications. Initially, short selections are assigned, until students have learned seminar methods. Later they may be asked to read longer works of fiction and nonfiction that require considerable reading time and organizational skills. To readily access a page, paragraph, or line in the work, students must be very familiar with the text. This familiarity does not come with hasty reading, but arises from concentrated effort involving note-taking and marking of the text.

Marking the text requires the reader to underline, highlight, or take notes on ideas, issues, and themes in the work. The physical act of marking the text locks information into the student's memory and allows for retrieval of the material during seminar. Figure 2.3 suggests various methods of marking a text.

FIGURE 2.3. HOW TO MARK A BOOK[2]

To find references quickly, students must be very familiar with the text. These are suggestions for marking their text as they read.

1. Highlight or underline passages that reveal crucial information, that show changes in character, or that trace the development of character.

2. Make notations in the margins as you react to passages that are unique or noteworthy.

---

[2] Adapted from Adler & Van Duren (1972).

3. Place a question mark (?) in the margin if you don't understand what the passage means.

4. Put an exclamation mark (!) in the margin to indicate something surprising or unusual.

5. Consider using these symbols:
   * to emphasize a statement already underlined or to denote a recurring idea
   + or ✓ to indicate something you want to remember

6. Use sticky notes for marking major ideas, for crossreferencing ideas, or for easy access to specific pages in the text. (Suggestion: use a variety of colors for different purposes.)

7. A smiling face, ☺, shows that you agree or like an idea.

8. A frowning face, ☹, shows disagreement or dislike.

9. Circle key words or phrases.

10. Underline vocabulary words you don't know. Jot down a brief definition in the margin, especially if the word is critical to your understanding of the passage.

While marking the text and traditional note-taking serve many students well, others are more visual learners who prefer using graphic organizers to trace issues, events, and character development. For the majority of students, a combination of marking the text and using graphic organizers is most effective. Failure to produce any preparation of the text is usually indicative of hasty, inadequate reading, which invariably results in poor seminar preparation.

A third way the student prepares for seminar is through reflection on the text before the actual seminar. The student can learn to reflect by processing questions such as these: "What is the author's purpose in writing. . . ?" "What are five main ideas in the reading?" "What can I learn from the way the character handles situations in his/her life?" "What relevance does this reading have to my life and the world in which I live?" By reflecting upon these questions or similar ones, young people develop critical thinking skills and use these skills to process and sort information.

A final step in seminar preparation is completion of preseminar tasks, which range from directed reading questions to inclass essays to artwork. Each task, which becomes a portion of the overall seminar grade, should focus the reader on the text and assist him with pulling his thoughts together in a logical way. When the teacher has thoroughly designed the task and the assessment rubrics, students will complete the tasks well and will understand their purpose. On the other hand, a poorly designed task may be perceived as busywork without value.

Students are better prepared for seminar when they have been taught their responsibilities and are held accountable for them. Figure 2.4 defines student responsibilities in a Socratic seminar.

FIGURE 2.4. RESPONSIBILITIES OF STUDENT IN A SOCRATIC SEMINAR

I am responsible for—

♦ Asking questions about what I have read, heard, and seen.
♦ Asking for clarification of any passage I have read but which I do not understand.
♦ Being courteous and respectful of my peers.
♦ Pausing and thinking before I respond to the facilitator's question or to a comment made by a peer.
♦ Giving my opinions clearly yet succinctly.
♦ Making judgments that I can defend with textual evidence.
♦ Explaining to others how I have inferred an idea by exploring the passage that has led me to this conclusion.
♦ Locating facts and examples in the text that can be cited as evidence for a particular argument.
♦ Listening attentively and patiently as peers share their ideas.
♦ Listening critically to others' opinions and taking issue with inaccuracies or illogical reasoning.
♦ Clarifying information and lending support to a peer's argument.
♦ Moving the seminar forward to new concepts.
♦ Maintaining an open mind to a diversity of opinions.
♦ Listening acutely to a peer's entire position before taking issue with it.
♦ Searching for connections with previous readings or prior studies.
♦ Avoiding repetitiveness by developing stronger listening skills.
♦ Being willing to change my opinion if more information is given

or if my reasoning has been flawed.

♦ Seeing the relevance of the reading to my world.

♦ Being prepared by having read my text thoroughly and reflect-ively.

♦ Having marked key issues in my text.

♦ Speaking loudly and articulating clearly.

♦ Exhibiting mature behavior with patience and self-control.

STEPS AND RULES FOR SEMINAR

WHAT DO SOCRATIC SEMINARS LOOK LIKE?

♦ Students arrive for the seminar, taking their places in a circle with the teacher. If the seminar text (an essay, poem, novel, primary document, artwork, etc.) has been preassigned, they arrive with their text marked and with notes and page references.

♦ The teacher asks an open-ended "opening question" to send the students into the text and then waits in silence.

♦ Now students respond, after teacher acknowledgment, to express a view, to cite evidence, and to examine, support, and disagree with the ideas of others. They look at each other, not at the teacher, unless they are seeking acknowledgement to speak.

♦ The teacher takes notes for evaluative purposes but provides no verbal or nonverbal feedback that either affirms or chal-lenges what the students say. The teacher may ask follow-up questions for clarification, or probing questions to push stu-dent thinking that is shallow or erroneous; however, questions are used sparingly and deliberately. The teacher is off this stage.

♦ When satisfied that the opening question has been thoroughly explored, the seminar leader asks one or more "core questions" to examine central points of the text.

♦ Students know this is their seminar. The teacher will ask the question, after which students direct most of the seminar. It is not uncommon for 15–20 student responses to arise from a single good Socratic question, or for the exploration of one question to last from 30 minutes to an hour.

◆ Once the text has been explored thoroughly (or time is running short), the teacher asks a "closing question," which springs from the text but which seeks to have students connect some issue from the text with their lives. At this stage, personal anecdotes may be shared, vulnerabilities may be exposed, real emotion may be expressed. This question is the one that often locks some ideas from the text to the students' long-term memories. Time and again, young people remember some idea about a particular text several years later because they recall something powerful a classmate said or something that was poignantly revealed in seminar.

◆ The seminar is over when it's over. For one class, the 5–7 prepared questions may take 45 minutes, with the teacher asking all 7 questions. Another class may talk for 60 minutes on the opening question. Seminars take on a life of their own because they are steered largely by students, with the teacher's occasional course corrections through questioning.

Teachers often report that a good class discussion feels much like a seminar when dialogue starts to flow and students engage each other; however, a regular class discussion achieves a high level of active engagement more by chance than by design. When students know the teacher is out of the discussion and won't agree or disagree, they rise to the occasion, carry on the dialogue, and, most importantly, prepare the assignment. In the seminar, there is nowhere to hide! Figure 2.5 lists differences between a seminar and a typical question-answer class discussion.

WHAT ARE THE RULES FOR THE SEMINAR?

FOR STUDENTS

The seminar establishes a setting where all must feel free to express their ideas without reprisal. Putdowns—through words, gestures, or even looks, are taboo. Good teachers don't tolerate personal insults among students anyway, but on seminar day, this rule must carry a heightened awareness. Even goodnatured, gentle teasing is out. Students are taught to disagree with someone's ideas, not with the person. Much as the lobster goes to the bottom of the sea to a recessed and protected area to shed its old exoskeleton and secrete

FIGURE 2.5. DIFFERENCES BETWEEN SOCRATIC SEMINAR AND CLASS DISCUSSION

SOCRATIC SEMINARS	CLASS DISCUSSIONS
Students and teacher in circle. All have eye contact; teacher is on the same level.	Students are in rows. Teacher is set apart and often higher on stool or behind podium.
97% student talk; students know teacher won't comment.	97% teacher talk, even if many questions are asked. Teacher elaborates and answers.
Average response for students is 8–12 seconds.	Average response for students is 2–3 seconds.
No verbal or nonverbal approval or disapproval is present. Affirming feedback by the teacher is taboo.	Teacher affirmation of correctness is critical. Sustaining feedback for incorrectness is critical.
Thinking, backed up with textual evidence, is paramount. Open-ended exploration, not rightness, is valued.	Rightness is paramount; thinking ends as soon as one is right.
Students listen primarily to peers.	Students listen primarily to the teacher, who has the answer.
Students have ownership for much of the flow.	Teachers have ownership for most of the flow.
Students are held accountable for contributions based upon preagreed criteria.	Students see discussion as a frill, a nebulous, negligible "participation grade." If you miss class, you didn't miss much.

a new one, students must be in a "safe" environment to expose their thoughtful vulnerabilities in an hour or two of dialogue. All it takes is one student's tolerated rudeness to another to shut down some in the seminar for the rest of the year. The risk is too great for them.

Another rule addresses general courtesy and self-control. Waiting one's turn, choosing disagreement language carefully, staying focused, and thinking before speaking are all expected of seminar participants.

Other than these affective rules, students must come to the seminar prepared, support their opinions with textual evidence where possible, and fully elaborate the points they make, raising new questions for their peers. They are expected to participate and know that alternative assignments await them if they do not. The rubric will later highlight specific exemplars for student behaviors.

The bottom line for seminar rules is that they must be thoroughly understood and consistently enforced. Most students will do what their teachers expect if these two factors are present. Appropriate behaviors must be specifically taught and modeled; inappropriate behaviors must be swiftly, gently, but always, corrected.

At-risk students particularly enjoy this process so much that they behave for the seminar and present challenges on most other days. They likewise will prepare their assignment for seminar but often do not complete other types of homework. It seems that the chance to be heard and to hear their peers is incentive enough for some students, once hooked on the strategy, to modify their behaviors and complete often challenging assignments.

For Teachers

The teacher's role in seminar, as previously described, shifts to listener, facilitator, enabler, clarifier, manager, and judge. The first five roles are overt, observable behaviors that direct the broad flow and some of the specifics of the discussion. All questioning and teacher comment should stimulate thoughtful discussion, draw out issues, request reasons or justification in the text, rephrase questions, or paraphrase answers for increased clarity. The teacher may begin, "Are you saying that. . . ?" and summarize his or her understanding of a student's 2-minute ramble. Such questions ask for clarification and may push circular thinkers to collapse their thoughts into succinct points. Asking, "Where in the text do you find evidence for that?" prevents a student from making a point just to hear the sound of his or her own voice. Follow-up questions that call for evidence ensure that the text is thoroughly explored, not just dusted in generalities. This is no bull session.

The "manager" function is met as the teacher enforces the rules, though the ultimate goal is for students to manage their own behaviors. There are times, however, when even well-trained seminar participants react to highly charged issues. The seminar leader must step in and uphold the rules about waiting for acknowledgement, thinking before speaking, and disagreeing with ideas, not people.

The toughest job of the seminar leader is to listen actively, take good notes, judge the responses of all speakers, but never engage in the dialogue to express an opinion. Teachers report sitting on their hands, biting their lips, and keeping their eyes down to avoid getting personally involved. Students are accustomed to answering a question in a class discussion and then looking to the teacher for validation or correction. Usually they can count on us for both! But any thinking about the question on the students' parts often ends as the teacher responds.

Seminar leaders must focus their energy on tracking and judging the student comments and remember that as long as teachers are not talking, students are still thinking and speaking! Seminar leaders must never agree or disagree, nod approval or look askance. All judgments are in the teachers' notes during seminar, not on their faces or in their voices.

For some, the "poker face" can prevail. Others find that their outgoing and nurturing personalities have difficulty with this part. These teachers might practice a pleasant "studied nod" that says, "Thank you for contributing; I understand what you are saying, but I'm not giving you any feedback about the quality of what you are saying." Of course, after seminar, teachers are free to praise, wink, hug, or otherwise engage individual students. It just cannot be done during the seminar, when the goal is for **participants** to explore the text thoroughly for understanding. Outward teacher judgment would interfere, changing the dynamic to teacher as keeper of the truth. Corrections and issues that should have arisen but did not, or ideas that were not explored fully, may all be placed in tonight's assignment or on tomorrow's lesson plan!

APPLYING THE SEMINARS TO THE DISCIPLINES

The seminar strategy is usable by all ages and in all disciplines; however, the frequency of use may be limited by the discipline. For example, science and math teachers usually spend a great deal of time in didactic instruction and modeling and spend less time in application and relevance. Though the time spent on discussing ideas often is less, using the seminar to explore science and math issues is an excellent way to get students to apply what they have studied. An example of an integrated lesson that culminates in the seminar might be a unit dealing with Darwinism, creationism, John Scopes, and man's right to think for himself. Realistically, this unit could encompass science, history, English, and possibly other curriculum areas. After examining these subjects in each class, students would read *Inherit the Wind* and come together for seminar, where the text could be explored from many perspectives, not just a literary one. This teaming approach demonstrates the interconnectedness of learning.

An integrated lesson for a middle school team may have many objectives, such as teaching reading skills, understanding historical or scientific significance, strengthening social interaction and communication, and broadening multiculturalism. All of these goals can be addressed in seminar through appropriate readings. A universal theme in many cultures is "how humans got fire." By reading myths from various cultures, students can compare their reasoning, scientific knowledge, and belief systems. Hopefully, they will begin to see the similarities and not just differences.

Sometimes teachers select a fable or other short reading to introduce a lesson. Because the purpose is to jump-start thinking, it may only be necessary to allot a short time to seminar. When a longer, sustained discussion is needed, add an article, essay, or short story that explores related issues. An introductory seminar serves well in eliciting what students know, believe, and want to know. The classic fable "Town Mouse/Country Mouse" is applicable to many disciplines. Suggestions are offered in Figure 2.6 for adapting "Town Mouse/Country Mouse" to specific teaching situations.

FIGURE 2.6. APPLYING SEMINARS TO THE DISCIPLINES:
EXAMPLE—"TOWN MOUSE/COUNTRY MOUSE"

SITUATION: HEALTH, PE, SCIENCE

You are teaching a lesson on stress management. Develop questions
that enable students to see that one person's happiness may cause
another person's stress.

SITUATION: HEALTH, PE, SCIENCE

You are teaching a lesson about stress and how different things
can cause stress depending on the individual. Use "Town Mouse/
Country Mouse" to discuss causes and reactions to stress.

SITUATION: ENGLISH, HISTORY

You are teaching a lesson about how one's individual perspective
on an event or issue can affect the decisions made and the outcomes
of those decisions. Focus on the way the two mice view life and
environment differently.

SITUATION: HOME EC., HEALTH, SOCIOLOGY

You are teaching a lesson on nutrition and food choices. What
connections can you draw between choice of food, lifestyle,
behavioral, and environmental factors associated with food?
Develop questions that cause students to explore these issues.

SITUATION: UPPER ELEMENTARY, MIDDLE SCHOOL

You are working with students on social skills, personal interactions,
and friendship-building. Focus on qualities of friendship.

SITUATION: ELEMENTARY, MIDDLE SCHOOL

You want students to come to appreciate their home communities,
yet to learn, with an open mind, about people who choose to live
in drastically different circumstances.

SITUATION: SOCIAL STUDIES, SOCIOLOGY

You are learning about historical migrations to cities and away
from cities. Use "Town Mouse/Country Mouse" to focus on why
such migrations may have occurred.

SITUATION: ENGLISH

You are preparing to teach a unit on American Romanticism and
the characteristics of this period, including distrust of city life.

SITUATION: ART
> Requires two versions of "Town Mouse/Country Mouse" with different illustrators.
>
> You are teaching a lesson about how readers are influenced by different illustrations of the same written text. Give half of the group one illustrated text and the other half a text by another illustrator. Develop questions that cause them to draw conclusions based on both the text and the illustrations.

TROUBLESHOOTING THE "WHAT IFS . . . "

WHAT IF THE OPENING QUESTION IS ASKED AND NO ONE RESPONDS?

Healthy wait time is always appropriate after asking a good Socratic question. In fact, there often is a correlation between wait time and the quality of thought required by students before answering. In a seminar on the bombing of Hiroshima, "A Noiseless Flash," the opening question was: "Light usually is associated with sanity; for example, 'I saw the light.' How is light in this case representing insanity?" The language was simple. The thought required was great. The students sat a full 30 seconds just soaking in the question. Then two or three at a time went to the text while others continued to ponder. Two minutes elapsed before anyone spoke, but it was apparent that thinking, not confusion, marked that 120 seconds of silence. The teacher softly repeated the question and waited patiently for a response.

If the teacher reads blankness or confusion after asking a question, a rephrasing of the question, breaking it down more specifically, or even trying an alternative opening, may help to jump-start the discussion. The toughest part of teacher preparation is to write good questions that challenge and provoke, are broad and open-ended, and use language understood by all. For a 9th grade heterogeneous class reading "Town Mouse/Country Mouse," "What's going on between these mice?" beats "What Platonic elements of friendship are explored in the rodents' interchange?" In the second question, the language barrier must be crossed before real thinking can begin for some students.

When no one responds to the opening question, it may be that students have not read their text. Reading together, "qualifying" for seminar, and showing their notes or text marking are ways to guarantee that students arrive prepared. If, however, students appear not to have read, and speak in generalization without textual evidence, the teacher should end the seminar promptly. Continuing on this line is now counterproductive, and an alternative teaching strategy is needed.

What if One Student Tries to Dominate the Seminar?

Overzealous speakers must be managed or the seminar is compromised. Since the seminar leader acknowledges each participant, a standing procedure can be always to recognize those who have not yet spoken before those who have, if several hands are up.

The talkative one also may "assist" the teacher by deliberately delaying his or her contribution until five classmates have responded to a question. This forces others to stop relying on the eager participant, and allows all to practice reflecting longer before expressing a view.

Another useful strategy is to help an extroverted student focus on listening, not speaking, by placing this child in the outer circle with responsibility for listening and taking notes on the entire seminar. For the last 5 minutes of class, the student summarizes the seminar. This child certainly has his turn to speak, but his contribution is tempered by acute practice in listening, reflecting, and synthesizing—skills he may well need to develop!

What if Some Students do not Speak During Seminar?

Many factors affect a child's willingness to speak. Naturally shy or insecure people will not speak easily until they are sure this is a "safe" place where no one is put down or otherwise judged for having a view. Gestures or words that mean "nerd," "goody two shoes," or "teacher's pet" are often more destructive than those that say, "That's stupid." All are intolerable and should result in ejection from seminar every time! The rules, as previously discussed, must be strictly followed. This settles the mind and reduces the risk for reticent young people. There always should be opportunity for those who do not speak in seminar to "make it up" in writing that night. While there is no seminar if all choose this option, it does provide an "out" for the painfully shy and for the natural introverts, who process information internally and often need more time to think before speaking. Natural extroverts, who process externally, figure out what they think by trying it out loud with other people. These students are first out of the blocks and get the seminar going. An hour later, the introvert has processed his thinking and may well make the most astute, well-substantiated comment of the seminar. As long as all have the option of writing for the seminar grade, the playing field is even for all personality types.

Several tricks often bring out reticent speakers. The round robin, moving one by one around the semicircle, may be used to solicit a response from "those who have not yet contributed." A teacher may call on a student who has not asked for acknowledgment but who obviously has some ideas by asking, "Mark, did you have something?" This needed, yet gentle, invitation helps nudge the student through his shyness to test his voice.

WHAT IF STUDENTS GO OFF ON A LINE OF REASONING THAT IS FAULTY OR INACCURATE AND START BUILDING ON IT?

The hope is that if an inaccuracy is voiced, another student will correct it. Because the teacher's role is not to judge outwardly, technical inaccuracies that are not built on should be allowed to pass. The teacher may note them and then correct them after the seminar. But if students develop dialogue around fallacies without dissent, the teacher may redirect the thinking with a follow-up question like, "Is there anyone who takes issue with this line of reasoning?" The teacher did not tell them they were on the wrong track; however, she did invite them to think about another side. This is often all it takes to have other views represented.

Another follow-up question, to call for evidence in text where none exists, should also short-circuit a faulty position. Occasionally, if these strategies do not work, the teacher may interrupt the seminar momentarily to establish facts before continuing with the seminar. This is only done if a key point, relevant for completion of the seminar, is incorrect, and subsequent discussion would be tainted without correction.

ASSESSMENT OF SEMINARS

Grading the seminar identifies the strategy as more than a class discussion and as an integral part of the learning process. Routinely, students ask, "Is this going to count for a grade?" If the answer is "No," many perceive that preparation for the assignment is optional. Seminars are doomed to failure as a learning strategy if this attitude exists. Students must know that they are accountable for their performance in the seminar itself and for completion of the preseminar and postseminar tasks. They also should be instructed on how the seminar is being graded and how it is weighted in final grades.

While suggestions and pointers on grading can be given, the ultimate method of grading must be designed by the classroom teacher. There is one absolute in grading: no student's grade should be determined merely on the number of times he speaks! While one student may speak five times, another may speak only once yet contribute more significant, more insightful information, or move the seminar into a new dimension. By using a rubric that targets the skill areas that are being assessed (conduct, speaking, reasoning, listening, and reading), teachers and students alike know that excellence in seminar involves a multitude of behaviors and responsibilities. Rubrics should state the point values of the preseminar and postseminar tasks and the specific things that the teacher expects to find in the assignment. Because these tasks comprise a large portion of the seminar grade, students must have clearly stated expectations before they do the assignments.

When a rubric is utilized, grading is not subjective but is based on the stated exemplars. Figure 2.7 illustrates a "design rubric" that states expectations for students on a preseminar activity related to Plato's *Apology*. Figure 2.8 is the "assessment rubric" for that task.

Figure 2.7. Task Design Rubric for Preseminar on Plato's *Apology*

GENERAL INFORMATION: A preseminar task is the first component in the seminar process. This task, whatever it may be, is intended to cause the student to think deeply about the seminar selection before the discussion begins. The task also allows the facilitator to assess the student's reading readiness by concentrating on information the student should possess if he or she is prepared for seminar.

SUGGESTED PREPARATION ACTIVITIES:
1. As you read, mark your text for main ideas and interesting facts.
2. Keep a note sheet where you trace significant ideas throughout the selection. Include page numbers.
3. Identify ideas that you want to explore in the seminar.

TASK:
1. You are to write for 20 minutes on Plato's *Apology*.
2. The form of the writing should be an extended paragraph supporting this topic sentence:
    Socrates was on trial because _____.
3. Give at least three reasons and an explanation of why he may have been on trial.
4. Conclude with a clincher sentence that pulls your response together.

ASSESSMENT:
1. This writing is worth 20 points of the total seminar grade.
2. All elements of proper paragraph writing will be assessed: topic sentence, supporting details, elaboration of ideas, and drawing a concluding inference.
3. Punctuation, spelling, sentence structure, and usage also are assessed.
4. MAJOR FOCUS will be your ability to answer the question of why Socrates was on trial and to give evidence from the text for support.
5. The writer must observe the time limits but may use the text.

FIGURE 2.8. PRESEMINAR ASSESSMENT RUBRIC
FOR PLATO'S *APOLOGY*

POINTS EARNED:

1. Form: topic sentence—5 points
           each supporting reason—2 points each (6)   _____
           elaboration of reasons—1 point each (3)   _____
           clincher sentence (inference)—1   _____

2. Accuracy of punctuation and usage: 5 points   _____

3. TOTAL NUMBER OF POINTS EARNED: (20)   _____

To use a rubric during the seminar itself, "charting" of student responses is necessary. Figure 2.9 suggests symbols for charting student responses.

FIGURE FIGURE 2.9. CHARTING STUDENT RESPONSES

These are the symbols used during seminar to record student responses. After the seminar concludes, the teacher transfers charted information to scores on the seminar rubric.

CHARTING:

Charting is a technique used by the facilitator to record what is actually occurring throughout the seminar. Symbols are used to indicate precisely what each participant has said or done. Charting is used after the seminar to assign the number of points earned by each student during the seminar. The facilitator also may elect to take notes on the comments made by each student.

✓9+   Student makes a comment, cites a page, and draws a conclusion.

✓9+   Student paraphrases and draws a conclusion.

✓9+   Student makes a comment, cites a page, but does not draw a conclusion.

✓+   Student makes an insightful comment but does not quote from the text.

H9   Student hitchhikes or piggybacks on someone else's comment and quotes the text to clarify a peer's comment.

✓-   Student gives his opinion and has no textual support; limited
            reasoning is evident.

✓R-   Comment is made that has little thought involved or that
            is a repetition of someone else's comment; weak listening
            skills may be apparent.

✓=   Student speaks just to get a grade.

Until the facilitator becomes adept at charting, he may choose to record
the seminar on audiotape and play the tape back to assist in grading. Students
need to be informed about how the tape will be used.

If another teacher is free, ask for help with charting comments.

✓   (student contributes)
9   (page number)
+   (clarification)
R   (repetition)
P   (paraphrase)
H   (hitchhike)

Later, charted information is transferred to the rubric. Charting
involves making notations or taking notes on students' participation
during seminar. While having complete notes on student comments
is desirable, many teachers find the task overwhelming and must
use symbols to denote established behaviors. Either technique may
be used; however, detailed notes allow the teacher to evaluate how
many objectives were covered during seminar and what objectives
need coverage in the next class session. For those who find the process
of charting too demanding when listening is so critical, running an
audiotape during the seminar and grading at a later time is a useful
option.

The seminar grade has three parts: the preseminar task, the
seminar, and the postseminar task. The length of the reading, the
length of the seminar, and the depth of the tasks should determine
the point value of each part. Grades on all three assignments must
be combined before the student's final grade is derived.

Grading seminars is not only difficult but also controversial.
Some teachers prefer not to grade seminars, arguing that grading
is too subjective. Other teachers contend that not grading devalues
the process. Caught in this dilemma, we have developed design and
assessment rubrics that we believe are fair and authentic grading

tools. Use of rubrics gives students and parents a better understanding of the teacher's expectations and grading methods. Only through clearly stated exemplars and thorough task design can fairness and consistency be maintained in grading. Figure 2.10 illustrates a seminar rubric.

FIGURE 2.10. SEMINAR RUBRIC

The second component of assessment is the seminar itself using the rubric. No, teachers do not fill out a rubric for each student while the seminar is in progress. That's humanly impossible. Instead, they chart student responses and later transfer these components to the rubric. Because students are taught what successful seminar participants look like by focusing on the "excellent" exemplars on the rubric, it is not necessary to complete individual rubrics each seminar. Students know how to apply the rubric for both self assessment and peer evaluation. For instance, a student can look at the breakdown of scoring and understand that a "3" in reasoning is good but that obviously something is missing in reasoning if the student has not received a "4".

When we first began leading seminars, we were not ready for a rubric as complex as the one that follows. Should any other leader feel as inept as we once did, we suggest choosing several of the exemplars in each area (speaking, listening, reasoning, conduct, and reading) and focusing attention on these; we have highlighted the exemplars which we believe to be most indicative of a particular level of performance with the "*". The value of the rubric comes from having stated expectations to increase fairness and lessen subjectivity in grading.

STUDENT _____ GRADER _____

DATE _____ TOPIC _____

DIRECTIONS: Identify the descriptors that best reflect the student's performance in each of the five areas.

(A) CONDUCT: _____ (B) SPEAKING: _____ (C)REASONING:_____
(D) LISTENING: _____ (E) READING: _____ TOTAL POINTS_____

SCALE: EXCELLENT: 4 GOOD: 3 FAIR: 2 UNSATISFACTORY: 1

CONDUCT:
    4   demonstrates clear respect for the learning process
        *exhibits patience with differing opinions and thought complexity
        *shows initiative by asking peers for clarification

attempts to draw others into the discussion
moves forward onto new concepts
recognizes his or her own nitpicking and avoids it
does not gain attention by inappropriate means
*exhibits control of potentially hurtful nonverbal behaviors
uses the hitchhiked symbol sparingly

3   shows composure but may sometimes show slight impatience
is not impatient while waiting to be recognized to speak
*demonstrates a respectful attitude towards others
may comment frequently but makes no attempt to involve others
*shows a desire to contribute responsibly to the seminar

2   *participates verbally but shows impatience with seminar process
may make insightful comments but does so sparingly
may be argumentative and generally lacks poise
may be unfocused because of depth or length of seminar

1   *shows no respect for the learning environment
is argumentative and rude
takes advantage of or causes distractions
arrives unprepared with text, paper, or pen
wants the floor for himself and not to further the seminar
is writing personal notes instead of seminar notes
may actually attempt to sleep during the discussion

SPEAKING:
4   *speaks to all participants, not just to the facilitator
*avoids the urge to talk too long
speaks loudly enough to be heard by all
avoids using slang and incorrect grammar
*articulates clearly and precisely
pronounces words accurately and appears to know meanings

3   *addresses the majority of comments to peers, not the leader
*attempts to move the conversation onto a new idea
does not try to say "everything" while he is recognized
tries to speak louder when signaled to do so
may mumble or stumble over unfamiliar words but does so sparingly

2   speaks directly to teacher
speaks too softly and needs to be reminded to speak louder
routinely lapses into use of slang or substandard usage
cannot pronounce key words in the text

*speaks only with prompting and has no sustainable point

1   *is reluctant to speak when called on or passes in "round robin"
     mumbles and mispronounces words
     cannot be heard at all
     shows absolutely no desire to contribute verbally

REASONING:

4   understands the question that has been posed before answering
     *cites logical, relevant textual passages to support views
     *relates the reading to other readings or studies
     expresses thoughts in complete sentences
     adds to the seminar significantly with insightful comments
     *makes connections between own thoughts and those of others
     resolves contradictory ideas of self and peers
     considers all sources, not just his or her own
     avoids piggy-backing on inaccuracies

3   responds to questions without any prompting
     demonstrates some reflection on the text but not mastery of it
     *can make limited connections with ideas of other speakers
     can somewhat relate own ideas to other readings or seminars
     uses quotes or paraphrases but inferences are underdeveloped
     *makes comments that are intriguing enough to merit reaction

2   may have read the text but has not thought about it before seminar
     may overlook important points, thus leading to faulty logic
     *may be accurate on minor points while missing the main concept
     contributes opinions that have no textual support for them
     has some difficulty in formulating understandable comments

1   makes illogical comments
     *says no more than "I agree"
     ignores previous comments and directional movement of the seminar
     attempts to use humor to avoid having to do serious thinking

LISTENING:

4   *listens for opportunities to respond to student-generated questions
     does not overlook details
     writes down questions, comments, or ideas
     *avoids repetition of previous remarks of self and peers
     *builds on and acknowledges what other participants have said
     points out flawed reasoning
     overcomes any distractions

3   *is generally attentive and focused
*responds thoughtfully to ideas and questions that are raised
may be too absorbed with own thoughts to hear others' comments
may write down some thoughts, though does not consistently do
so

2   responds only to ideas that are personally interesting
asks for repetition of questions or for rephrasing of questions
takes very limited notes
may be easily distracted or may be the source of distraction
does not look up the text as it is cited by another student
*does not visibly respond to cited text; may be unaware of location

1   is inattentive to other speakers
exhibits the body language: "I'd rather be anywhere but here."
*makes comments that show total misinterpretation of material
may not listen well enough to understand points of others
takes no notes during the seminar

READING:

4   demonstrates the ability to pass a reading comprehension test
*is familiar with the text and can quickly locate quotations
*has marked the text or has a note sheet
*understands major concepts in the reading
identifies any contradictions in the reading

3   demonstrates ability to pass a reading comprehension quiz
*has marked the text or prepared notes
*can locate most references in the text when needed
demonstrates knowledge of facts, but may lack mastery of concepts
acknowledges difficulty with reading and asks for clarification

2   appears to have skimmed the selection and knows minimum on quiz
has little or no marking of text and has scanty notes
*is confused about key concepts because of hasty reading
makes comments that reflect shallow knowledge of first few pages

1   is clearly unprepared and fails reading quiz
*is unfamiliar with the text
has no notes or marking of text
asks for no help with the reading

Finally, it is often appropriate to provide postseminar activities. Figure 2.11 is an example of a task design rubric for such an activity; Figure 2.12 is the assessment rubric.

FIGURE 2.11. TASK DESIGN RUBRIC FOR POSTSEMINAR ON PLATO'S *APOLOGY*

GENERAL INFORMATION: A postseminar task is the third component of the seminar process. This task is designed to showcase what the seminar participant has learned from reading, discussing, and analyzing the text. The length of the task and the point value of the task may vary.

SUGGESTED PREPARATION ACTIVITIES:

1. Review the notes you took during the seminar.
2. Think about what each contributor said and the reasons for his or her position on issues.
3. Think about issues that received superficial coverage in the seminar.

TASK:

1. You are to write a response essay reflecting on what characteristics of Socrates you would like to possess in your own life.
2. The form of writing should be four or five paragraphs.
   a. The introduction should hook the reader, state the source, and present the thesis statement.
   b. Each body paragraph should explore a characteristic of Socrates that you want to have. State the characteristic and elaborate fully.
   c. The concluding paragraph should redirect attention on Socrates as an admirable character who has qualities worthy of possessing in a modern society.
3. Purpose: to explain and to reflect.
4. Point of view: first person.
5. Tone: Formal, standard English.

ASSESSMENT:

1. Total point value for seminar: 30 points.
2. Major focuses: essay writing form, elaboration of ideas, punctuation, usage, spelling, sentence structure, and originality of thinking.

FIGURE 2.12. POSTSEMINAR ASSESSMENT RUBRIC
FOR PLATO'S *APOLOGY*

We inform students of their final seminar grades by using this form. Copies of pre- and postseminar assessment rubrics are included with student writings.

POINTS EARNED:

1. Essay form (15)   _____
    a. paragraphing and sentence style
    b. thesis statement
    c. elaboration of reasons
    d. coherence and unity

2. Grammatical and mechanical accuracy (5)   _____
    a. spelling
    b. usage
    c. punctuation

3. Originality and depth of thought (5)   _____
    a. Factual accuracy
    b. Relevance of yourself

4. Point of view (3)   _____

5. Tone (2)   _____

6. TOTAL NUMBER OF POINTS EARNED: _____

TOTALS

_____ Preseminar (20)

_____ Seminar (50)

_____ Postseminar (30)

_____ FINAL SEMINAR GRADE

MODEL LESSON

Incorporating the seminar strategy into lesson plans is more complex than forming a circle and tossing out questions. Following specific steps ensures that students are prepared and facilitators are comfortable. The following model lesson culminates a unit on international diplomacy for sophomore world history and literature.

STEP 1: LESSON OBJECTIVES

Through text exploration, students will recognize that many principles that govern a healthy friendship are principles that need to be present in international relationships.

STEP 2: TEXT SELECTION

Seminar text includes both the "Town Mouse/Country Mouse" and an excerpt from Cicero's *On Friendship* (which gives his definition of a friendship). Additionally, students need their history notes on international diplomacy.

STEP 3: STUDENT PREPARATION

Students have two central responsibilities—first, to read and mark the text; second, to complete preseminar tasks.

STEP 4: TEACHER PREPARATION

The facilitator's task is to design questions based on lesson objectives. When teachers have several opening, core, and closing questions prepared, their confidence as leaders is enhanced. This models shows only one opening and one closing question.

Opening question
　　Which mouse in "Town Mouse/Country Mouse" would make
　　　　the better friend?
Core questions
　　What behaviors of the mice are desirable or undesirable
　　　　in friends?
　　In Cicero's *On Friendship*, what is his definition of a friendship?
　　What, according to Cicero, are the benefits and responsibilities
　　　　of a friendship?
Closing question
　　Ideally, how should principles of friendship be present
　　　　in international diplomacy?

STEP 5: SEMINAR

The facilitator leads the seminar and charts student responses. (Figure 2.9 provides a charting model.)

Students practice their skills in listening, speaking, reasoning, reading and conduct.

STEP 6: FOLLOW-UP

When the seminar ends, students complete postseminar tasks that enrich and extend learning. The length of these tasks may vary.

Providing a workable seminar model is never simple nor followed verbatim. It is a guide and nothing more. Teachers who rely heavily on prepared study guides don't do a great deal of original thinking. Likewise, a seminar leader who tries to use someone else's questions hasn't really prepared through reflective thinking. Students and teachers must learn from the seminar experience. For the teacher, much of this learning occurs during question development and anticipation of student responses. No two teachers will phrase questions the same or have identical objectives; consequently, there is no "crutch" on which teachers can lean for seminar preparation. It's hard work, but the results of lively seminar are payment enough. We recommend that teachers get feedback on their seminars both from students and colleagues. Figure 2.13 provides an instrument for self- or peer-assessment.

FIGURE 2.13. SELF-ASSESSMENT INSTRUMENT FOR FACILITATOR OR PEER COACH

Yes	No		
_____	_____	1.	Teacher collected preseminar assignments before beginning the seminar.
_____	_____	2.	Teacher asked for a moment of silence to allow students to block out extraneous conversations and to focus in on the text.
_____	_____	3.	Teacher had all charting and recordkeeping materials ready.

_____   _____   4. Teacher reminded students of at least one rule and one expectation before asking the opening question.

_____   _____   5. Teacher was seated on the same level as students.

_____   _____   6. Teacher refrained from giving his or her own opinion.

_____   _____   7. Teacher stated the opening question in clear and simple language.

_____   _____   8. Teacher asked follow-up and clarification questions.

_____   _____   9. Teacher listened well to students and allowed his or her questions to build on a student comment.

_____   _____   10. Teacher was comfortable with silence and allowed for wait time.

_____   _____   11. Teacher called on all students, recognizing new participants before calling on those who had already spoken.

_____   _____   12. Teacher firmly but gently corrected misbehavior by restating seminar rules.

_____   _____   13. Teacher spoke infrequently and then only briefly, thereby enabling students to feel in control of their seminar.

_____   _____   14. Teacher, by example, created an atmosphere of trust and respect.

_____   _____   15. Teacher clearly explained the requirements of the postseminar task and stated his or her expectations.

THE BOTTOM "LINE"

While Socratic seminars are manageable in any school structure, they offer schools with longer blocks of uninterrupted time a more natural and effective strategy for extended discussion. It is neither a simple nor entirely predictable strategy to facilitate when students are "on," speaking 97% of class time.

Leading Socratic seminars is akin to fly-fishing. The teacher throws out a question and floats the line, seeking a wide range of comments and evidences by students. Discussion may resemble Faulkner's stream of consciousness as one speaker's thoughts follow another, not always logically, but always moving, doubling back, subject to the prevailing winds. But then the fly fisherman reels in, tightens the slack by asking a follow-up question or returning to the original question. He pulls the line to the right or left with another core question and casts again with a closing question.

This is the skill of the bass master and the seminar leader. What they do looks easy, even effortless. It takes energy, intuitive listening, lots of practice and even a little faith to do it well. And the beneficiaries? Our "fish" are hungry. The pond is fully stocked. We need only have the proper bait and skilled fishermen to get them hooked. Socratic seminars are proving to be a most potent lure!

Finally, no teacher should assume that reading about how to conduct seminars is sufficient. That's comparable to a doctor performing heart surgery without ever having seen surgery or practiced it. Teachers need to attend workshops where they can practice leading seminars and have their questions answered by an experienced facilitator. Although seminar models may be useful, they cannot substitute for practice.

REFERENCES

Adler, M.J. (1982; 1984). *The Paideia proposal*. New York: Macmillian.
Adler, M.J., & Van Doren, C. (1972). *How to read a book*. New York: Simon & Schuster.

OTHER SOURCES

Adler, M.J. (1983). *How to speak, how to listen*. New York: Macmillian.
Briggs, I.M. (1980). Gifts differing. Palo Alto, CA: Consulting Psychologists Press.
Goodlad, J.I. (1984). *A place called school*. New York: McGraw.
Weiss, P.F. (1987). *Great ideas: A seminar approach to teaching and learning*. Chicago: Encyclopedia Britannica.

3

THE COLLABORATIVE CLASSROOM[1]

INTRODUCTION

The extended period challenges the classroom teacher to create an interesting learning environment that engages the attention of the student for a longer period of time, rather than providing an opportunity for the best nap of the day. Ninety or more minutes can be an eternity in some classes, but the lengthened period also offers the opportunity to create and execute activities that are engaging, exciting, and productive. One extremely valuable tool in any classroom is cooperative learning. Although effective in the shorter period, it is especially powerful for the block schedule. Approaching lesson planning with a cooperative mindset helps the teacher to construct a class where the students experience increased interaction with each other.

Cooperative learning strategies can provide different modes of learning. Lecture is still important, but it is not all that is done; shorter times of lecture are interrupted by having students work in pairs or small groups, discuss ideas together, check one another's understanding, and share conclusions with other groups and pairs in the classroom. Often, in a cooperative classroom, when an idea is presented, every student responds verbally to someone else, and many times students move around the room to discuss and gather information. Varying the modes of learning can increase the effective-

---

[1] This chapter was written by John D. Strebe, Math Teacher, Mt. Hebron High School, Howard County, MD.

ness of the learning environment, while making learning more fun for everyone.

Cooperative learning is a model of teaching that has received considerable attention in recent years. Educators such as Robert Slavin, Spencer Kagan, and David and Roger Johnson have written volumes on its use (Slavin, 1990; Kagan, 1990; Johnson, et al., 1990). The use of cooperative learning in the classroom involves implementing a process that creates a collaborative classroom environment. The basic steps of the cooperative learning process are introduced briefly in the first section of this chapter. Second, this process is applied to the messy reality of the classroom, an altogether more complex task.

COOPERATIVE LEARNING: THE PROCESS

The basic formula for implementing cooperative learning includes these steps:[2]

CLASS BUILDING

In this step of the process it is critical for students in a class to bond together as a cohesive group. All too often we leave this step to chance—hoping that the class will develop into a "good group." Get-to-know-you activities and group successes are proactive techniques that can be utilized to facilitate a positive classroom environment and esprit de corps.

It is unreasonable to expect students to work together cooperatively on content if no level of trust exists. Thus, activities are needed that enable students to learn each others' names, interests, likes and dislikes, to help develop a level of comfort among students that will make the success of cooperative teams more likely. Two sources of such activities are *Community Building in the Classroom* (Shaw, 1992) and *Schools Without Fear: Group Activities for Building Community* (Lehr & Martin, 1994).

Anytime a group meets with success, or for that matter cohesively weathers a failure, the group members become closer. Thus, challenging groups to achieve a certain attainable level of excellence and then helping the groups meet that challenge will draw the members closer together.

---

[2] Adapted from Kagan (1992).

TEAM FORMATION

Cooperative learning teams can be composed in three different manners: teacher selection, student selection, or random selection. Teachers often create cooperative learning teams by dividing students into groups of three, four, or five students. It is recommended that each team be heterogenous in composition, based primarily on the most important abilities or skills in a particular subject area, as well as on gender, racial or ethnic background, socioeconomic status, and/or a variety of other student characteristics. Student-selected teams, which may be more homogeneous, occasionally are used, especially when the focus of the teams' efforts will be a project requiring substantial effort outside school. Finally, teachers occasionally will create teams through random procedures such as lineups and numbering-off (Kagan, 1990). These groups typically are formed for the sole purpose of class building and stay together only a short time. Playing cards are used later in this chapter as a means of creating somewhat random teams.

TEAM BUILDING AND TEAM IDENTITY

Just as class building is utilized to draw the entire class together, the steps of team building and team identity are employed to bond a four- or five-person cooperative learning team together. Typically, get-to-know-you activities and activities that emphasize commonalities of the team members are employed to facilitate positive student interaction. Team identity is developed through the use of team names, team signs, team handshakes, team pictures, and a host of other strategies.

COOPERATIVE LEARNING STRUCTURES

"Structures" are activities that may be utilized and adapted to any grade level and any subject matter. Cooperative learning is far more complex than simply throwing an activity at a group of students and saying: "Work together on this task." We know what happens when this occurs. Certain students take over, either through force of their personality, or because no one else exhibits much interest in the task. Other students become "freeriders," do nothing, and create animosity because of their refusal to participate. Thus, structuring activities carefully is an important aspect of the successful cooperative learning classroom. To be effective, cooperative learning structures, at a minimum, must meet the following four criteria:

- The structure must have a **group goal**. A task must be created for students which results in a group product or group evaluation of some sort.

- The group goal must be met through the **face-to-face interaction** of all team members. In well-designed structures, team members do not toil in total independence. At least part of the work must be completed through discussion and interaction among members.

- The face-to-face interaction must result in a state of **positive interdependence** in which all student contributions are necessary and no one contribution is sufficient. This is the idea that the participation of all team members is necessary for success. If even one member does not pull his or her weight, the team cannot be successful. We sink or swim together.

- Finally, and perhaps most overlooked, although students are somewhat dependent upon each other, **individual accountability** is emphasized and carefully orchestrated. The essence of cooperative learning is that **"We work together, we learn together, but we are held individually accountable for our own learning."**

CELEBRATION AND REWARD

The final step of the process of implementing cooperative learning in the classroom is for team members to celebrate the group's successes. Often, as part of this step, group rewards and recognition are awarded.

APPLYING THE COOPERATIVE PROCESS
TO THE CLASSROOM

Ideally, the cooperative mind set is instilled beginning on the first day of school. There is no one right way to accomplish this goal; each individual teacher must find his or her own path. Trial and failure is a wonderful way to discover an appropriate means to establish a cooperative classroom, especially if an initial failure is followed by persistence and finally success. Do not try too much all at once, but do try something manageable that can be mastered to a high degree of excellence. Repeat the process with another cooperative structure until you possess a library of tools that can be pulled from the shelf with ease.

CLASS BUILDING

Spending longer blocks of time together can increase the importance of peer relationships in the classroom. A necessary activity for creating a cooperative environment is for students to develop respect for themselves and an appreciation for their classmates. Part of this process is accomplished best by allowing students to know each other multidimensionally, to see below the surface, beyond hairstyle, clothes, and shoes. Students need to consider other students as additional resources towards successful learning. Students must recognize the importance of individual talents, yet realize they are better together than they are apart.

FORMING INITIAL TEAMS

One way to help students experience a cooperative environment on the first day of school is to organize them into groups of four, after first allowing them to sit wherever they wish. Usually, students will choose to sit with their best friends; however, this seating arrangement will be changed almost immediately. Classroom furniture is arranged in a way that encourages students to sit in groups, either four desks together or small tables with four chairs or large tables with eight chairs, four at each end.

Playing cards can be used effectively to help students to get to know each other and to establish informal, but temporary, groups. For example, in a class with 24 students, the cards numbered two through seven (24 cards, 6 per suit) are distributed to students sitting in the groups which they have chosen. To ensure that new acquaintances are made, the first four students sitting together are given the two, three, four, and five of hearts and the next table of four is given the six and seven of hearts and two and three of clubs. This pattern continues until all the cards have been issued. Students are asked to stand up and find a partner from a different group who has a card of a **different color and different value**. The pairs are asked to face each other and think silently about something memorable from the summer. In pairs, the partner holding the red card shares the summer memory with the partner with the black card and then the black card partner shares a summer memory with the red card partner. They thank each other and are told to find a new partner who is holding a card of the **same color and different value**. The thinking-sharing-thanking process is repeated with a different question such as, "What was your favorite class last school year and why did you like it?" Now students are instructed to find the other people holding **the same value card**, to stand in a group of four, and to memorize the month and day (not the year) of the birth date of all four members of the group. The last task for each group is to decide where to sit together and move themselves and their belongings to the new location.

This process "randomly" forms new groups; all the friends who chose to sit together when they arrived are now spread throughout the classroom in different groups. At a later time, when students better understand productive cooperation, good friends can and should be in the same group. Often, a month of cooperative experience is sufficient time for students to reach this point.

When the administration does not cooperate and sends a number of students other than a multiple of four, a slight modification needs to be made. If 25 students are in the class, you might want to create four groups of four students and three groups of three students by using the cards numbered two, three, four, and five from all suits and three cards each numbered six, seven, and eight. Make sure to use four reds and five blacks among these nine cards. The extra black card can pair with the teacher during the sharing or one trio of students can be allowed. Similar adjustments should be made for other numbers of students. If you have an even number of students, then have the same number of black and red cards. If a five-member group is desired, then for 24 students hand out the cards from all suits numbered two through seven and one ace. The ace is assigned to one of the groups making a group of five members. What is wonderful about this activity is that even when completely wrong categories of cards have been distributed, it still can be made to work. Personal experience of the author validates this, but a bit of spontaneous creativity is required. Students are very forgiving and often will enjoy helping the teacher become skilled at these new ideas.

One helpful suggestion is to have laminated numbers hanging from the ceiling over each table or cluster of chairs for easy identification of a particular group of students. Additionally, the hanging numbers identify centers where the students can arrange furniture into groups, which is especially helpful when changing from a pairs task to a team activity. Because furniture sometimes is rearranged the morning after a rug cleaning or floor waxing, the identified locations allow teams to reform without chaos or confusion.

TEAM BUILDING

Now that the students are together, a sense of oneness must be established. Sometimes a group of people determine very quickly that they cannot possibly work together because they do not share anything in common. One thing to share is the great feeling of group success. At this point the teacher might ask, "Does anyone want to take a risk and recite all the birth dates of your team?" Usually a student, like Jon, will volunteer and correctly give the dates. The teacher might say to the class, "Tell Jon, great job!" The class responds and the teacher should say something like, "Jon, could you have done that without the help of your team?" Of course, Jon needed his team to accomplish the task. The teacher might say, "That is how we are going to learn in here this year! We will get help from others and we will give help to others. We will accomplish more together than we could have apart." At this point another person might be given the opportunity to give the birth dates. Rewards at this time should be team rewards. If tangible rewards are used, such as lollipops, let Jon distribute them to the entire team to reinforce the team contribution.

All of us have much in common; bringing students to this realization greatly contributes to their effectiveness as a team. One way to accomplish this is to have each team complete a "Things in Common" (TIC) sheet (Fig. 3.1). A TIC sheet asks students to agree upon a list of common likes and dislikes for a variety of categories such as foods, movies, actors, music groups, or TV shows.

FIGURE 3.1. THINGS IN COMMON SHEET

TEAM #_____

TEAM NAME _____

WE ALL WE ALL WE ALL WE ALL WE ALL WE ALL WE ALL

                    LIKE   DISLIKE

One
Food

One
Place To Go

One
Activity

One
Movie Or TV Show

One
(Your Choice)

To begin the activity the teacher might say, "Send me the person from each team whose birth date comes earliest in the year." This group of students, one from each team, is given 2 minutes to return to their respective teams and use the TIC sheet to gather common likes and dislikes from the team members. One sheet is used for each team. The interviewer asks his or her team for a food they all like. They all must like this food, although it does not have to be everyone's favorite. Then a food they all dislike is shared. If three people dislike liver, but one likes liver, then this food cannot be written. This continues for each activity, movie or TV show, place to go, and so on, until the TIC sheet is complete. The team is told to crowd over their completed lists and reflect that they share 10 or more things in common. Some teams finish early and are encouraged to obtain additional results for some of the categories.

At this point the interviewers bring the completed sheets to the teacher, who shuffles the papers, chooses one, and encourages the class to guess which team is being described as the teacher makes up a story using the TIC sheets. For example, one team's sheet might inspire the following ad-libbed story: "This team could go out for dinner together and have pizza, but they would never have brussels sprouts on their pizza. Where would they eat pizza without the sprouts? Why, at the beach of course; but while at the beach they would not go to school. What would they do? They would shop, but they would not do homework. In the evening they would all watch *Forrest Gump*, but if *Mary Poppins* came on, they would turn it off. They would then hop into their Firebird to get more pizza, but no one would go to bed early. Which team is it?"

Encourage the teams to talk about their choice so they can make a team guess as to which team has been described. (Remember, numbers are hanging above the teams for easy identification.) When a team correctly guesses the identity of the team being described, a team reward can be given; or if the guess is incorrect, the team described in the reading can be given the reward. Usually, students beg to try again with another team. After a few days, all teams have been described using the TIC sheets. More importantly, teams are beginning to break down barriers and increase communication. This increased awareness of others happens not only within the teams but among the entire class as well.

TWO COOPERATIVE LEARNING STRUCTURES

There are hundreds of cooperative learning structures. Round-table and Think/Pair/Share offer easy implementation and powerful results.

ROUNDTABLE

A simple way for students to realize the value of teamwork and achieve team excellence is to play roundtable sums. Ask the students to be completely quiet. The student with the latest birth date in the year is instructed to take out a piece of paper and put the team number at the top. Directions for roundtable sums are given. The teacher writes a two-digit number on the board, and when it is each team member's turn, a number, a plus sign, and a number are written by the student such that the sum equals the number on the board. After writing, the student passes the paper to the next team member in the circle, who writes a sum using different addends. The goal for each competing team is to write the most number facts without duplication in the allotted time. Students are not allowed to communicate in any way. The roundtable continues for 60 seconds, allowing for several cycles of the paper. A signal to stop is given and the score for each team is determined.

For example, if the teacher gives the number 64, one team's response might be:

$$20 + 44 \qquad 35 + 29$$
$$2 + 62 \qquad 16 + 48$$
$$29 + 35 \qquad 20 + 44$$
$$38 + 36 \qquad 63 + 1$$

This team's score is 6, since 20 + 44 is listed twice and 38 + 36 is not 64. The team records its score.

Now the teacher might say, "Do you think if you were given an opportunity to strategize, you could improve your score?" The teams are given a chance to talk and to agree upon a different way to do the activity. Students may need to be reminded that each student must write a number, a plus sign, and a number each turn. More than one wily team has tried to have one student write all the plus signs, another write one column of numbers, another write another column of numbers, and the last student pass the paper! This strategy is illegal!

Make sure the teams agree on their new strategy, give them a different number, and start the clock. After 60 seconds, determine each team's new score. Then compute the difference between the first score and the second score (the improvement score). In most cases, the second scores are much better. This allows students to experience how team interaction improves performance. The teacher might say something like, "That's the way we are going to learn this year—together. If you will work together, generally you will do better." Rewards and recognition can be given to the team that scores the highest as well as the team that improves the most.

THINK/PAIR/SHARE (TPS)

Since questions are a part of every teaching situation, how questions are asked is a vital area of concern. Many times students answer before giving adequate thought to the real content of a question. Often students give ridiculous answers to questions, sometimes sincere and sometimes not. Several years ago, Frank Lyman studied how to ask questions cooperatively; the outcome was a method called Think/Pair/Share (McTighe & Lyman, 1988). Classrooms where Think/Pair/Share is correctly used foster deeper thinking, greater student response, a reduction in risk and embarrassment, and less panic among the students. Additionally, more students feel included in the learning; in fact, because each student is accountable to someone else, more of them are involved in the learning. Every student reacts to the question and interacts with a partner. This method is so powerful that it should be taught beginning the first day of kindergarten!

The concept can be briefly described in this way. Each person in the classroom picks or is assigned a partner. The teacher asks students to enter the Think Mode and then poses a question. After 3 seconds of "wait time," students are instructed to enter Pair Mode and discuss possible responses with their partners. Students then "Share" their responses as the teacher calls upon students randomly or solicits volunteers.

FIGURE 3.2. THINK/PAIR/SHARE

THINK MODE

- The teacher instructs students to enter Think mode by pointing to the head, pointing to a THINK sign in the room, saying "Think mode," holding up a ping pong paddle with "THINK" on it or through some other signal.
- The teacher asks a question and establishes wait time.
- Students do not communicate to anyone (may write ideas down).
- Students refrain from shouting out.
- No hands are raised (too distracting, causes panic by others).
- Students who finish early are asked to create a defense for their answers.

PAIR MODE

- Teacher indicates Pair mode by raising two fingers, another paddle, etc.
- Students lean toward each other and communicate with their partner about the question.
- Students discuss a defense for their conclusions, rehearsing their response.
- Students use a "whisper voice" to discuss.
- Students refrain from shouting out.
- No hands are raised.
- Students come to agreement or they agree to disagree.

SHARE MODE

- The teacher indicates Share mode with a hand up, a paddle, etc.
- Teacher calls on students randomly or students raise hands to respond.
- Students refrain from shouting.
- Students share responses and defenses with the class in a variety of ways.

and Sometimes
TEAM MODE (or SQUARE MODE)

- Teacher indicates Team mode by a stirring motion with the hand.
- Students lean toward the center of the group and do everything that is done in Pair mode, attempting to arrive at a "team answer."

Not all questions need to be asked using this structure, but certainly key questions, at least, deserve this treatment. Students are protected in Think and Pair mode; they gain confidence during discussion with their partners and are more willing to respond before the entire class. Perhaps two of the most outstanding qualities of Think/Pair/Share are that students begin to view each other as resources and that no students are left out of the learning activity. There should be no outcasts in cooperative learning. The Pair Mode brings every student into the fray. Additionally, the opportunity is provided for the teacher to assist the students in the development of social skills. It is truly a cooperative activity that allows all students to address and respond to questions. Think/Pair/Share helps to create a cooperative climate in the classroom.

Students must be taught this approach to thinking and responding; with repeated practice, maximum benefit can be experienced in each mode. Each mode stands alone and can be taught and practiced independently. When cooperative teams are present in the classroom, an additional mode called Team (or Square) Mode is required. Often this step, which involves all team members conferring together, either follows or takes the place of Pair Mode.

These modes can and should be used in various combinations. For example, the sequence Think/Pair/Think/Square is effective for "tough" questions, with more clues given during the second Think time. Think/Pair/Share/Think helps students to reflect upon what was shared. Occasionally, it may be advisable to employ Think Mode and then immediately move to Share Mode, so that students cannot always rely upon a peer (in Pair or Team Modes) to provide them with an answer.

Teachers are often the culprits when Think Mode is violated. Some will ask, "What is the theme of this book?" Students will immediately raise their hands or blurt out an answer. After all, the teacher did ask for an answer to a question. Instead, a teacher could say, "Let's think about the theme of this book." Now, students are more inclined to think rather than answer. It is good to have a nonverbal cue to remind students to lower their hands when they forget and raise them prematurely. One cue is for the teacher to have arms and hands extended to silently "push down" the students' arms. Using Think/Pair/Share encourages teachers to ask carefully constructed higher order questions requiring deeper student thought. With practice, TPS becomes less artificial, more natural and internalized, for both the teacher and students.

TEAM FORMATION REVISITED: MOVING TO MORE PERMANENT TEAMS

The initial teams formed on the first day of school were constructed without attention to personality or ability and will probably not be as effective as desired. Teacher observation and student performance will allow the teacher to reform the class into new, well-balanced groups. Until that occurs, the first teams could sit together each day, or students might sit in their teams just at certain times to accomplish group goals. In any case, at some time goodbyes should be said and new teams allowed to get to know each other. Again, a new team might learn one another's birth dates and do a "Things In Common" sheet to see how much they do have in common.

Using the completed "Things in Common" sheets, teams can be encouraged to create a team name that describes their group. The team name becomes a focus for team pride; everyone wants to achieve excellence so the team will look good. The members of the "Sleeping Pizzas" help each other study for the quiz so the number on the scoreboard next to their team name will be the highest one. Some examples of team names are: The Beach Bums, Pizzerias, The Snow Skiers, The Gump Group, The Mountain Climbers, and The $ Seekers. Team names should be uplifting, decent, and agreed upon by the entire team. Several days may be needed for some teams to arrive at just the right name. While they may work unnamed for a while, the name finally agreed upon will instill pride. Occasionally, a team will need the teacher's assistance in obtaining a name.

After the name has been chosen, a means to display the team name becomes necessary. One way is to have the students use magic markers and artistically display their name with artwork on a piece of paper that is then posted (using tape rollbacks) on a laminated "scoreboard" with the other team names from the class. After a while, students begin to love that name and work for team glory as the teacher uses remarks like, "Wow, The Chocolate Lovers were awesome this week!"

As new teams are formed throughout the year, new and

different ways of creating team names can be used. In February as "March Madness" approaches, college and university names can be used for team names. Students can be allowed to create names from a list of topics from the next subject unit. Given a Greek alphabet students will generate some memorable names like "The Mu Cows" or "The Apple Pi's." Professional sports teams can be used as the sources for team names. Use your own creativity and wondrous ideas come forth. Identification with a team is crucial and should be encouraged by the teacher. Unlike a baseball team, students do not wear team uniforms, but like a sports team, the team's success is made up of individual excellence and cooperative accomplishment. When a student correctly answers a question or makes an outstanding point, a good response might be, "Sara, you really have made an excellent observation. You and your team, The Licorice Lovers, are something else!" The individual student is given recognition, but within the context of the team.

The team names become rallying flags for good performance. Often, gentle team competition can be an asset to increased study and effort on the part of students who wish their team to have success. This can be accomplished in several ways, three of which are briefly described below: the raw score competition, improvement points, and Carolina Teams. In all approaches, the team performance is described by a number of points which is posted next to the team name. Points are allowed to accumulate for a short period of time, perhaps 1 or 2 weeks, after which a champion is crowned. The old points are erased, the teams remain the same, and a new competition is begun, with another champion crowned after 1 or 2 additional weeks. In classes where six or more teams are required, it may be helpful to have two divisions, crowning a champion in each, rather than one per class. The teacher must decide which type of competition best suits a particular class, perhaps consulting the class for input that will be helpful in making the right choice. Once a decision has been made, learning activities are designed, learning opportunities presented and assignments given. At some point, evaluation of learning occurs, often measured by a numerical rating (i.e. a quiz score).

RAW SCORE COMPETITION

Each student receives a numerical grade, which is recorded in the gradebook. The individual grades of each team member are averaged for a team score and this team score is posted on the scoreboard. Team recognition is given using praise and/or some reward or special privilege. Although students have cooperated during the learning process, they usually take the quiz without the help of a teammate. This preserves individual accountability, which is essential if everyone is to master the necessary skills. At times it is appropriate to take pair quizzes or team quizzes, but a regular use of this method can result in some students "riding on the coattails of others" as well as some students feeling used by teammates. The result can be a decrease in team interaction as one or two students do all the work.

Team competition with raw scores requires that teams be formed with a balance of scoring power in mind. Try to have the teams as equal as possible with regard to team scoring potential.

Raw score teams are not appropriate when one or more students score extremely low, even though great effort has been expended by the student and the team. Generally, classes of homogeneous ability, like a calculus class, are best suited to this type of scoring.

IMPROVEMENT POINTS

Another option that can be used in all classes, but especially in those with heterogeneous composition, is to measure and record the improvement of each team member, posting the combined improvement total on the scoreboard. One classroom proven structure is Student Teams Achievement Divisions (STAD), developed at The Johns Hopkins University under the direction of Robert Slavin (1986, 1991). Each student is assigned a target score that reflects the student's past performance, yet can be beaten with reasonable effort. One version of STAD restricts that target to a multiple of 5. For instance, a student with an 83 average could be given 80 as a target. Depending on how that student does relative to the target, improvement points are earned by each individual for the team. One example of a STAD-type scoring system (Fig. 3.3) is applied to the performance of the "Four Wonders" in Figure 3.4.

FIGURE 3.3. STAD SCORING SYSTEM

Student Performance	Improvement Points Earned
A Perfect Paper	30 Points
Beat target by 11 or more	30 Points
Equal target or beat it by 1 to 10	20 Points
Fall short of target by 1 to 10	10 Points
Fall short of target by more than 10	0 Points

The team improvement average is recorded on the scoreboard. For example:

FIGURE 3.4. THE 4 WONDERS

Student	Target	Quiz Score	Improvement Points
Katie	95	100	30
Nathan	90	96	20
Matt	85	80	10
Anna	80	69	0

The team average of improvement points is 15, a number which is written next to their team name on the scoreboard.

Targets can be altered after every two evaluations to provide proper incentive for the student. STAD is a wonderful creation that encourages the best students to be better and nudges low-achieving students to excellence. It creates a level playing field for all students to be able to contribute to team success equally. A student with a 55 target, due to past performance, can contribute 30 points to the team by earning a 66, the same as a student with a 95 target who scores 100. We do this in several competitive sports so that all players have hope for success. In golf, handicaps are determined based on past performance so that any of us, with a proper target, can compete evenly with Greg Norman on an 18-hole round. Without a proper scoring allowance, the match would be over quickly, incentive would be missing, and failure imminent. Many students also feel that they cannot have success, ever! We all can improve, especially when we have the opportunity to contribute. STAD offers this possibility to all students.

STAD teams should be formed by grouping one High achiever,

two Average achievers and one Low achiever per team. For three- and five-member teams, use HAL and HAAAL composition. The sum potential for improvement should be approximately equal on all teams. A HHAL team has less improvement potential than a HAAL team. The high-achieving student has less "room" above the target than a low-achieving student. As with all team formation, give special attention to personalities and team dynamics. Always ask the question, "Do I think that this team will work well together or will learn to work well together?"

When student papers are returned, both the grade and the improvement score are recorded on the paper. Students soon will begin to work to become a member of the "30-Point Club," and the 30 on the paper signifying maximum improvement (and therefore, maximum contribution to the team) becomes the greater goal. The earning of a 30 for improvement results in congratulations by the team. Of course, the teacher sets the proper stage for this to occur, by encouraging the team to recognize the 20- or 30-point scorers. Teams need to be reminded of the contribution of the entire team to the learning success. Additionally, the team that may have groaned at the placement of certain classmates on their team now values the contributions of these lower achievers.

Imagine a student who has always failed in math who now receives 30 improvement points for the team by beating the 55 target by 11 points. That student is a superstar for the day. This can incite excellence by that student. In the past, a 66 would deserve no special recognition, but STAD rewards the improvement. Soon the target will go up to perhaps 65, requiring a score of 76 to earn 30 points. The student becomes hungry for the 30 and is nudged to success.

Students who are top performers feel the necessity to submit quality work and are more careful so that perfect papers can be submitted, resulting in 30 points for the team. STAD is a structure that can give every student a sense of worth.

CAROLINA TEAMS

Rather than assigning individual target scores for each team member, another choice is to assign a team target score, a number that reflects the combined performance of the individual team members prior to being placed on the team. This target becomes the goal for the team, a target achieved through cooperative effort, but individual test taking. For a team of four people with the averages of 90, 80, 96, and 90, the team target might be 89, the average of these scores. The team strives to be the best for the glory of The Pizza Eaters, and the individual test scores are 95, 87, 98, and 92 for an average of 93. That is fine improvement. The Carolina System provides both a team reward and an individual reward. Individual students receive bonus points added to the grade before the score is recorded in the gradebook. The bonus for reaching the target is set by the teacher and may vary according to the composition and/or level of the class. For example, if a 3-point bonus is offered, the scores recorded would be 98, 90, 101, and 95. The team is rewarded for being better together than they were apart. If the team does not equal or exceed their target, there is no penalty; points are not deducted from their grades, and scores without bonus are recorded.

The team performance can be recorded by computing a simple percent—that is, the percent of the team target that the team achieved. The formula is:

Team Score = $\dfrac{\text{Team Quiz Average}}{\text{Team Target}} \times 100$

For the team performance described above, the computation of team points would be:

Team Average = (95 + 87 + 98 + 92)/4 = 93.
Team Score = 93/89 x 100 = 104.5

A score of 105 would be posted next to this team's name on the scoreboard.

The students soon realize that a score of 100 means that the team hit its target exactly; a score less than 100 means a disappointment of having fallen short of the team target, and a score greater than 100 indicates that the team exceeded the target and should celebrate! As with STAD, after a week or two team scores are compared and a champion is crowned. The scoreboard is then erased and a new competition begins between the same teams.

When papers are returned to a Carolina Team, the student on a team who has earned the bonus receives a paper that looks like this:

	John Strebe		Unit Exam	
	~~95~~	98!		
1.	6.	11.	16.	
2.	7.	12.	17.	
3.	8.	13.	18.	
4.	9.	14.	19.	
5.	10.	15.	20.	

The 95 changed to a 98 becomes a beautiful sight, a status symbol, and a reason for team celebration. A good question to ask a student who has received such a paper is, "Why is your original grade changed to a 98?" The answer reminds the entire team that they have worked well together. Often the question needs to be asked, "What is the best way to improve your grade?" This is followed by the team or the class shouting the answer in chorus, "By helping my teammates!"

After every two quizzes or evaluations, a new team target needs to be computed. This number will tend to follow the team performance. One method is to compute the average of the two team scores and the team target. For example, suppose a team with a target of 90 had team quiz averages of 92 and 94. We could compute the new team target as follows:

$$\text{New Target} = \frac{92 + 94 + 90}{3} = 92$$

Generally, this method proves quite satisfactory, although common sense should be the major resource for establishing new scores.

A place to record these Carolina points needs to be located. Sometimes, a folder with score sheets inside is a simple solution. Such a score sheet is shown in Figure 3.5 (on pages 90–91).

The Carolina system seems to be more flexible for forming teams than the STAD system; it allows for more homogeneous teams at times. Sometimes it is especially profitable for high-achieving students to work together. After all, someday in the real world they will work together with other high achievers on sophisticated projects. Heterogeneous teams also are appropriate for Carolina Teams.

Once teams have been formed, it is important to help the students experience the value of team interaction. These team-building experiences are an essential aspect of developing effective teams.

One effective team-builder can occur after the return of a quiz. Students are encouraged to work with their teammates to completely and thoroughly correct mistakes on the quiz and to submit the corrections to regain a percentage of the points lost. Through this process, students discover their peers to be valuable resources and are motivated to work together more powerfully before the next quiz to reduce errors. Usually the corrected papers are not rewarded with additional team points on the scoreboard.

1–2–4 ACTIVITY PLAN: COOPERATIVE WORKSHEETS

"One, two, four" (1–2–4) is a wonderful team builder in which students complete worksheets cooperatively. Often when such a task is attempted by a group, one dynamic person takes leadership at the expense of other students' contributions. To make this activity truly cooperative, each student is instructed to complete the assignment individually. After an appropriate length of time, students are allowed to pair with a teammate to discuss their independent work, achieving consensus in some cases and disagreeing in others. Now the teams form and a discussion leader is appointed to help each team decide upon final team conclusions, after which a class sharing is conducted. Each person has been able to address the assignment without interruption, knowing that the accountability of a partner's questions was coming in the near future. A final defense of answers to the team results in a deepening of thought for this activity. 1–2–4 is the application of Think/Pair/Team/Share to an activity, enabling worksheets to be done cooperatively in much the same manner that questions are asked cooperatively in TPS.

FIGURE 3.5. CAROLINA TEAMS SCORE SHEET

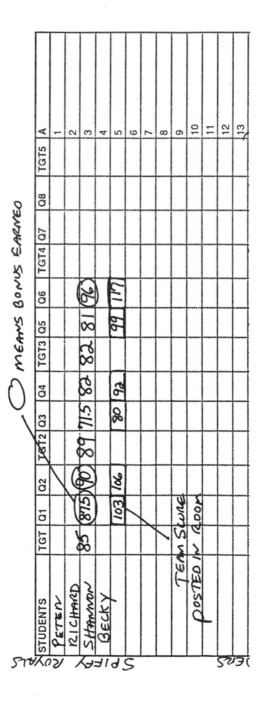

STUDENTS	TGT	Q1	Q2	TGT2	Q3	Q4	TGT3	Q5	Q6	TGT4	Q7	Q8	TGT5	A
PETER	85	87.5	90	89	71.5	80	82	81	96					1
RICHARD														2
SHANNON														3
BECKY		103	106		80	92		99	117					4
														5
														6
														7
														8
														9
														10
														11
														12
														13

○ MEANS BONUS EARNED

TEAM SCORE POSTED IN ROOM

SPIFFY ROYALS

THE 4 WINDS

TARGET MET (BONUS GIVER)

Minki													
Wade	85	96	98	90	99	97	95.5	95	100	105	95	91.5	95.8
Tim													
David	113	115	110	106		107	111		96	101			
Sam	88	90	88	89	86	98	93	90	90	94	95		
Lori													

TEAM POINTS PUT ON CHART IN ROOM

KEPT AT 95 BECAUSE I WAS STOPPING EXTRA CREDIT QUESTIONS FOR NEXT 2 QUIZZES.

THIS IS A CAROLINA PAIN; NO TEAM POINTS.

To introduce students to the procedures and value of this activity, a fun competition can be conducted using a series of questions requiring diverse knowledge and some critical thinking. One example is a series of questions about the Toronto Skydome (Fig. 3.6). Ten points are awarded on the team scoreboard for each correct team answer and the top-scoring team is rewarded for its excellent work. Only team answers are valid. To protect all students, especially those less inclined to dominate a discussion, students should work a short time on their own. They then pair up to make decisions, and then have a team discussion. Students experience the value of working together after being allowed to think on their own. They also see the need to consider everyone's opinion and arguments, especially when a correct answer is ignored due to personality.

The 1 mode can be a homework assignment, occurring in the evening. The 2 mode can occur at the beginning of class, followed by a team consensus, the 4 mode. Learning deepens for the individual student and the number of students involved increases. The multimodality of the activity keeps the extended period from becoming monotonous and boring.

PERSONAL SHARE PAIRS

Getting students to work well together can be a difficult task. Students often see one another superficially, never moving beyond the outward appearances of hairstyle and clothes. This lack of understanding keeps biases and prejudices in place and makes it difficult to work together effectively. Students need to understand that people have many more commonalities than differences. At the same time, we need to help them appreciate one another's differences, changing them from barriers that separate to windows of relationship which enlighten. Team builders enable this process. The following activity is an effective team builder.

Students sit in their cooperative teams and observe while the teacher models parts of the activity. A student is asked to be the timekeeper and to signal when a minute has passed. The teacher creates a T chart on the board or on newsprint; the two columns are labeled LIKES and DISLIKES. The teacher's name is written at the top of the chart. When the class hollers "Go!," the teacher writes

FIGURE 3.6. 1–2–4 USING THE TORONTO SKYDOME

THE TORONTO SKYDOME IS A FABULOUS ARENA WITH THE WORLD'S
FIRST FULLY RETRACTABLE ROOF. IT HOUSES SEVERAL ATHLETIC TEAMS
AND SERVES AS A MUSIC PALACE. SEATING OVER 50,000 PEOPLE, THE
SKYDOME, LOCATED IN TORONTO, CANADA, ALSO CONTAINS
RESTAURANTS, STORES, A HOTEL AND OFFICES. IT IS TRULY A WONDER
OF ENGINEERING AND CONSTRUCTION.

HERE ARE 10 MULTIPLE CHOICE QUESTIONS ABOUT THE SKYDOME.
THINK CAREFULLY, BECAUSE <u>YOUR TEAM WILL RECEIVE TEAM POINTS</u>
FOR EACH <u>CORRECT</u> ANSWER. WHEN IT IS TIME FOR CONSENSUS,
<u>CONSIDER EACH PERSON'S RESPONSE</u> BEFORE SELECTING A TEAM
RESPONSE.

A) The Skydome is the home of the   1. Astros   2. Mariners   3. Expos   4. Blue Jays

B) The Dome is located on Lake   1. Ontario   2. Erie   3. George

C) The roof can be closed only when it rains.   1. True   2. False

D) In 1991 the Dome hosted the All-star Game. Who won the homerun contest and also
    hit a homerun during the actual game?   1. Mark McGwire   2. Cecil Fielder
                                                              3. Cal Ripken, Jr.

E) How long does it take for the roof to open or close as it moves 71 feet per minute?
           1. 5 minutes   2. 20 minutes   3. 1 hour

F) At its highest point, how tall a building could fit inside the Dome?
           1. 100 stories   2. 31 stories   3. a 2 story colonial and no higher

G) Of the 88 washrooms, how many are for women, if you know that 6 are
    'Family Service' facilities for the care of children and infants? Hint: That leaves 82
    adult bathrooms.
           1. 41   2. 39   3.   43

H) How many Boeing 747's can fit on the Skydome's playing field?
           1. 20   2. 4   3.   8

I) What is something that is never allowed in a seat at the Skydome?
           1. smoking   2. holding hands   3. drinking alcohol

J) The hydraulic pitcher's mound is elevated to field level and locked in place for the
    baseball game. After the game, the liquid is drained and the mound is lowered to make
    the field level. What liquid is used to fill the chamber?
           1. oil   2. beer   3. water

<u>ANSWERS</u> a)4 b)1 c)2 d)3 e)2 f)2 g)3 h)3 i)1 j)3

as many personal likes and dislikes as time permits, probably stretching the minute a bit. The result looks something like Figure 3.7.

Figure 3.7. Likes and Dislikes T-Chart

JONATHAN YEUNG

Likes	Dislikes
WIFE	RUDENESS
KIDS	BAD DRIVING
GARDEN	WEEDS
BASKETBALL	LOSING
ORIOLES	INTENSE NEATNESS
GOLF	WHINING
ROMANTIC MOVIES	SNOWMEN (a golf term)
NEATNESS	BROKEN MACHINES
USC	CELTICS

Now the teacher asks students to make a T-chart on pieces of their own paper, writing neatly. Several minutes are allotted for individuals to complete this task. Students then are asked to consider other interesting preferences, such as a famous historical or contemporary figure with whom they would enjoy spending a day. Typically, names of athletes, war heroes, inventors, Hollywood stars, artists, leaders of movements, authors, musicians or musical groups, characterize the students' responses. Sometimes an appropriate question to have students think about is, "What would you hope to gain from being with that person for a day?" Students also could be asked to write a brief statement of their purpose in life. Sometimes this evokes an interesting discussion about purpose, with many examples, and the observation that today's purpose could very well change next week. Hopefully, students begin to think about living directed, purposeful lives. The students may go back and add information as time permits.

At this time students are asked to stop writing and enter Think mode to focus on the teacher's list and possible questions that could be asked about the various likes and dislikes. Students pair up and share their questions with their partners while in Pair mode, after which they raise hands and in rapid fire fashion ask the teacher about likes and dislikes. For example, "What kinds of things do you grow?" or "What is the difference between neatness and intense neatness?" or "What's this about snowmen?" This part of the activity is fun for everyone and helps students to feel closer to their teacher as well as to understand that teachers are human too.

After a while, it is the students' turn to read each other's lists and ask questions. Remember, the purpose of this activity is for students to know each other better, to lower the barriers to conversation, and to lessen biases so they will work together more effectively with the subject matter being taught.

With three-, four-, or five-person teams, three rounds are required to complete the sharing session. Figure 3.8 illustrates possible rotations. In each phase, the teacher should instruct students to do the following: Exchange Papers; Briefly Gaze at Your Partner; Read Your Partner's Paper; and Take Turns Asking and Answering Questions About Each Other.

During this questioning period, the teacher walks around the room, listening to conversations, learning about students, and assisting students in asking questions. As each round comes to a conclusion students are encouraged to return to the Think mode to Reflect upon the uniqueness of their partner, after which they express thanks for the sharing and perhaps even shake hands. Papers are returned and the next round ensues.

Perhaps all papers can be collected by one person in each group and given to the teacher for some enjoyable private reading. Generally, after this activity has been completed the members of teams feel much closer to each other and group efficiency is vastly improved. Although the extended block provides sufficient time for this activity as well as significant subject matter study, an attractive option is to divide the activity into segments and stretch the process over several days. Often the middle of a 90-minute block is a profitable time to complete part of this process.

In some classes, students are not eager to write about themselves on totally blank paper. Prepared sheets can be used instead (Fig. 3.9).

A very similar activity can be accomplished without writing. The team is given a piece of poster board divided into quadrants (teams should be no larger than 4) and each person is assigned one of the quadrants. Using scissors, glue, and magazine pictures,

---

FIGURE 3.8. POSSIBLE TEAM ROTATIONS

Teams of 4

Round 1: Your partner is opposite you. (1 & 2; 3 & 4)
Round 2: Your partner is next to you. (1 & 3; 2 & 4)
Round 3: Your partner is diagonal from you. (1 & 4; 2 & 3)

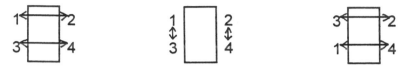

Teams of 5

Two people are "twins" and function as one person. The partner matched with the twins must read 2 papers and question 2 people at the same time.

Round 1: Your partner is opposite you. (1 & 2; 3 & 4, 5)
Round 2: Your partner is across from you. (1 & 3; 2 & 4, 5)
Round 3: Your partner is diagonal from you. (1 & 4, 5; 2 & 3)

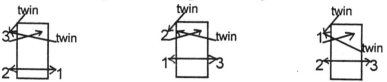

Teams of 3

Each person is assigned the number 1, 2, or 3.

Round 1: Students 2 and 3 question student 1.
Round 2: Students 1 and 3 question student 2.
Round 3: Students 1 and 2 question student 3.

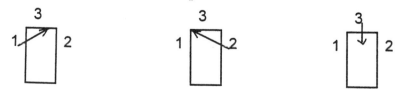

FIGURE 3.9. "WHO I AM" PREPARED SHEET

NAME _____

<u>FAVORITE THINGS</u> (COLORS, FOODS, PLACES TO GO, THINGS
TO DO, TV SHOWS, HOBBIES, MOVIES, MUSIC, ETC.)

<u>THINGS I DON'T LIKE</u>

<u>WHAT I LIKE TO DO IN SUMMER</u>

<u>MY FUTURE HOPES</u>

<u>THE PERSON ALIVE NOW OR WHO LIVED IN THE PAST WHOM</u>
<u>I WOULD LIKE TO SPEND A DAY WITH</u>

each team member creates a collage in the assigned quadrant, reflecting his or her personal "likes." Each teammate is questioned individually by his or her partners regarding this collage in a pattern similar to that suggested in Figure 3.8 for "Teams of 3." A space in the center of the poster may be left blank for a team name chosen to reflect the pictures, perhaps something the students have in common. This team poster can be displayed in the room to foster the team bonding.

ALPHABETIC FOODS

Another activity that generates both team and class unity centers around foods and the alphabet, and makes use of the roundtable strategy. A recorder is "scientifically" appointed for each team, such as the person who has the shortest hair. The recorder is instructed to write all the letters of the alphabet in a column on a paper containing the team name. Using whisper voices, the team leans in and brainstorms the names of 26 foods, each beginning with a different letter of the alphabet. Some letters require some pretty fancy creativity, and teams are permitted to invent foods where needed. The team then studies its list, after which it is put out of sight. This "warmup" activity prepares the team for the competition.

A second recorder makes a list of all 26 letters of the alphabet on another sheet of paper containing the team name. Students are told that in a moment, a signal will be given and the second recorder will write a food beginning with "A" on the sheet. The sheet is passed to the next person, who writes a food starting with the letter "B," after which the roundtable continues. Rules to follow are these:

- The foods do not have to be from your team list.
- Spelling does not count except for the first letter.
- You may not skip a letter or go back to a previous letter.
- No communication can occur, including writing, lip synch, and speaking.
- The team may pantomime (act out) a food.

This is a timed activity, so students are encouraged to pantomime. If even after pantomime, the writer cannot think of a food, the word "SHUCKS" can be substituted. Although this entry will not count in the scoring, the next person can go on to the next letter. The teacher walks around the room, calling time when every team is finished.

Teams exchange their papers with another team and judge the validity of each of the foods on the list. A "?" is placed next to any suspect food, indicating that the team challenges this entry. One by one the challenges are presented to the class for their consideration. "Is tea a food?" one team asks. All teams lean in and come to consensus. "Let's vote," says the teacher. If a team thinks tea is a food, they put their thumbs up. If the team thinks tea is not a food, they energetically shout "WAAAH!" The majority rules; ties are granted the benefit of the doubt and the food is counted as valid. Once all challenges are considered, each team sheet is tallied and the amounts placed on the scoreboard.

Students enjoy this team-builder and pull together as a class and as a team. Note that the votes indicate class opinion and not necessarily the truth. For the remainder of the year, the class can use "thumbs up" for approval and "WAAH" for disapproval.

INSTRUCTION WITH TEAMS

Cooperative teams that have been wisely selected and carefully built become small companies where excellence can be better achieved and interpersonal skills can be improved. The team setting provides a natural setting for projects, research, and performance activities. Lecture, discussion, and review can also be accomplished with the students in teams. Having formal teams does not restrict the learning environment to a singular arrangement; students can be taught to quickly rearrange the furniture into pairs, into rows of singles, and back into teams for optimal learning. For example, if a heavy content lecture is scheduled, the students respond to a request for pairs by changing from groups of fours to sets of twos, each pair being from the same team. Think/Pair/Share is used for key questions. Perhaps later in the period, group discussion is used to cement learning, and the pairs quickly reform their team of four. Another approach would be to have students sitting in rows without regard to team membership for most class sessions and just use the formal teams on review and activity days. Of course, teams should be sitting together when team-influenced graded work is returned, so they can celebrate and comfort each other as appropriate.

Sometimes classrooms can become stagnant and lethargic towards learning because students are responding in the same old ways to the same old stimuli. At such a time, team-building activities may infuse students with a fresh outlook. Another strategy for reenergizing the classroom is to mix or to stir the class by using a different seating arrangement for a day or two. Students are moved to temporary teams without names and usually not with anyone from their formal team. Sometimes the result of such a stirring is a great increase in productive work. When these temporary teams are dissolved and the students return to their established teams, there seems to be a new energy, even a sense of coming home again.

TEAM DISCUSSION AND CIRCLE OF KNOWLEDGE

The presence of teams provides a wonderful opportunity for in-depth analysis by students. Once a poem has been read, a math problem posed, a science question raised, or a German sentence given for translation, students are allowed to think, write, and work individually without interruption until each has determined a response. A team leader is appointed and a group discussion is conducted, with each team member discussing the question with the leader. The team considers the contribution of each person, examining the defense of different conclusions. A team decision is made and consensus achieved. At this time, one possible way to hear from the teams is to use an activity called "circle of knowledge," in which the leader from each team gives the team conclusion and, where appropriate, the team defense. Responses are heard one at a time from each team in order of seating until the circle is complete.

Another effective way to respond after individual thinking and team discussion is to use erase-and-write boards, one board per team. A board writer is appointed and the team leader coordinates the accurate transfer of the consensus to the board. At a given signal each board writer holds the board high for the entire class to see. Sometimes, to assure ownership of the result on the boards, each team member can initial the result, indicating agreement with the statement on the board (erase-and-write boards are available from World Research Company, 1–800–843–9737).

The roles of team leader and board-writer can be rotated with each question or with each new day. The boards offer an opportunity for the teams to communicate with the teacher in a noiseless fashion. The teacher also can use a board to communicate with the class in a nondisruptive way. For example, a board with "6 minutes left" written on it can be held up to communicate silently the close of an activity.

No one has to be embarrassed by an incorrect public response, because team conclusions are being reported. The blame for incorrect results and the glory for offering perceptive thoughts are shared. Sometimes a quiet student will comment when an incorrect team response is, "I had that right, but you wouldn't believe me." A teacher can encourage students to consider the importance of convincingly defending what they believe to be true. Additionally, teams learn that it is not always the forceful personality who is the guardian of truth, and that all opinions must be considered equally. Using this format provides all students the opportunity to share their thoughts, especially those who would never speak out in front of an entire class of peers.

One key question on most any day in a classroom can be, "Students, what did we learn today? Give examples and recall situations." Proceeding in the manner described above by using circle of knowledge allows a summary of a lesson by the students rather than by the teacher.

CELEBRATION AND REWARD

Whether in a block schedule or not, celebration of team or pair accomplishment motivates and energizes students towards excellence. Such behavior in an academic setting may have to be demonstrated and taught. When a teacher celebrates learning and accomplishment, students are more likely to take pride in learning and model the teacher in their own celebration. The teacher might ask this question in Think mode: "How can we celebrate excellence of a pair or team?" Students Pair up and then Square up to generate a list of behaviors and expressions, after which, using circle of knowledge, the class compiles their ideas on a piece of newsprint. Examples include the following: Do a team "high 5." Say YESSSSSS! Make an agreed upon team gesture or sound. Say sentences like, "We are awesome."

Students must be instructed on the difference between celebrating and gloating. How vital it is for teams and pairs to learn to love achieving excellence! We need to celebrate learning!

Rewards can be used to celebrate the success of a team or pair. Rewards can be simple words of praise, points awarded to the team on the scoreboard, pats on the back, or handshakes. Also effective are tangible team rewards such as lollipops, special privileges, or Polaroid pictures taped on a Wall of Fame. Rewards given to the entire team are the most effective, even if only one student seems to have been responsible for the team's achievement. For example, if a student from The Fab Four makes an insightful point after a team discussion, that student should receive glory for the idea and the team should be recognized as well. "Wow, Susan, that is a wonderful thought. Boy, those Fab Four are awesome!" Susan and her three teammates feel a sense of pride and accomplishment, strengthening their bond together. The individual is important. The team is important. Individual brilliance often arises out of team interaction and contributes to team accomplishment. The desire for tangible team rewards seems to decrease as the team's desire for team accomplishment increases.

PAIRS NOT TEAMS?

Often an effective starting point for the use of cooperative learning in the classroom is to create pairs of students instead of teams. Early in the year, even on the first day, pairs can be formed and taught Think/Pair/Share. Pair-building can be done with any of the previously described team-builders. For example, Things-in-Common sheets are powerful tools for bringing two students together. Roundtable sums is adapted by simply having partners pass the paper back and forth.

One way to form temporary first pairs is to place slips of paper in a tub with the first and last names of famous people written upon them. Students draw slips randomly and pair accordingly. For example, the student who picks the ELVIS slip must locate the student with the PRESLEY slip. In a math class, one slip of paper might have on it the equation $2x + 12 = 22$ and another slip $3x - 11 = 4$. Both equations have 5 as the solution. The students solve the equations, then find each other. Similar pairing tools can be used in other disciplines. Again, if the class has an odd number of students, plan ahead and have one trio of slips that match up. Three slips might include one with CAL, one with RIPKEN and one with JR. or three slips with equations having 5 as a solution. The classroom will then be organized into many pairs and one threesome.

After pairing students could exchange birth dates, take turns sharing information about their summer vacations, and do a TIC sheet. Once TPS is mastered, the pair becomes a learning team.

Motivating pairs to interact can be difficult; one extremely effective tool is a strategy called Carolina Pairs. Similar to Carolina Teams, each pair of students is given a numerical target that reflects their past academic performance before they were partners. The target should challenge the pair a bit, but it must be reasonably attainable if the students work well together. Students work and study together, but are evaluated individually. When and if the average score of the teammates equals or surpasses the target, the pair is recognized, and 3 points are added to their quiz scores. Remember, in Carolina Pairs points are never subtracted from a student's score. For example, a pair with a target of 85 might have quiz grades of 90 and 76, giving them an average of 83. They receive no bonus and the actual grades of 90 and 76 are recorded in the gradebook.

Successful pairs celebrate and are reminded that the best way to improve their grade is to teach their partner. Outstanding pairs can be rewarded in many other appropriate ways, including the taking of "celebrity" photographs which are displayed on the Wall of Fame or highlighted as "Pairs of the Week." Scores are recorded on the score sheets and new targets are computed after two evaluations.

Forming the right pairs is important for success. Teachers who use Carolina Pairs need to ask the question, "Do I think that this pair will work well together, or can they learn to work well together?" Carolina Pairs cannot be used until information has been gathered concerning students' achievement and personalities. Students may be allowed to select their own partners once they have experienced working cooperatively in teams or teacher-created pairs. When student-selected pairing is allowed, the teacher must roam the classroom playing the part of matchmaker for certain students, making sure that everyone is happily paired and that no one feels slighted or left out.

When using Carolina Pairs, special emphasis must be placed upon the benefits received by both the student who is teaching and the one being taught. The student being taught obviously gains much, but the student who teaches cements his or her understanding of concepts and gains a deeper grasp of what has been taught. The student who takes the time to teach a partner will probably achieve better than if not given this opportunity.

Apparently, something special occurs when students' grades are interdependent, because actual grades always seem to increase even before the bonus points are added. Using Carolina Pairs seems to result in genuine cooperative learning.

PEER COACHING

An effective tool with a class organized in Carolina Pairs is peer coaching; one of the students is the player and the other is the coach. The pair is given a short activity. Partner "A" begins working on the task while partner "B" leans over to observe what is written. The coach directs the player to successful completion of the task using encouragement, praise, and guidance. The coach must learn to lead and not do the task for the player, being a good teacher who nudges the student to the truth. For each succeeding activity, the students switch roles.

Peer coaching can be effectively done at the blackboard or with newsprint on the wall, with the coach standing behind the player who is writing on the board. The coach is like a supervisor, evaluating the player's performance. This structure is helpful in a keyboarding class, for example; the coach observes the player's technique and fills in a critique sheet, later discussing the observations. By evaluating the partner, the coach learns to be more sensitive to good typing form when the two change roles.

CONTRACTS FOR CAROLINA TEAMS AND PAIRS

Making agreements, commitments, and promises is an important part of employment, business, and marriage. Contracts are instruments of accountability and serve as reminders of obligations. Contracts can be valuable tools when used with

Carolina Teams and Pairs, especially when the students choose their partners. Students take blank contracts overnight to think about promises that will be made to help and cooperate with a partner or several team members. Once agreed to, the contracts are signed and submitted to the teacher for approval. The contractual process seems to help students focus on the mutual responsibility and can be used to refocus pairs or teams if cooperation begins to wane. Having a contract gives students the opportunity to experience being faithful to what they have promised, even when difficult circumstances arise. Maintaining the contract can encourage students to be creative in making the pairing effective. Figure 3.10 is a sample contract for use with STAD groups and Figure 3.11 is a sample contract for Carolina Pairs. These may need to be modified for other age groups.

STUDENT DISCIPLINE

Many teachers' good plans are foiled and enthusiasm dimmed by a constant need to reestablish the focus of the class and bring students to order. Using cooperative learning encourages students to increase their interaction, which can make it more challenging to focus the class on a singular point, such as the teacher. Constantly reminding students to return to task or to be quiet for a 90-minute class will exhaust even the most patient and controlled teacher. The concept that the cooperative class is "our" class and that both students and teacher are responsible for the class activities allows for a powerful solution. We must teach students how to bring their teams to focus, to get on task, and produce quality work. One means of accomplishing this goal is to assign one student in each team that responsibility, the role of being the team "enforcer" or "captain." Establish an agreed upon signal to return to Think mode, such as counting down "3–2–1," raising a hand, ringing a bell, or saying a key word like "Clemson." When the signal is given, enforcers bring their teams to a quiet focus by some audible or visible team cue, such as shushing or stretching hands out in front. This is most effective if the teacher teaches the enforcers the response to the quiet signal and then the enforcers teach their teams.

FIGURE 3.10. SAMPLE STAD GROUP CONTRACT

WE AGREE TO HELP EACH OTHER TO HAVE MAXIMUM SUCCESS BY LISTENING PATIENTLY TO ONE ANOTHER'S QUESTIONS, BY ASKING EACH OTHER FOR HELP, BY ASKING IF SOMEONE NEEDS HELP, BY ANSWERING QUESTIONS IN A CAREFUL AND THOUGHTFUL MANNER, BY HELPING EACH OTHER TO LISTEN IN CLASS AND BY ENCOURAGING ONE ANOTHER.

WE PROMISE TO CALL EACH OTHER WHEN POSSIBLE IN ORDER TO PROVIDE MISSED ASSIGNMENTS AND ADDITIONAL HELP.

WE WILL RECEIVE TEAM POINTS IF WE CAN IMPROVE, IF WE CAN BE BETTER TOGETHER THAN WE WERE APART.

WE PROMISE TO COOPERATE IN AN EFFECTIVE MANNER.

MY SIGNATURE_____

PARTNER SIGNATURE_____

PARTNER SIGNATURE_____

PARTNER SIGNATURE_____

ONE PERSON HAS TO TAKE ON THE RESPONSIBILITY TO MAKE SURE THE ENTIRE GROUP IS ON TASK. THIS PERSON IS YOUR ENFORCER. PICK ONE PERSON FOR THAT ROLE.

OUR ENFORCER IS_____

FIGURE 3.11. SAMPLE CAROLINA PAIRS CONTRACT

WE AGREE TO HELP EACH OTHER TO HAVE MAXIMUM SUCCESS BY LISTENING PATIENTLY TO ONE ANOTHER'S QUESTIONS, BY ASKING EACH OTHER FOR HELP, BY ASKING IF MY PARTNER NEEDS HELP, BY ANSWERING QUESTIONS IN A CAREFUL AND THOUGHTFUL MANNER, BY HELPING EACH OTHER TO LISTEN IN CLASS AND BY ENCOURAGING ONE ANOTHER.

WE PROMISE TO CALL EACH OTHER WHEN POSSIBLE IN ORDER TO PROVIDE MISSED ASSIGNMENTS AND ADDITIONAL HELP.

WE PROMISE TO COOPERATE IN AN EFFECTIVE MANNER.

WE WILL RECEIVE BONUS POINTS ADDED TO OUR GRADE IF WE CAN IMPROVE, IF WE CAN BE BETTER TOGETHER THAN WE WERE APART.

THIS AGREEMENT IS MADE BETWEEN THE PARTNERS AND THE TEACHER.

MY SIGNATURE_____

PARTNER SIGNATURE_____

TEACHER SIGNATURE_____

Giving students responsibility for discipline yields many benefits. Students learn to be responsible for themselves and others. Students experience both the success and failure of attempting to influence another person positively. They learn interactive skills that will be essential for relationships with employees, employers, friends and parents. Stress is reduced for the teacher, freeing more energy for building relationships and teaching the love of the subject matter. The class is focused and ready to learn. Rotating the role of enforcer until each team member has had this responsibility results in a classroom of enforcers. After 4–8 weeks, the enforcer role can be put on the shelf, because the students have become responsible for the class behavior.

VALUING ONE ANOTHER

Establishing a cooperative classroom requires students to develop sensitivity, empathy, a willingness to accept and give help, and a perception of classmates as valuable resources. Time, thought, and energy must be devoted to helping students acquire a proper view of themselves and an elevated view of their peers; they must come to believe that every student is unique and valuable.

To establish these ideas in a cooperative classroom, the teacher must serve as model and leader. Resolving to treat all students as valuable, no matter what the situation, is the first step. Sharing personal experiences that support these principles is another vehicle. A teacher who vividly describes the joy of learning that he is finally going to become a parent, or shares the pain of losing a precious infant, strongly communicates the value of each human life. It is not too much to come right out and tell your students, "You are unique and valuable." Do this often enough, and they will repeat it about themselves, say it to one another, and come to believe it.

Being unique and valuable is not an entitlement, but a responsibility. To be less than your best, to miss homework, to accept mediocrity is not to act in a unique and valuable manner. The goal for every student is excellence. The expectation for every student is to be treated in a unique and valuable way by everyone in the classroom. As a result, any occurrence of the words "shut up" should be followed by a sincere apology. Some of our most entertaining class moments occur when a student creates an elaborate apology for uttering the "S" word, or when the teacher apologizes for violating the uniqueness promise. Establishing such a foundation in the classroom contributes to increased cooperation and caring actions. It becomes a natural thing to help someone in need.

Raw score teams, Carolina Teams, and STAD bring competition into the environment to promote increased cooperation, yet in these classes some teams do lose, albeit only for a week or two. Students who are reminded continually that they are unique and valuable are motivated to achieve and are consoled in defeat. When your team loses, you are disappointed, but you are still worthy of respect. Competition and cooperation can work together to create a productive learning environment as long as students have a setting in which they can respect themselves and their classmates.

GOODBYES

After 8 or more weeks of working together, a team of students often grows very close. They have experienced victory and defeat. Together they have celebrated as well as encouraged each other. They have come to know each other more than superficially and have become primary resources of learning for one another. Before new teams are formed, the old teams need to be allowed to say "goodbye" and "thanks" to each other.

One way to let students express their farewells is to have each student create a paper fan of nice notes using a roundtable format. Each student takes a sheet of paper, printing his or her name on the top. On signal the papers are roundtabled; each team member writes something positive about the teammate whose name appears on the sheet. The paper is creased just under the name, folded back, creased under the nice note, folded forward so only the name is showing. At this point the papers are passed in the roundtable. Writing, creasing, and folding, first back, then forward, allows each person to see only the name on the paper. At the end of the activity each person receives his or her own paper, which is opened and read. Sometimes additional thank-yous and shaking hands happen before the team is dissolved.

Saying goodbye in a serious way allows the class to grow closer, cementing good memories for future enjoyment. Creative ways to say goodbye should be used to bring effective closure to team life together.

REACHING THE GOAL

Establishing a cooperative classroom is not an easy task, but it can be a worthy goal. I recommend the incremental approach to introducing classroom change. Try something cooperative, like Think/Pair/Share, and become an expert with that particular strategy. Next, perhaps, learn to be comfortable with the 1–2–4 activity structure; then explore team discussion with circle of knowledge. Following this approach allows a teacher to build confidence and provides momentum for additional successes.

There is no one correct way to do cooperative learning. The results will vary as greatly as the personalities of teachers, the needs of students, the furniture and room size, school policies, and the nature of the subject matter. However, most successful cooperative environments will include team interaction, positive interdependence, group goals, social skill training, and individual accountability.

When a truly cooperative classroom has been established, learning remains hard work, but working hard together is more pleasant. Cooperative learning within the longer block provides a setting in which students can grow to their fullest potential and teachers can experience the true satisfaction of their calling.

REFERENCES

Johnson, D.W., Johnson, R.T., & Holubec, E.J. (1990). *Circles of learning: Cooperation in the classroom.* 3rd ed. Edina, MN: Interaction Book Company.

Kagan, S. (1990). *Cooperative learning: Resources for teachers.* San Juan Capistrano, CA: Resources for Teachers, Inc.

Lehr, J.B. & Martin, C. (1994). *Schools without fear: Group activities for building community.* Minneapolis, MN: Educational Media Corporation.

McTighe, J. & Lyman, F.T. Jr. (April 1988). Cuing thinking in the classroom: The promise of theory-embedded tools. *Educational Leadership*, 18–24.

Shaw, V. (1992). *Community building in the classroom.* San Juan Capistrano, CA: Kagan Cooperative Learning.

Slavin, R.E. (1986). *Using student team learning.* 3rd ed. Baltimore, MD: The Johns Hopkins Team Learning Project, Johns Hopkins University.

Slavin, R.E. (1990). *Cooperative learning: Theory, research, and practice.* Englewood Cliffs, NJ: Prentice-Hall.

Slavin, R.E. (1991). *Student team learning: A practical guide to cooperative learning.* Washington, DC: National Education Association.

4

FOUR MODELS OF TEACHING[1]

INTRODUCTION

As schools change from single-period, daily schedules to schedules that provide blocks of time, a major concern for teachers, students, and administrators is how the time will be spent. In particular, teachers and students often are concerned about sustaining an interest in learning. Teachers question the students' abilities to attend to information for long periods of time, and students doubt the teachers' abilities to maintain interest. One goal of the scheduling reform movement has been "to allow and encourage the use of active teaching strategies and greater student involvement" by providing longer periods of time for instruction (Canady & Rettig, 1995, p. 12). The converse is equally true; faced with longer blocks of time, teachers must have and use a repertoire of teaching strategies that involve students actively in the learning process. A lecture may be boring for 45 minutes, but it becomes deadly when continued for 90 minutes or more!

Another concern for teachers changing to a form of block schedule is the issue of short-term and long-term retention of material. Teachers often believe that to be remembered new information must be practiced daily. Those working in an alternate-day schedule sometimes wonder whether new learning will be affected negatively. For those involved in the 4/4 semester schedule, the concern is more likely to be the ability of students to retain

---

[1] This chapter was written by Brenda M. Tanner, Assistant Superintendent, Louisa County Schools, and Deborah D. Pettit, Principal, Louisa County Middle School, Mineral, Virginia.

information over time; students may complete a subject such as Algebra I in a semester and may decide not to take another math course until the following year.

Both of these concerns are addressed by the models of teaching presented in this chapter. Designed specifically to help students acquire and process information, these models enhance student thinking and learning, not by teaching and telling, but by questioning and involving students in the learning process. These models of teaching are "models of learning" by which students can process information and increase their capabilities "to learn more easily and effectively in the future" (Joyce, Weil, & Showers, 1992, p. 1).

The models described in this chapter are based upon the work of Gunter, Estes, and Schwab (1995), and are derived from the work of Joyce and Weil (1986), who, for over 25 years, examined models of teaching from academic, clinical, athletic, and military fields in a search for "promising approaches to teaching" (p. 2). The strength of these models lies not only in the experiences of practitioners, but also in the strong research base that serves as a foundation for each.

Four information-processing models have been selected for inclusion. These models focus on the acquisition and organization of data, the formation of concepts, the use of creative thinking, and the enhancement of general intellectual ability. Concept development, the first model presented, is designed to guide students through a process of categorizing information and synthesizing this information in order to make generalizations. The second model, concept attainment, requires students to develop a definition of a selected concept through the examination of critical attributes. Synectics, the third model, relies on the use of analogies and metaphors to encourage creative thought. Finally, the memory model provides students with association techniques to link new information to that which is familiar.

When teachers add these models to their repertoire of teaching strategies, the longer blocks of time afforded by new forms of scheduling become a boon rather than a challenge. Students are actively involved in the learning process, and the likelihood that knowledge will be retained is increased.

CONCEPT DEVELOPMENT

DESCRIBING THE MODEL

The concept development model leads students through the process of organizing and refining information into categories and finally synthesizing the information by forming generalizations. Adapted from teaching strategies developed by the late curriculum theorist Hilda Taba, the concept development model mirrors the inductive thinking processes involved in categorizing and manipulating categories. The steps in the model, as noted in Figure 4.1, are designed to support Taba's belief that specific strategies can be used to teach thinking skills and that the strategies should be used in a specific sequence so that one thinking skill builds on another (Taba, Durkin, Fraenkel, & McNaughton, 1971). It has been reported in the research that practice with the concept development model increases retention of information and that students can learn to carry on these thinking processes independently (Bredderman (1981) and El Nemr (1979) in Joyce & Weil, 1986; Worthen, 1968).

FIGURE 4.1. STEPS IN THE CONCEPT DEVELOPMENT MODEL[2]

1. **List** as many items as possible
2. **Group** the items.
3. **Label** the items by defining the reasons for grouping.
4. **Regroup** or subsume individual items or whole groups under other groups.
5. **Synthesize** the information by summarizing the data and forming generalizations.
6. **Evaluate** students' progress by assessing their ability to generate a wide variety of items and to group those items flexibly.

This model is appropriate for use in any subject area in which students must organize and manipulate large amounts of raw data into concepts. It is used most effectively in a whole-class

---

[2] Gunter, Estes & Schwab, 1995, p. 117.

setting because students benefit from hearing a variety of data presented by others. Concept development is valuable when used at the beginning of a unit of study for determining students' prior knowledge and is particularly effective as an end-of-unit review.

PREPARING FOR THE LESSON

Preparation for a lesson incorporating concept development requires that the teacher determine the appropriateness of the model relative to learning objectives. Of primary importance is the teacher's familiarity with the steps of the model and with the wording of the questions. The teacher's role is to facilitate and record student exploration of information leading to development of a concept.

The model is useful in assessing student knowledge and under-standing, both before and after a unit of study. If used as a pretest, student preparation is unnecessary, except that students understand the expectations for participation in the steps of the model. When used as a postassessment, student preparation involves the student having previously studied the material related to the concept.

Materials needed include chart tablets, transparencies, or a large amount of chalkboard space, because the items listed in Step 1 and manipulated throughout the model must be visible to all students. As the students group items in Step 2, colored chalk or markers are helpful in delineating groups. Additional paper, transparencies, or chalkboard space is necessary for Steps 3 and 4, in which the groups are labeled and regrouped or subsumed, either by small groups of students or by the whole class.

USING THE STRATEGY

STEP 1: LIST AS MANY ITEMS AS POSSIBLE

In Step 1, the teacher asks, "Tell me what you know about _____." As students give responses, the teacher lists them on the chalkboard or on an overhead transparency. Another method of generating a list of items is to ask students to write three sentences about the topic and to underline the most important words. Until students become familiar with the model, the teacher encourages further listing, even when students seem to have run out of items. This database forms the information from which later generalizations will be developed.

The responses of an 8th grade science class in their first experience with the concept development model are used to illustrate the steps in the model. The teacher's objective was to assess the students' existing knowledge regarding electricity in order to frame the areas of study during the unit.

The teacher introduced the lesson by telling the class they were beginning a unit on electricity and she wanted to find out what the class already knew about the topic so that she could determine which areas to emphasize during the unit. The teacher stated, "All responses will be accepted, no response is wrong, and items about which you have questions will be investigated during the unit of study." She continued with the statement, "Tell me what you know about electricity." The response "makes lights run" triggered a list of items powered by electricity; however, the teacher accepted all responses and encouraged the group to continue in order to develop a comprehensive database which included 60 items, some of which are listed here:

can shock you	runs by the sun	makes stuff run
makes lights run	heat	power plant
stove	air conditioning	molecules
telephone	fire	electric fences
all appliances	fan	lightning
washing machine	stereo	refrigerator
vacuum cleaner	t.v.	deep freezer
makes dryer run	current	curling iron

STEP 2: GROUP THE ITEMS

Step 2 begins with the question, "Which of the items on our list seem to belong together because they are alike in some way? Tell why you think those items go together." As students offer groups of items, it is helpful to ask them to tell why those items go together, because the whole class gains insight through hearing each other's reasons for grouping. Older students and adults tend to apply a label, so it may be necessary for the teacher to discourage labeling in this step and to encourage explanations. To indicate the grouping combinations, the teacher uses numbers or symbols, circles the items in colored chalk, or rewrites the items in groups.

Items often will be included in several groups.

Students in the science class grouped the items in the database using nine different combinations. Some items were included in several groups; for example, "motor" was included with "things which run by electricity," "things that move," and "things that make stuff run."

STEP 3: LABEL THE ITEMS BY DEFINING THE REASONS FOR GROUPING

Step 3, the "labeling" phase in the model, is conducted as a whole-class activity, or the class may be divided into student teams, to respond to the questions, "What would you call the groups that have been formed?" and "Why do you think the items in the group go together?" With the whole class, the teacher discusses one group of items at a time by reading the items to the class, asking for someone to provide a label and an explanation, and displaying the labeled group in a place visible to the entire class. The teacher does not judge, but accepts all student responses and encourages class discussion. From discussion in Step 2, students have some ideas about connections within groups; through group discussion in Step 3, however, more complex connections can be drawn.

An alternative to the whole-class activity is to allow student teams to complete the labeling by rewriting the groups of items on transparencies or on sheets of chart paper. It is likely that students are ready to move around, as the listing and grouping steps may take as long as 30 minutes. After labeling, all teams explain their choice of labels to the whole class.

With the science class, the teacher divided the students into teams who listed and labeled the items for their assigned group on large sheets of paper. The examples listed below include some of the labeled groups, which were displayed for the class.

THINGS THAT SHOCK YOU

    gets to you by power line
    sparks
    electric fences
    battery
    lightning
    socket plug

THINGS THAT GIVE ELECTRIC ENERGY

static
socket plug
fire
current
can shock you
transformers
kilowatts
sparks
electric fence
batteries

COLOR WORDS

red
blue

THINGS INSIDE ELECTRICITY

kilowatts
atom
molecules

STEP 4: REGROUP OR SUBSUME INDIVIDUAL ITEMS OR WHOLE GROUPS UNDER OTHER GROUPS

In Step 4, students examine different relationships among the groups following the teacher's questions, "Are there items in one group that you could place in another group?" and "Are there whole groups that could be placed under another one of the labels?" Asking for student reasoning in this step is important so that the class can move beyond superficial relationships to examine relationships from different perspectives. Often in this step, whole groups are subsumed within other groups.

The science class formed a new group by combining THINGS THAT GIVE ELECTRIC ENERGY and THINGS THAT SHOCK YOU, with the latter title indicating that the first group was subsumed within the second.

STEP 5: SYNTHESIZE THE INFORMATION BY SUMMARIZING THE DATA AND FORMING GENERALIZATIONS

In Step 5 the teacher states, "Look at all of the groups we have made and make a statement about all of them." Drawing generalizations through examination of the grouped data is difficult for many students until they become familiar with the thinking processes involved in concept development; therefore, teacher support through examples is critical.

These are examples of student responses from the science class:

Electricity is very useful and it is dangerous.
Electricity helps us a lot.
Electricity can make many things move.

STEP 6: EVALUATE STUDENTS' PROGRESS BY ASSESSING THEIR ABILITY TO GENERATE A WIDE VARIETY OF ITEMS AND TO GROUP THOSE ITEMS FLEXIBLY

Step 6 requires that the teacher consider student progress in the thinking skills involved in the model. Student responses offer insight into skill development as well as into student knowledge of a concept. This assessment step leads to further instructional decisions, including reteaching or the design of further study of a concept.

The science teacher decided that the students' responses indicated the need for additional experiences with the thinking processes involved in concept development. Their skills in analyzing the information and regrouping could be improved. Most importantly, she learned that the students needed to study basic information about electricity and that it would be helpful to relate this information to what they already knew.

TROUBLESHOOTING POTENTIAL PROBLEMS

Upon their first experience with concept development, teachers sometimes voice concern about the length of time needed to complete the model. Generating a comprehensive database of knowledge and categorizing the information necessarily requires time and may be uncomfortable for students who are unaccustomed to thinking in new ways. After three or four trials with the model, both students and teacher become familiar with the process and it proceeds more quickly.

When using the model, it is critical that items listed in the database generated in Step 1 be specific; otherwise grouping in the next step will be confusing. It may be necessary, therefore, to prompt students to be more specific. Equally important is the generation of a comprehensive list of items in Step 1, so that generalizations may be based on a variety of data; therefore, teacher encouragement to continue listing may be necessary.

ASSESSING AND GRADING STUDENT LEARNING

The emphasis of the model is on ascertaining student knowledge and thinking about a topic; therefore, it is not recommended that student responses be graded. Student concern with grading could stifle the responses and limit the database. Used as a review, the model can be followed by a test in order to measure individual student knowledge. Another assessment option is to follow the model with a writing activity that may be graded.

EMPLOYING APPROPRIATE FOLLOW-UP ACTIVITIES

If the model is used as an introduction to a unit of study, then follow-up includes proceeding through the unit with labeled categories forming areas of study. Charts containing the original database and labeled groupings can remain on display throughout the unit of study so that students can confirm, refute, or add to information in the database during the unit. The model can be used at the conclusion of a unit of study for test review or to help students organize information for oral or written presentations. In performing the steps of the model, students list, group, label, analyze, and synthesize, thereby developing skills important in the thinking process.

CONCEPT ATTAINMENT

DESCRIBING THE MODEL

The concept attainment model is designed to help students define a concept by identifying those attributes absolutely essential to its meaning through the comparison of examples and nonexamples. Based on the research reported in *A Study of Thinking* by Bruner, Goodnow, and Austin (1977), and first described as a teaching model by Joyce and Weil (1986), concept attainment leads students through the thinking processes involved in examining and categorizing data to develop concepts. The model (Fig. 4.2) involves the teacher choosing a concept, determining its definition through identifying distinguishing attributes, and selecting examples. Students then are presented with the series of examples, some of which contain all of the attributes of the concept (positive examples) and some of which contain only some of the attributes (nonexamples). The students examine the examples for likenesses and differences to identify the essential attributes of the concept and to formulate a definition for the concept using those attributes.

FIGURE 4.2. STEPS IN THE CONCEPT ATTAINMENT MODEL[3]

---

1. **Select and define** a concept.
2. **Select** the attributes.
3. **Develop** positive and negative examples.
4. **Introduce** the process to the students.
5. **Present** the examples and list the attributes.
6. **Develop** a concept definition.
7. **Give** additional examples.
8. **Discuss** the process.
9. **Evaluate**.

Concept attainment is appropriate within any subject area in which students must identify and understand a concept or compare concepts. Use of the model affords students practice in the thinking process involved in forming a concept, as well as in teaching the meaning of the concept. Given the numerous abstract concepts found in secondary curricula, such as justice, symmetry, metamorphosis, or irony, concept attainment is a valuable tool in clarifying both teacher and student understanding. Additionally, arriving at a definition and discussing how the process unfolds enhances retention of information. Used in a whole-class setting, the process enables students to learn from each other as they develop a definition together and discuss their thinking.

---

[3] Gunter, Estes & Schwab, 1995, pp. 98–99.

PREPARING FOR THE LESSON

Teacher preparation for the concept attainment model involves choosing a concept that can be clearly defined, writing a definition, selecting its essential attributes, and developing positive examples and nonexamples. Selecting and defining a concept requires extensive thought on the part of the teacher and should be of central importance to the learning objective. The teacher's definition is important in planning the examples; however, students will generate their own definition as they examine the examples. The success of the model depends on the quality of the examples. Each positive example must contain all of the attributes of the concept; each nonexample must contain **some** of the attributes in order to help students focus on essential attributes. It is recommended that the examples be "tested" prior to use by actually listing the attributes of each example and comparing them to the essential attributes of the definition.

Materials needed include chalkboard or overhead transparency to list student responses. It is important that all information generated during the model be seen by all students to facilitate their input into development of the concept definition.

USING THE STRATEGY

STEP 1: SELECT AND DEFINE A CONCEPT

Careful consideration must be given to the selection and definition of a concept, so that the examples developed will have clearly defined attributes. A dictionary definition may not yield the level of understanding or meet all of the criteria that the teacher wishes students to gain through the model; therefore, a teacher-generated definition may be best.

Throughout the description of the steps in concept attainment, the concept of "commutative," taught to a math class, will be used as an example. The teacher defined the concept as follows:

combining elements or having elements that combine in such a manner that the result is not affected by the order in which the elements occur.[4]

STEP 2: SELECT THE ATTRIBUTES

It is essential to list the defining attributes in order to check them against the examples before beginning the model. The defining attributes of "commutative" are:

- ◆   Order or sequence of elements or events; and
- ◆   An intervening operation that does not change the original element or event.

STEP 3: DEVELOP POSITIVE AND NEGATIVE EXAMPLES

It is crucial to have a sufficient number of appropriate examples as defined above. Examples for the concept "commutative" are listed here and could have been represented to the math class pictorially, described verbally, or demonstrated for maximum effect:

POSITIVE EXAMPLES (+)
> Putting on two socks
> Studying math and science
> Walking in a circle
> Eating cake and ice cream

NONEXAMPLES (-)
> Putting a sock and a shoe on one foot
> Cooking and eating a hamburger
> Reading the first to last chapters in a book

STEP 4: INTRODUCE THE PROCESS TO THE STUDENTS

The following is a sample teacher explanation:

> Our class is going to form a definition today. The process is called "concept attainment." I will be giving you examples of the concept which you will define. This most likely will involve a different way of thinking for you, because the teacher usually gives the definition of

---

[4] The idea for this lesson came from Kathy Pierce, Assistant Principal, Louisa Middle School, Mineral, Virginia.

a concept before discussing it. With this method, you gradually will develop your own definition for the concept.

There are two columns on the board (transparency)—one for attributes (traits, features) of the positive examples and one for attributes of the nonexamples. As each example is shown, you will name its attributes, and I will list them under the appropriate column.

Positive examples contain all of the attributes of the concept.

Positive examples also may contain some nonessential attributes, which we will eliminate as we examine several examples.

Nonexamples may contain some, but not all, of the attributes of the concept. Attributes of the nonexamples will be used for comparison with those of positive examples and to highlight features of positive examples.

Nonexamples do not eliminate any attributes from the positive list.

An attribute can be crossed off the positive list only if we see a positive example that does not contain an attribute on the list.

STEP 5: PRESENT THE EXAMPLES AND LIST THE ATTRIBUTES

The teacher begins with a positive example and lists all student responses in naming attributes under the "positive" column. Although some attributes, such as color or size, may be nonessential to the definition, they are listed at this point because they eventually will be eliminated through other positive examples. The second example is also positive, and is carefully chosen to eliminate some of the "nonessential" attributes from the first example. Then, a nonexample is shown, to help students focus on attributes they may have missed in the positive examples. The process continues with examples until the teacher determines that there is an adequate list of attributes essential to the definition of the concept.

In our "commutative" example, the math teacher presented the first POSITIVE EXAMPLE by demonstrating "someone putting on two socks." The attributes listed from this example included, "two," "socks," "feet," "hands," "legs." When the second POSITIVE

EXAMPLE, "studying math and science," was described, the words "math," "science," "paper," "pencil," and "book" were listed as attributes. When the teacher reminded the class that each positive example must contain all of the attributes of the concept, the class immediately crossed out "math," "science," "paper," "pencil," and "books" along with "socks," "feet," "legs," and "hands." Attributes were crossed-out, not erased, so that students could see how they were arriving at their definition. The essential attribute remaining on the list following the second example was "two" and the teacher asked the class to think about the order of the two activities described in the examples.

Next, a NONEXAMPLE, "putting a sock and shoe on one foot," was presented. Attributes listed under the NONEXAMPLE column included "one sock," "one shoe," and "one foot." At this point in the lesson, the students were focused on the idea of one action versus two. The next NONEXAMPLE, "cooking and eating a hamburger," resulted in a list of the attributes "eating," "cooking," "hamburger," and "two actions." This example forced the math students to examine the idea that two items were mentioned (as in the positive examples), but that the two activities could not be changed without affecting the results.

The teacher then presented a POSITIVE EXAMPLE, "eating cake and ice cream," and the class then identified an essential attribute as "you can do either thing first." The teacher determined that the class was ready to develop a definition when the next example, "putting a stamp on an envelope and sealing the envelope," was presented and correctly identified as a positive example.

STEP 6: DEVELOP A CONCEPT DEFINITION

This step requires the teacher to encourage students to state a definition using the list of attributes. As they become more experienced with the model, students will develop definitions that are more complex and comprehensive than those in a dictionary.

In the math class, the teacher identified the concept as "commutative" and explained that the students were now ready to develop a definition based on the attributes listed on the board. The class used the NONEXAMPLES to help formulate the definition, as they discussed the idea that the actions in those examples had to be performed in a certain order. The initial definition created by the students was stated simply as, "you can do either action first."

STEP 7: GIVE ADDITIONAL EXAMPLES

This step is used to check student understanding of the concept by giving them several additional examples of the concept and asking them to identify these as positive or nonexamples. Having the students explain their choices provides insight into their thinking and level of understanding of the concept at this point. Additionally, students should be asked to provide their own positive examples of the concept.

Additional examples given to the math class for "commutative" included:

POSITIVE EXAMPLES (+)
> Washing your face and brushing your teeth
> Putting on two gloves

NONEXAMPLES (-)
> Washing clothes and folding them
> Washing the dishes and putting them away
> Starting a car and driving it

POSITIVE EXAMPLES provided by the students included, "going to your locker and going to the bathroom," and "combing your hair and brushing your teeth."

STEP 8: DISCUSS THE PROCESS WITH THE CLASS

In this step, the teacher reviews the process with the students to help them understand how they developed the definition. It is helpful to have students explain when they understood the essential attributes of the concept and which examples were most helpful. By means of this discussion, students gain an understanding of the thinking process—analyzing likenesses and differences—involved in defining a concept.

STEP 9: EVALUATE

Asking each student to provide a positive example of the

concept provides a check of understanding. Having each student write a definition of the concept periodically following the concept attainment process will provide review as well as insight into whether the process helped with retention of information. Once students are familiar with the model, the teacher may challenge them to define a concept and to develop positive and nonexamples to determine their level of understanding of the process.

TROUBLESHOOTING POTENTIAL PROBLEMS

Two major problems associated with the concept attainment model lie in the choice of a concept that can be defined clearly and choosing positive examples that are true examples of the concept. If a clear definition is not established, it is impossible to select examples. The choice of a definition is necessarily time-consuming and thought-provoking for the teacher; however, the reward in learning for students is worth the investment. Each example also should be "tested" against the concept definition before use with students, to avoid confusion with attributes that may not be readily recognized or that may become confusing during the process. It is important that the teacher's data set contains enough examples to provide students adequate information to analyze and compare attributes.

Until they become accustomed to the process, students may become frustrated and resort to blind guessing. It is important that the teacher provide support and encouragement during the first attempts with the model, as students wrestle with a new way of thinking.

ASSESSING AND GRADING STUDENT LEARNING

As noted in the evaluation step of the model, comprehension of the concept will be assessed by determining the quality of the students' definition as well as their ability to identify additional positive examples or nonexamples and to explain their thinking (Step 7). It is not recommended that students be graded on their participation in the model itself, as the primary emphasis is on group participation in the process to arrive at a comprehensive definition of a concept. Grading students on their knowledge of the concept may be accomplished through a test or assignment in which students define and give examples of the concept after it has been discussed in the context of the unit.

EMPLOYING APPROPRIATE FOLLOW-UP ACTIVITIES

If used as an introductory activity to the study of a concept, follow-up activities may include having students generate their own positive examples and nonexamples throughout the unit to insure continued understanding of the concept. After students have become familiar with the model, they may be able to formulate a definition for a concept and to create several positive examples and nonexamples to demonstrate their understanding of the thinking processes involved in attaining concepts.

SYNECTICS

DESCRIBING THE MODEL

Synectics is a structured group activity in which students learn to think creatively and to solve problems through the use of analogies and metaphor. The term was coined by William J. Gordon (1961) from Greek roots, and means "the joining together of different and apparently irrelevant elements" (p. 3). The process itself was developed by Gordon and his associates beginning in 1944 for use in industry with groups of individuals who were responsible for the development of new products. It is based on Gordon's study of creativity in inventing art, philosophy, psychology, and science. Gordon later published materials for use in schools (Gordon, 1968; Gordon & Poze, 1971).

There are several versions of the Synectics model (see Gunter, Estes & Schwab, 1995). The Synectics model presented in this chapter is designed to "make the familiar strange." The steps involve students in drawing three types of analogies, leading them to view a familiar topic in an unfamiliar way.

Synectics is effective in a variety of subject areas when the objective is to develop creative insight and deeper understanding of a topic by looking at it from a variety of perspectives. It is most effective when used with a whole class, because new ideas are sparked as thoughts are shared. Student writing becomes more descriptive through the use of metaphors generated in the model. Students also gain new insights and deeper understandings of a literary character's thoughts and feelings, of scientific phenomena and mathematical concepts, or of human problems and abstract ideas such as democracy, prejudice, poverty, and justice.

FIGURE 4.3. STEPS IN THE SYNECTICS MODEL[5]

1. **Describe** the topic.
2. **Create** direct analogies.
3. **Describe** personal analogies.
4. **Identify** compressed conflicts.
5. **Create** a new direct analogy.
6. **Reexamine** original topic.
7. **Evaluate**.

PREPARING FOR THE LESSON

Teacher preparation includes determining the appropriateness of the model for the learning objective and choosing the analogies for Steps 2 and 5. Materials needed include chalkboard space, transparencies or chart tablets, so that all information generated throughout the steps of the model is visible to students.

STEP 1: DESCRIBE THE TOPIC

In this step, the teacher asks students to describe a topic either orally or in writing. It is helpful to ask students to write several sentences or a paragraph about a topic and to underline the important words and phrases. The teacher then lists the descriptive words or phrases on the board or overhead as the students give responses from their paragraphs. All responses are accepted by the teacher without evaluation.

A senior English class listed these words from their descriptive paragraphs on the subject of "war":

bloody	proud	hell
destructive	necessary	deadly
heartache	waste	inhumane
patriotism	evil	innocent

---

[5] Gunter, Estes & Schwab, 1995, p. 137.

STEP 2: CREATE DIRECT ANALOGIES

In this step, the teacher asks the students to examine the list of descriptive words and to form an analogy between the words and an unrelated category such as plants, animals, or machines. After rereading the list of descriptive words or having a student do so, the teacher states, "Look at our list of descriptive words and think of a plant that reminds you of those words. Please explain why you chose that plant." As students offer names of plants, the teacher lists them on the board under the heading PLANTS. After all students have had an opportunity to name a plant and to explain their reasoning for the analogy, the teacher asks the class to vote on the analogy that best represents the sense of the words listed in Step 1.

Following the English class example, the students named these plants:

ivy	rosebush	dogwood
hydrilla	Venus Flytrap	cactus
crabgrass	marijuana	oak tree

Explanations for the analogies included ivy, because it takes over an area and, therefore, is destructive; marijuana, because it causes heartache and can be destructive; dogwood, because it has a symbol in the flower which represents Christ on the cross, the blood of Christ, and blood is shed in war. The explanation for the dogwood appealed to the class; it was chosen through the class vote as the analogy which best represented the words listed in Step 1.

STEP 3: DESCRIBE PERSONAL ANALOGIES

In this step, the teacher asks the students to think about what it would feel like to be the object chosen in Step 2 and to tell why they have that particular feeling. Student responses are recorded on the board. Responses from the English class to the question, "How would it feel to be a dogwood?" included:

bored	proud	conceited	exploited
admired	beautiful	loved	needed
poisonous	symbolic	strong	adaptable
powerful	innocent	evil	secure
sad	adapted		

STEP 4: IDENTIFY COMPRESSED CONFLICTS

The teacher asks the class to review the list of words from Step 3 to find pairs of words which seem to "fight" or are in "opposition to each other" and to explain their reasoning. The class then votes for the pair of words that represents the best compressed conflict. The English class generated these pairs of words in opposition and voted for "evil and innocent" as the pair that expressed the best compressed conflict.

> loved — lonely
> exploited — admired
> exploited — secure
> evil — innocent
> lonely — needed
> poisonous — innocent
> sad — proud
> power — innocent
> sad — strong
> adaptable — secure

STEP 5: CREATE A NEW DIRECT ANALOGY

The teacher then names another category (plant, animal, machine, or other) for a direct analogy and asks the class to think of examples of that category which are best described by the compressed conflict chosen in Step 4. The students then vote for the object best described by the compressed conflict.

Using a machine as the analogy, the English class chose these examples as embodying the characteristics "evil and innocent" and chose "television" as the best direct analogy:

car	gun	electric chair
cotton gin	artificial heart	television
chipper	wrecking ball	blender
government	nuclear bomb	

STEP 6: REEXAMINE THE ORIGINAL TOPIC

The class returns to the original topic by comparing the last direct analogy to the original topic. This will be the first time during the process that the original topic has been mentioned since Step 1. As the students have "moved away" from the original topic, they have listened to each other develop analogies and images that will enable them to think about the original topic in new ways. At this point, it is effective to have the students write sentences or a paragraph describing the original topic to compare to their original writing. Allowing the students to choose from all the analogies generated during the process will enhance the quality of the descriptions.

An image generated by the English class in comparing a television and war included "war is like a television because its intent may be honorable or good, but the results of what it does may be harmful." Another image chosen from the analogies compared "war to an ivy plant that entangles and strangles living things."

STEP 7: EVALUATE

A comparison of writings completed before and after participation in the model provides insight into student ability to consider a concept in a more creative manner. The teacher may choose to evaluate the use of metaphor and imagery in writings or discussions following the Synectics model. Discussion with the class about their thoughts during the model helps students to analyze images and to recognize thought processes involved in creative thinking.

TROUBLESHOOTING POTENTIAL PROBLEMS

Problems may arise when the direct analogies chosen in Steps 2 and 5 do not yield a sufficient number of student responses. If the chosen analogy is not working, the teacher should substitute another analogy, so that students can generate as many comparisons as possible. In Steps 2, 4, and 5, students' votes may be influenced by peers. For this reason, it is sometimes helpful to have students close their eyes or put their heads down on their desks when voting. In the case of a tie, the class votes a second time on items receiving the most votes. The benefit of the model is realized through student comparison of unlike items and discussions of the tension developed in compressed conflicts.

ASSESSING AND GRADING STUDENT LEARNING

As noted in Step 7, evaluation of student learning in the Synectics model may take several forms. Pre- and postprocess writings may be compared for use of more complex analogies, improved description of a topic, or increased use of metaphor. As students become more proficient with the model, the teacher may note improvement in their ability to think flexibly and in more complex terms, especially in discussing compressed conflicts.

EMPLOYING APPROPRIATE FOLLOW-UP ACTIVITIES

Synectics can be combined with other models to expand student thought about concepts being explored through concept development or concept attainment. Because the Synectics model allows students to gain another perspective, a new dimension is added to the study of abstract ideas such as prejudice or democracy. It is effective both as an introductory activity or as closure to a unit of study. It is particularly effective in improving creative writing.[6]

MEMORY MODEL

DESCRIBING THE MODEL

For years, memory enhancement techniques have been explored both in and out of the classroom. Long before students concerned themselves with memorizing the amendments to the Constitution or the lines in the next school play, Greek and Roman orators applied memory techniques to the learning of lengthy speeches. In more recent years, many systems for improving memory have been developed (Lorayne & Lucas, 1974; Buzan, 1983; Clark & Clark, 1989; Carney & Levin, 1991). Numerous research studies support the educational benefits of using mnemonic techniques to facilitate memory (Peters & Levin, 1986; Levin & Levin, 1990, Carney, Levin, & Levin, 1994).

In their book, *Instruction: A Models Approach*, Gunter, Estes, and Schwab (1995) provide four basic models for improving the

---

[6] For materials in the area of language development contact SES Associates, 121 Brattle Street, Cambridge, MA 02138.

recall of information: the link model, the loci model, the memory through motion model, and the names and faces model. The link model provides an easy-to-follow guide for those interested in exploring memory models with students. This model is based on the process of associating or linking new information that is to be memorized to something that is already known. The teacher initially guides the model by selecting and organizing information that is to be learned and by modeling and explaining the process of making associations. The model shifts from being teacher-centered to being student-centered as students are provided with opportunities to practice developing their own associations (see Fig. 4.4). Rather than being an instructional strategy used solely by teachers, with sufficient practice this model can become an effective study technique for students.

FIGURE 4.4. STEPS IN THE MEMORY MODEL[7]

1. **Select** the items.
2. **Organize** the material.
3. **Prepare** the associations.
4. **Explain** the process and present the associations.
5. **Practice** creating associations.
6. **Evaluate**.

Before examining the model and its use in the instructional program, it is important to point out that the focus of this model is not on the rote memorization of facts and skills, but on the logical association of facts with information that is already in the mind. Even though the memorization of basic facts may at times be necessary, in general, the rote memorization of information does not facilitate the transfer of learning (Caine, et al., 1994). The memory model is primarily a process of associating and linking the unfamiliar with the familiar, thus linking the "to-be-acquired information" meaningfully to the "previously acquired information" (Levin & Levin, 1990, p. 316). This model is appropriate for use in any content area where students are asked to memorize information.

---

[7] Gunter, Estes & Schwab, 1995, p. 251.

PREPARING FOR THE LESSON

Before using the memory model, the teacher and/or students must identify the information that is to be memorized (plant classifications, a poem, famous people and their deeds, etc.). To "convince students of the utility" of the technique, it is important to provide demonstrations of how the model can be applied directly to course content (Carney, Levin, & Levin, 1994, p. 171). The teacher must be familiar enough with the model to demonstrate the strategies and explain his/her thinking to the students. It is important that the associations that are made provide strong visual images, linking familiar information to the new data. In other words, students must be able to connect the new learning to something that is already in their minds if "memory links" are to be established.

The teacher should maintain a goal of developing student independence with this model. Once the students have developed an understanding of this model, the teacher primarily serves as a facilitator, providing materials and assistance as needed. Although no special materials are required to implement this model, the use of pictures, objects, or other materials that increase sensory experiences will help to develop stronger images for memory links. Drawing paper and color markers are suggested for activities that encourage students to link new information to strong visual images.

USING THE STRATEGIES

Presented next are the six basic steps of the link model as described by Gunter, Estes, and Schwab (1995). It is important that the teacher become familiar with the entire model before demonstrating the process to students. To practice and check for understanding, it is helpful to rehearse the model with friends, family, or peers before working with students. Following the list of basic steps, an example of a memory lesson is provided.

STEP 1: SELECT THE INFORMATION

The first step in teaching this model is to select the information that is to be memorized. Although something as simple as a grocery list may be used as an example, it is important to help students define key concepts, facts, or other pieces of information from their studies that need to be remembered. The teacher provides the items to be memorized or students are asked to identify the information by underlining, circling, highlighting, or listing the ideas from materials selected by the teacher. It is suggested that the first time this model is used the teacher generate the list of items to be learned.

STEP 2: ORGANIZE THE MATERIAL

Once the information to be learned is selected, the teacher analyzes the information to determine if the items could be categorized in a manner that would facilitate the memory process. Even though it is possible to use the link method to memorize information that is listed randomly, it is helpful to list the items alphabetically, numerically, chronologically, or in any grouping appropriate to the learning.

STEP 3: DEVELOP ASSOCIATIONS

After the information has been organized, the next step involves the creation of strong visual images that link what is to be learned to something that is already known. Additionally, these images must somehow connect the items to be remembered, the first to the second, the second to the third, and so on. The first time this model is used, the teacher develops the visual associations in order to model the thinking process for students.

It is important that familiar information be linked clearly to the new information and that the items to be remembered are securely linked to one another. To make strong visual links, Buzan (1983, p. 65) suggests the images must be one or more of the following:

+ **Exaggerated**—exceptionally large, loud, etc.
+ **Absurd**—humorous, ridiculous.
+ **Sensual**—associated with any of the basic bodily senses.
+ **Moving**—not static.
+ **Colored**—bright, showy, gaudy.
+ **Imaginative**—creative, imaginative in any way.

♦ **Pure**—clear, not too abstract or complicated.

The purpose of this activity is to create intense visual images that "stick" in the mind and are easily recalled.

STEP 4: PRESENT ASSOCIATIONS TO THE CLASS, MODELING THE PROCESS

The teacher explains the need for the model and outlines the steps. It is important that students hear about the thinking that occurred as the teacher selected and organized the information and prepared visual associations. Once the associations have been presented, students are asked to examine them to determine which of the images are exaggerated, absurd, colored, moving, etc. Students also can be asked to make suggestions as to how the associations could be enhanced.

During this stage of the process, the teacher can elect to involve students in the creation of images for several items. It is important that the teacher remind students that, for this technique to be most effective, the images must have personal meaning.

STEP 5: PRACTICE USING AND DEVELOPING ASSOCIATIONS

After all of the associations have been created and presented, students are given time to practice recalling the items. This practice may come in the form of verbally repeating the associations to a partner, drawing the images, or visualizing the associations and jotting down key words that will provide memory assists. Students then "quiz" each other, or the class can be challenged as a whole, to see how many of the items can be remembered using the associations.

Next, students are given the opportunity to practice using the model. Depending upon the class and the information used as a model, the teacher can decide to have students generate new associations for the same list of information or create new images for a different list. In either case, time needs to be provided for student practice as part of the instructional period or as a homework assignment. After the associations have been created, students should be allowed time to share their images with others.

STEP 6: EVALUATE

To evaluate use of this model, students should be asked to recall the information in some manner. It is suggested that, rather than simply asking students to list the information, the teacher design evaluation strategies that require application of skills. Problem-solving activities and written assignments are examples of measures that can be used to go beyond the simple listing of facts.

The second stage of this process involves student self-evaluation. To do this, students examine the effectiveness of the process and analyze the images that were retained and those that were forgotten. This evaluation must be an ongoing process if students are to improve in their use of the model.

APPLYING THE MODEL

The memory model is appropriate for use in any content area where students are asked to memorize information. The following lesson links the names of the thirteen original colonies to strong visual images that are connected in a story format. Using this model, students not only memorize the colonies, but also the order in which they gained statehood. The example is appropriate for use in a social studies class or as part of a unit designed to teach memory improvement strategies.

Lesson: The Thirteen Original Colonies

Objective: The student will memorize the 13 original colonies in the order in which they became the first 13 states.

Step 1: The 13 original colonies are selected as the information that is to be learned.

Step 2: The colonies are organized according to the order in which statehood was gained.

Step 3: The teacher develops strong visual images for linking all 13 colonies. Associations are made that are vivid, yet direct. Images that are too complicated or detailed confuse students and tend to inhibit rather than enhance learning.

Step 4: The teacher begins the lesson by explaining the objective and discussing the importance of learning this information. The teacher then describes the techniques that are useful in enhancing memory, explaining how these techniques have been used to develop strong visual images that will help students remember not only the colonies but also the order in which they gained statehood.

The lesson proceeds as follows:

Teacher talk: Think of a blank stage. On this stage we are going to create a pile of items, one on top of the other. When I finish describing the items, I will call on several of you to try to recall everything I have described.

1. On the stage, spinning on its edge like a coin, is a huge white dinner plate, from the Dollar General Store. Let's call it "dollarware." (Delaware)

2. Right in the middle of the spinning dollarware is a gold pencil, piercing like an arrow through the bull's eye of a target. (Pennsylvania)

3. Standing on the end of the gold pencil, where the eraser usually is, is a newborn Jersey calf trying very hard to keep its balance. (New Jersey)

4. The tail of the newborn Jersey calf is sticking straight out; on the end of its tail, where the tuft of hair usually is, is a big, ripe, juicy, Georgia peach. (Georgia)

5. Piercing right through the middle of the ripe Georgia peach, making it inedible, is a greasy connecting rod from a tractor trailer. (Connecticut)

6. On top of that very greasy connecting rod is balanced a massive, not big, not large, but MASSIVE, block of ice. (Massachusetts)

7. Slipping and sliding and trying to keep his balance on that MASSIVE block of ice is a recent graduate from medical school; we know that because he's holding a white diploma with red letters that say "MD" on it and he's waving it to his mother. (Maryland)

8. Perched on top of the medical school graduate's head is a large ocean liner headed south for the winter. (South Carolina)

9. Sitting on the deck of that south-bound ocean liner is a brand new, freshly smoked ham. (New Hampshire)

10. Balanced on that new ham is Miss Virginia, wearing a shimmering dress and a large strangely shaped crown.

11. If you look closely at Miss Virginia, you can see that her crown is shaped just like New York's Statue of Liberty. (New York)

12. Balanced on the very tip of that New York landmark is the sister ship of the ocean liner, but this one is returning to the north carrying its cargo of sunburned tourists. (North Carolina)

13. The deck of that north-bound ocean liner is covered with tourists rubbing lotion over their burns. It seems that they would have known better than to ride in the sun all the way back from the islands. (Rhode Island)[8]

Step 5: After presenting all the images, the teacher asks students to repeat each of the images, individually, in a small group, or with a partner. The teacher should make sure that key words, such as "pencil," "massive," "new ham," etc., are included in each student's oral response. Students can also draw the images as a means of rehearsing the information.

At this point students may be encouraged to "personalize" the images more by creating new images to replace any of the original that are unclear to them. Here the emphasis is on making associations that have personal meaning for each student.

Step 6: The ability of the students to recall the information may be evaluated by several methods, the

---

[8] The idea for this lesson came from Ed Buhrer, English teacher, Louisa County High School, Mineral, Virginia.

simplest of which is to have students list the colonies in the order in which they were presented. A more advanced form of evaluation requires the students to utilize the information to solve a problem or answer a question. For example, in the 13 original colonies lesson, rather than listing the 13 colonies, students might be asked to describe how the growth of the nation would have changed if the three southernmost colonies had not been part of the original 13. Another task might be to have students plot the 13 original colonies on a map and explain why these colonies were first to establish statehood.

A second part of the evaluation procedure involves self-evaluation on the part of the learner. Students are allowed time to discuss the model, what they found to be effective and ineffective strategies, and how they might use the model in the future.

TROUBLESHOOTING POTENTIAL PROBLEMS

For students to maintain interest in learning this model they must see the benefits of devoting time to the creation of associations. If students perceive this as a game rather than a purposeful learning activity, they may decide they do not want to "play." It is then that problems in the form of inattention and disruptive behavior are likely to occur.

It is important that the teacher have clear examples to provide during the introduction of the model. If associations become too abstract or complicated, students may be lost. The teacher also must explain his or her thinking during the creation of the images and stress the importance of students developing images that have personal meaning. Some students may at first have difficulty developing visual images and, if asked to draw images, those who do not consider themselves to be artists may resist. For this strategy to be added to their repertoire of study skills, extra encouragement and practice may be needed.

ASSESSING AND GRADING STUDENT LEARNING

As previously outlined, evaluation is included as part of the memory model. **In Step 6,** students are assessed on their recall of information and on their ability to utilize the model. If the purpose of the lesson is to have students memorize information, then it is appropriate, following opportunities for practice, that students be assessed and graded. The teacher also may evaluate the students' understanding of the model by asking them to explain their use of images and to discuss the effectiveness of memory techniques. To promote the use of the model, it is suggested that student self-evaluation be encouraged.

FOLLOW-UP ACTIVITIES

Following the initial teaching of the memory model, the teacher should look for additional information that could be presented or studied effectively with the use of the model. Students should be encouraged to utilize this method in their studies of all content areas. The techniques used in developing associations should be reviewed periodically to promote retention. One means of reviewing association techniques is to select a popular commercial and examine it to determine which techniques were utilized to encourage consumers to remember the product. This activity provides a clear demonstration of the fact that memory techniques are useful and effective.

CONCLUSION

The models presented in this chapter are designed not only to enhance teaching, but also to improve thinking. Longer periods of instructional time in a block schedule invite teachers to design lessons that actively engage the learner in processing information. Although learning and teaching new models will require time and effort, the teacher will be rewarded by increased student interest and improved learning.

REFERENCES

Bruner, J., Goodnow, J., & Austin, G. (1977). *A study of thinking.* Huntington: Robert E. Krieger.
Buzan, T. (1983). *Use both sides of your brain.* New York: E.P. Dutton.

Caine, G., Caine, R., & Crowell, S. (1994). *Mindshifts*. Tucson: Zephyr Press.

Canady, R.L., & Rettig, M. (1995). *Block scheduling: A catalyst for change in high schools*. Princeton: Eye on Education.

Carney, R., & Levin, J. (1991). Mnemonic techniques and art education: get the picture. *College Student Record, 25(3)*, 318–324.

Carney, R., Levin, J., & Levin, M. (1994). Enhancing the psychology of memory by enhancing memory of psychology. *Teaching of Psychology, 21(3)*, 171–174.

Clark, C., & Clark C. (1989). *Hassle-free homework*. New York: Doubleday.

Gordon, W.J. (1961). *Synectics*. New York: Harper & Row.

Gordon, W.J. (1968). *Making it strange*. Books 1 & 2 and teacher's guide. Evanston: Harper & Row.

Gordon, W.J., & Poze, T. (1971). *The metaphorical way of learning and knowing*. Cambridge: Porpoise Books.

Gunter, M.A., Estes, T., & Schwab, J. (1995). *Instruction: A models approach*. 2nd ed. Boston: Allyn and Bacon.

Joyce, B., & Weil, M. (1986). *Models of teaching*. 3rd ed. Englewood Cliffs: Prentice Hall.

Joyce, B., Weil, M., & Showers, B. (1992). *Models of teaching*. Boston: Allyn and Bacon.

Levin, M., & Levin, J. (1990). Scientific mnemonics: Methods for maximizing more than memory. *American Educational Research Journal, 27*, 301–321.

Lorayne, H. & Lucas, J. (1974). *The memory book*. New York: Ballantine Books.

Peters, E., & Levin, J. (1986). Effects of a mnemonic imagery strategy on good and poor readers' prose recall. *Reading Research Quarterly, 21(2)*, 179–192.

Taba, H., Durkin, M., Frankel, J., & McNaughton, A. (1971). *A teacher's handbook to elementary social studies*. Reading: Addison-Wesley.

Worthen, B. (1968). A study of discovery and expository presentation: implications for teaching. *Journal of Teacher Education, 19*, 223–242.

5

SIMULATIONS[1]

Historically, having the "time to teach" and to use techniques such as the simulation has been one of the most compelling problems faced by teachers. The traditional fragmented school day has strongly reinforced teacher-centered, teacher-dominated classroom instructional techniques. Now, with the increasing availability of block scheduling in middle and high schools, teachers can and should use more and more interactive teaching strategies with their students. Such strategies include cooperative learning, Socratic seminars, role-playing, academic games, and simulations. Simulations are particularly promising and hold great potential for increasing student learning because they include many aspects of other interactive learning techniques. The Chinese proverb which proclaims that "I do and I understand" is a relevant message to educators concerned about student achievement.

The purpose of this chapter is to help teachers make informed decisions about the use of simulations as an interactive instructional method. Through an increased awareness of the educational potential of simulations, teachers will gain an understanding of what they can and cannot do to enhance student learning outcomes.

WHAT CONSTITUTES A SIMULATION?

A basic definition of simulations describes them simply as "reality." Cruickshank (1968, pp. 190–191) depicts simulations as a teaching strategy where a scenario or model has been created to be played out by participants to provide them with lifelike problem-solving experiences.

A simulation is described by Klietsch (1972) as "a replica of

---

[1] This chapter was written by Elizabeth D. Morie, Associate Professor, School of Education, James Madison University, Harrisonburg, Virginia.

a real world situation worth learning. An educational simulation permits a person to become a working member of the system, to set goals, to develop policies, and to analyze information." For Jones (1987, pp. 9–18), the simulation is "an untaught event in which sufficient information is provided to allow the participants to achieve reality of function in a simulated environment." And finally, Bloomer adopted the definition that simulations must include two essential elements. First, the simulation must represent a "real" situation; second, it must be "operational" or involve an ongoing process (1973, p. 224).

A "simulation game," according to Cruickshank (1977, p. 27), is an academic game in which students use prior knowledge in a specific subject such as math, English, or economics to solve problems related to that discipline. *Scrabble* and *Monopoly* are examples of simulation games related to the fields of spelling and economics.

An illustration of an early simulation appropriate for middle and high school students is "Caribou Hunt" from the social studies series, *Man: A Course of Study* (Educational Development Center, 1968). The purpose of the simulation is to encourage students to study man in a very different cultural setting. The simulation enabled players to project what it was like to be an Eskimo hunter trying to survive in an arctic land. Students worked in groups of five, with one member of each group representing the caribou herd, two students acting as beaters, and two as kayakers. The game was played on a game sheet; the object of the simulation was to have the beaters pursue the caribou and force them into the water where kayakers could overtake and kill them. Special dice were used to determine the movement of the beaters and kayakers. The game proceeded quickly and permitted players to see how difficult it was for Eskimo hunters to accumulate enough food to survive, and how much time would be taken up by hunting. As students continued to play the game, they usually developed more effective hunting strategies (Cruickshank & Telfer, 1980, p. 77).

USES FOR CLASSROOM SIMULATIONS

Classroom simulations are designed for a variety of instructional purposes, extending from introductory exercises to culminating activities that follow extensive student research and classroom preparation. The following are examples of specific purposes for which simulations can be used (Shay, 1980, pp. 26–27).

ICEBREAKERS

Simulations are an effective team-building or "warm up" activity for students (See Chapter 3 for other team-building activities). They also can provide a means of introducing course content. Simulations have been used effectively to create a learning environment that encourages a high level of class participation and interaction. Such an environment is particularly productive in disciplines such as social studies, where class discussions and group projects are valuable in teaching course content. Simulations for team-building and enhancing classroom interaction should be fairly brief, imaginative, and involve communication skills. An example of such an activity, developed by Ken Jones (1991), is "Detective Story." The simulation requires the participants to become actual ideas for characters in an unwritten detective story in the mind of a famous author who has a mental block. The writer's block prevents the ideas from joining together as a group—the participants must meet in pairs and negotiate ideas to try to get the story moving again.

DEVELOPING EMPATHY AND UNDERSTANDING

Many simulations will involve students in situations where they will need to make critical choices and deal with social conflict with diverse people and diverse cultures. Such "real" experiences appear to be an effective method for broadening students' perspectives and developing greater sensitivity to and understanding of social, cultural, economic, and political problems. "Tenement," a British simulation, is a good example of a caring simulation which can elicit great empathy and understanding along with denunciations of injustice. It concerns the problems accompanying life in a large-city tenement. The tenants do not compete for benefits; they apply for benefits. There are 14 roles: seven tenants, six public agencies, and one landlord. The purpose is to make students aware of the difficulties of living in such a situation and to point to ways some of these difficulties might be solved (Jones, 1987, p. 23).

ANALYZING SOCIAL PROBLEMS

Often simulations are designed to immerse students in the scope, causes, and effects of certain social problems. Within the context of simulations, it is possible to prescribe solutions and to study their impact or consequences. The "Tenement" simulation, described above, also could be used effectively as a means of analyzing social problems.

EXPLORING THE FUTURE

Predictions or exploration of the future are possible through complex computer simulations. Students are encouraged to think like creative problemsolvers and to develop the capacity to manage and cope with continuous change. "Cities" is an example of such a commercially available simulation game where the player(s) make decisions regarding the future of the city (Lewis, et al., 1974, p. 97). Other examples are discussed under the section "Using Simulations in the Content Areas."

DEVELOPING ANALYTICAL AND RESEARCH SKILLS

Simulations which involve any degree of problem-solving will develop students' skills in analysis. It is especially valuable when simulations also allow the application of analytical and research skills across the curriculum.

DEVELOPING ORAL AND WRITTEN COMMUNICATION SKILLS

Teachers who use simulations believe that oral and written communication skills are improved as a result of student involvement in activities that stimulate them to use the skills of analysis, evaluation, and extrapolation. Most simulations require effective oral communication skills, and teachers can work on writing skills by requiring individual papers on such topics as comparing the simulation with reality (Shay, 1980, pp. 26–27).

One of the advantages of simulations is that students learn by using a wide range of communication skills: negotiating, arguing, interviewing, note-taking, drafting, editing, organizing, public speaking, and listening. They get to practice communication skills.

SELECTING A SIMULATION

When choosing an appropriate simulation, teachers need to ask themselves nine specific questions (Shay, pp. 29–30).

FIGURE 5.1. BASIC STEPS IN SELECTING A SIMULATION

---

1. What is the instructional objective?
2. What problem or process is represented?
3. Where in the course content should it be placed?
4. How much class time will the exercise require?
5. How many class members can participate?
6. Who will fill what roles?
7. What is the composition of the teams?
8. What does the debriefing include?
9. What financial and classroom resources are needed?

---

1. What is the instructional objective? This is the first and most critical decision in the entire selection process.

2. What problem or process is represented? A simulation should never be selected merely for "fun;" rather, the simulation should relate to the course content or objectives.

3. Where in the course content should the simulation be placed? Running a simulation at the beginning and at the end of a course has certain advantages. At the beginning, the simulation may establish an open or participatory atmosphere, and it also may be used as a basis for discussion throughout the course. At the end of the course, the simulation may be used as a culminating activity following quite a lengthy preparatory process involving teacher lectures and student research. However, the teacher needs to ensure that sufficient time has been allowed at the end of the course to complete the simulation, including sufficient time for a quality debriefing.

4. How much class time will the exercise require? Teachers are advised to begin with a brief simulation that can be completed in one class period; the debriefing may be carried over into the next class. An alternative is to select a simulation that can be completed entirely during an extended class period or block. As the teacher becomes more proficient in selecting and implementing simulations, he/she can move on to one which requires several days. Eventually, some highly experienced teachers are able to build an entire course around the extended simulation.

5. *How many class members can participate?* Simulations generally will recommend an optimum number of players; most, however, can be expanded or contracted depending on total class size. Avoid those simulations that involve a small number of participants and thereby exclude much of the class.

6. *Who will fill what roles?* Consider carefully the possible consequences of how students are allocated to certain roles. An example of an important decision is determining how high status roles should be distributed.

7. *What is the composition of the teams?* If the simulation is a team activity, consider whether the simulation is appropriate for the class's ability. Is there sufficient heterogeneity in the class to build teams capable of functioning adequately in the simulation?

8. *What does the debriefing include?* Does the simulation include a debriefing guide, with appropriate questions that help accomplish the objectives of the activity? How much of the debriefing is teacher-focused and how are students involved? What further learnings should result from the simulation?

9. *What financial and classroom resources are needed?* Preview the materials needed, physical space requirements, and all other resources required to enable the simulation to proceed successfully.

DESIGNING A SIMULATION

Teachers who are simulation novices are well-advised to begin with commercially developed materials that will lead them through the implementation steps. As they become more proficient with this teaching strategy, many teachers will prefer to develop their own simulated activities based on the course content. Surveys have found that teachers are more likely to use their own simulations longer, and they believe them to be academically more relevant than those that are commercially developed. Teachers can use the steps below and in Figure 5.2 as a guide for designing their own simulations (Shay, 1980, pp. 30–31).

1. *Define the educational objective.* Decide if the purpose of the activity is to be conceptual learning, skills acquisition, or empathic insight.

FIGURE 5.2. DESIGNING A SIMULATION

---

1. Define the educational objective.
2. Define the model to be represented.
3. Outline the dynamics of the model.
4. Delineate the rules of play.
5. Develop discussion questions for debriefing.

---

2. Define the model to be represented. What area or problem will be the focal point for the simulation? What types of organizations, groups, or people will be involved? During this step, create the environment and the initial scenario.

3. Outline the dynamics of the model. What roles will the players and the teacher assume? What types of interaction will take place between individuals, the environment, and groups? What behaviors will the simulation seek to reveal or encourage?

4. Delineate the rules of play. Begin with procedural rules such as length and sequence of events. Then determine behavioral rules, such as the type of behavior required, what restraints will be on behavior, what will motivate the players, and what are to be their goals. Decide how resources will be distributed initially and what will determine changes in resource allocation. Establish evaluation rules to determine how feedback on behaviors and decisions will be provided and how goal attainment will be measured. Finally, how will conflicts be resolved and how will rules be enforced?

5. List discussion questions for debriefing. Some sample questions include the following:

♦   What were the reactions, perceptions, and interpretations of the actions of others?

♦   Analyze and compare individual or group objectives and strategies in light of the outcomes.

♦   Consider cause and effect; what might have been done differently?

♦   Make a careful comparison of the simulation model with real world for the purpose of assessing its accuracy (Shay, 1980, pp. 30–31).

IMPLEMENTING SIMULATIONS

Whether the simulation is teacher-made or commercially developed, specific decisions must be made before implementing the simulation.

First, what role will the teacher play during the simulation activities? Will the teacher be merely an observer, or act as an umpire? The teacher should not become an active participant, as this changes the dynamics of the activity. The teacher also must guard against being too dominant or attempting to overcontrol the students' interactions.

A second important decision is whether and how the simulation will be graded. Teachers are urged to use their own judgment in this regard; however, they need to assess closely whether grading will distort student behaviors and outcomes. One recommended alternative for lengthy simulations that do require some grading is to base grades on the planning phase, such as on a preliminary research paper, or on a postsimulation analysis paper.

Jones (1987, p. 101) deals extensively with the question of assessment because it is an area of controversy in simulation literature. Figure 4.3 represents an example of how a teacher might wish to formally assess student behavior during a simulation.

Another important consideration is to determine how the educational value of the simulation will be assessed. As stated earlier, commercially developed simulations generally are recommended for beginners because, among other considerations, they have been pretested, and they contain valuable planning and debriefing guidelines. Additionally, all teachers should use the debriefing discussions to glean modifications which might make the simulation more realistic or more educational. Student feedback should be a continuous source for modifying future simulations, whether commercial or teacher-designed.

Still another critical task for the teacher in implementing a simulation is to ensure that students perceive a challenging goal and are encouraged to find ways of reaching that goal through their own efforts. One method for achieving challenge is to build a carefully structured, yet flexible plan for student participation in the simulation event. A knowledge base is essential before beginning the simulation; facts, attitudes, and values must be

FIGURE 4.3. ASSESSMENT OF STUDENT BEHAVIOR

Assessment of Student Behavior				
	Standard Achieved			
Criterion	Above Average	Average	Below Average	Remarks
Level of Interaction				
Clarity of Expression				
Courteous				
etc.				

explored using all possible sources, such as lectures, readings, films, observations, and interviews. Moreover, the instructions for the simulation must be studied carefully before beginning the activity. This preparation also provides students the opportunity to accept individual responsibility for their involvement.

Grouping is an important consideration if the simulation is to proceed successfully. Whenever possible, divide the class into many small groups. A great deal has been written regarding optimum group size. There appears to be consensus that the ideal group size is four to five members. Studies have found that interaction drops considerably among secondary students when groups exceed nine members; the larger group tends to split into small subgroups.

The composition of groups also should be considered carefully. McKinney and Dill (1969) reported that students performed better when they were given the opportunity to decide for themselves how team assignments should be made and how they should be organized. A formal method for accomplishing this would be the use of a group preference questionnaire. Certain guidelines for teachers are quite important, however. Group membership should change over time as topics change. Homogeneous groups are not as effective as heterogeneous groups, which are more lifelike. Motivation is also higher in mixed groups. The "natural leader phenomenon" suggests that groups interact better when the leadership has been selected by the group rather than assigned by the teacher.

A final step, and possibly the most important one in the implementation process, is planning and executing a thorough and careful debriefing. The debriefing exercise is critically important in determining the effectiveness of the simulation event. The process should move fairly rapidly from the specific to the general in the following sequence (Jones, 1987, pp. 86–87):

> Go around the table and have participants explain their own parts in the simulation, problems they encountered, and how they solved them. Then enter into a general discussion on:
>
> ◆ How did the groups organize?
>
> ◆ Was the organization effective?
>
> ◆ What alternatives were there?
>
> ◆ Did the group or individuals explore the options, analyze the situation, and plan accordingly?
>
> ◆ How effective was the communication?
>
> ◆ Were the language and behavior suitable and appropriate?
>
> ◆ What lessons did the participants learn?
>
> ◆ Would they act differently when faced with a similar situation in the future?

Using Simulations in the Content Areas

Teachers wishing to include simulations among their instructional strategies should begin with a review of current textbooks to determine what might be readily available from the publishers. Should recent texts fail to produce relevant materials, and many will, a review of the literature on simulations should be the next step in search of simulations which would help meet the requirements of the local and state curricula and the interests of the students. Unfortunately, most handbooks and directories on simulations were published two or more decades ago, which makes availability of the materials problematic at best. See the list of references and resources accompanying this chapter for sources of simulations.

SOCIAL SCIENCES

Whereas simulations can and have been used in all content areas, a literature review confirms that the greatest volume of materials has been developed in the social sciences. Some relevant simulation topics might include such issues as the effect of rapid social change on life in American cities, how Athens lost her Empire, dissension among the early Greek states, the rise of the United States, federal versus state power, national priorities—the list is endless, depending upon the teacher's imagination.

Goodsell (1972, p. 44) developed a typical social studies simulation around the issue of the arms race since 1939. Six weeks were spent in the traditional study and classwork dealing with the facts and issues. During the seventh week, five small teams were set up to represent five countries' views on the arms race: The People's Republic of China, the USSR, the United States, India, and Pakistan. The class was then told that Pakistan had invaded Kashmir. Each team was assigned to prepare a position statement relative to this problem. Each team's statement was read to the class for comment. The position statements were revised and again presented to the class. The India representative suggested that Kashmir not be given up without a fight. The moderator responded that Pakistani troops were killing Hindus trying to flee India. The Indian delegate had no comment. Such moves and countermoves continued until it was decided that a U.N. peacekeeping force should occupy the border.

The format used in this example could easily be adapted for a number of similar issues, including the Bosnian conflict. Goodsell reported that student interest was outstanding and students became fully informed about the issues involved and the complexity of international relations as a result of their participation in this activity.

Simulations in economics are plentiful; many are readily available from the Council for Economic Education, located in a major college or university in every state. Materials and other support are made available to schools upon request.

The simulation "Balance" (Lewis, et al., 1974, p. 93) is an activity involving ecology, economic goals, and decision-making. Intended for senior high school students, the first hour simulates the last 150 years of U.S. history. Fifteen participants are animals; four are Indians; the rest are settlers who destroy the animals, fight Indians, and tame the wilderness until their population exceeds 100,000. The participants then are divided into families of four members each, who live in Ecopolis, an ecologically troubled city. Students interview parents and adults, read about pollution, and attempt to develop a plan for social action to address their problems. Participants conduct an ecological survey of their community and a forum on the ecological balance in their local environment. The simulation concludes with an essay-style evaluation.

"Community" involves both economics and local governmental affairs. This simulation helps participants become aware of specific economic principles and problems involved in running a community, the relationship between wages and profits generated by local industry, and the tax expenditure problems of local government. The objective of the simulation game is to create the most progressive community possible. Success is measured by the number of improvements in the community, by wage rates and by the prosperity of local industry. Students become aware of the public sector of the local economy and discover the problems of selecting and financing public services (Lewis, et al., 1974, p. 98).

Birt and Nichol (1975, pp. 1–7) have compiled an interesting book containing "how to" guidelines for simulations as well as several detailed simulations that can be used readily by novice teachers. They envision simulations as an exciting teaching strategy that brings the past to life by enabling students to see history through the eyes of those who made it.

"Frontier" is a simulation that places students in positions found in early colonial America, such as merchants, tobacco planters, shipbuilders, and fur traders. The objective is to show students some of the problems and opportunities facing early settlers at various stages of colonial development from 1690 to 1783, while demonstrating the concept of the Frontier in American history. The colonists may settle in the regions shown on the simulation map, which depicts the five main colonial areas for settlement in the 1690s. Among the questions dealt with are the establishment of trade and commerce, the danger of Indian wars, the question of French intervention in alliance with the Indians, the changing fortunes in the production and sale of colonial commodities, the danger of natural disasters, and the outbreak of hostility between the colonists and the British government (Birt & Nichol, pp. 45–64).

SCIENCE

Simulations can be used in three ways in science education: (1) to teach the basic science content, (2) to educate through science to develop basic skills and desirable attitudes, and (3) to teach about science and technology and their impact on modern society (Ellington, et al., 1981, p. 25).

Ellington, et al. (1981), recommend that simulations not be used as a front-line teaching method, but as a complementary and supportive strategy for reinforcing basic facts and principles. Rather than the traditional paper-and-pencil exercises required by students to demonstrate their understanding, simulations could achieve the same objectives. An example of a simulation game is "The Young Chemist," which was developed to help students master the complexities of the periodic table (p. 177). The class is divided into groups of four, within which there are competing pairs who have to pick up question cards in numbered order and discuss the question in an attempt to reach the right solution. The answer agreed upon is then compared to that of the opposing pair, and the two answers are checked against the answer sheet. Clues can be taken in trying to find the correct answer and a scoring system is used on each item. The winning pair is the one scoring the most points over the entire game, which ends with the successful construction of the first 18 elements of the periodic table.

For developing laboratory skills, computer-based simulations offer the most interesting possibilities. Computer simulations can expand the range of experimental opportunities in situations where a conventional experiment is quite difficult; where experimental apparatus is not available, or too complicated, or too expensive for general laboratory use; where actual experimental work could be dangerous; or where a conventional experiment would take an unusually long time to complete.

Two Mesa, Arizona, public high schools are examples of schools that have turned to computer-based simulations when required experiments were too dangerous and too expensive. Some physics and chemistry courses are currently using the Universal Lab Interface (Vernier Software, Portland, OR) and the HyperCard hypermedia software (Apple Computer, Inc. Cupertino, CA). Classes also use the Personal Science Laboratory software and LinkWay Live! hypermedia software (EduQuest, Atlanta, GA) to conduct experiments (Stinson, 1993, p. 24).

ENGLISH

The literature is primarily silent with regard to simulations and simulation games appropriate for secondary English students. As simulations are noticeably absent from comprehensive source books, journal articles, and books dealing generally with simulations, one might conclude that this discipline does not readily lend itself to such a teaching strategy. However, teaching literature through role-playing (one facet of simulations) and using simulated events to motivate students in creative and descriptive writing appear to offer excellent possibilities for secondary English teachers.

As a role-playing example, a Shakespearian news conference might be held, with participants playing Friar Lawrence, Benvolio, Montague, Capulet, Lady Capulet, and the nurse. The characters are asked questions by the audience (reporters) requiring that they describe the play's events and their feelings or views, make comments, or answer questions about their relationships. The news conference might take place in the graveyard immediately after the end of the play, with the ghosts of Romeo, Juliet, and Tybalt present.

"Captions" (Jones, 1991, p. 185) is an appropriate simulation for a journalism class. The simulated event is the annual convention of the Reporters, Authors, and Photographers Society (RAPS); delegates are anxious to photograph each other and write captions for their pictures, which they hope will be included in *Rapture*, the society's journal. During the debriefing, the discussion could cover journalism issues concerned with news sense, eye-grabbing captions, publicity, invasion of privacy, libel, etc.

"Monolith" (Jones, 1991, p. 215) offers potential for public speaking and writing activities. The simulation requires participants to be archaeologists and sociologists who must theorize about a round stone object that has been found in a clearing in a jungle in a South American country. Participants are divided into pairs and work cooperatively to determine their approach to the problem, how to investigate without destroying the evidence, and what actions should be taken. The pairs must advance theories about the origin and the purpose of the stone. The debriefing could discuss the theories, the presentations, or historic preservation.

MATHEMATICS

Simulations can help students learn to apply mathematics using a simplified real-world event or computer-generated data which is then interpreted by the students. Prealgebra and algebra texts generally contain simulations to teach probability, but more sophisticated simulation games in mathematics are also plentiful. One of the oldest and best known is Allen's "WFF'n Proof," a game of modern logic, which he developed while a law student at Yale in the 1960s. The purpose of the game is to provide practice in abstract thinking and learn mathematical logic by constructing logical systems (Jones, 1988, p. 115). Allen also has authored various other mathematical games, including "On-Sets," the game of set theory, and "Equations," the game of creative mathematics (Zuckerman & Horn, 1970, pp. 211–212).

SOME ADVANTAGES OF USING SIMULATIONS

While there are certain concerns among teachers over the use of simulations, such concerns are diminished by the number of compelling advantages for students. The following areas are those in which simulations appear to be particularly effective as an instructional technique.

STUDENT INTEREST

There is ample evidence that simulations increase student involvement with the course content both within the classroom and outside. Simulations tend to motivate students and generate enthusiasm for the content, the teacher, and learning in general.

ATTITUDINAL CHANGE

Anderson's research (1970) revealed that simulations were better able to produce attitudinal changes than conventional classroom techniques. Many simulations deal with social and political issues, and following student involvement in such simulations, teachers report a moderate attitude change for students, who appear to become more empathetic, tolerant, and sensitive to the needs and demands of others. Simulations also tend to encourage increased peer- and student-teacher interaction and a more relaxed, open, and interactive classroom.

SKILLS ENHANCEMENT

Simulations tend to improve bargaining, persuasion, and decision-making skills. Students learn that society is complex and requires careful study and analysis. There is also some evidence that simulations promote student understanding of the relationships among ideas, people, and events.

COGNITIVE LEARNING

Simulations are not the optimal teaching strategy if the objective is factual learning outcomes. This does not mean, however, that some factual learning does not take place. In fact, it can be said that the vicarious and realistic experience of the simulation will make knowledge more relevant and understandable (Shay, 1980, pp. 27–28).

VARIETY AND CHANGE OF PACE

Simulations add variety to classroom activities and increase the opportunities to immerse students in realistic learning experiences. Such diversity is especially valuable for teaching in the longer block.

REALISTIC EXPERIENCES

Simulations guarantee participants a life-like experience. For example, during "A Caribou Hunt," students experience more realistically what it would be like to have to subsist as a primitive hunter.

PROBLEM-SOLVING EXPERIENCES

Simulations provide students the rare opportunity to solve difficult problems themselves rather than observe how someone else would solve them. Researchers have found that simulations in math and vocational education significantly increased students' problem-solving skills.

TRANSFER OF LEARNING

Studies have revealed that a simulation involving problem-solving tasks could develop students' ability to apply (transfer) knowledge of concepts and principles. Moreover, when simulations are used in such courses as driver education, the potential is greater for good transfer from the training situation to the real-life situation.

RESPONSIVE ENVIRONMENT

Students receive immediate feedback or knowledge of how they are doing. They know if they are catching caribou or if they are able to operate the automobile simulator.

SAFETY

During simulations, students are safe to make errors. For example, many errors can be made in a driving simulator without suffering the actual consequences.

FUN

Simulations are enjoyable. Students experience enjoyment beyond what is usually found even in the most interactive classroom. Teachers report that simulations promote greater student motivation and interest in academic subjects that many students typically dislike.

DEMOCRATIC

Simulations are in accord with democratic ideals. Authoritarian procedures are deemphasized as students are provided with opportunities for focused conversation, intense dialog, and the consideration of the social consequences of alternative policies or actions.

ADDRESSING LIMITATIONS AND CONCERNS

Even the strongest advocates for classroom simulations are aware of certain limitations. The following concerns need to be considered by teachers when evaluating when, where, and how to use simulations effectively.

UNPREDICTABILITY

Simulations will not have uniform results each time they are used, nor are they intended to do so. Outcomes will vary with different groups. By their very nature, simulations are intended to be quite flexible and to allow for considerable risk-taking. Confident teachers are not dissuaded from using simulation because of this characteristic. Rather, they welcome the flexibility and freedom provided by such an interactive learning activity and they value the benefits to their students.

LACK OF TEACHER CONTROL

Hustle and bustle, low-level chaos, and lack of certainty are all present from time to time during student involvement in simulations. Teachers who find interactive learning environments intolerable will not be comfortable, nor should they feel compelled to use classroom simulations. Before excluding simulations from their classroom, however, these teachers are urged to attempt a few short and simple events. They can still require, as should all competent teachers, the setting of ground rules and standards of behavior at the outset of every simulation in order to minimize inappropriate behavior among students.

COSTS

Whereas many commercially developed simulations are costly,

most are quite reasonable. Advance planning can get the expenditure for simulations included in the school budget and the cost can be justified on the basis of their effectiveness. Teacher-made simulations can bypass expensive materials and are often superior, as they relate more directly to the course content.

COMPLEXITY

Overly complex simulations include those with too many rules and too many details. These are cumbersome and distracting to participants and should be avoided (Shay, 1980, pp. 28–29).

TEACHER RESISTANCE

Although the simulation movement began during the early 1960s, many teachers remain unfamiliar with simulations as a teaching strategy and are naturally reluctant to use them. Teacher surveys have revealed that a primary reason for not trying simulations has been the need for training in the effective use of simulations and assistance with how to acquire them. Instructional leaders, including principals and central office staff, should take note of this need for help and provide workshops, follow-up support, and assistance in locating appropriate simulations in the content areas.

TIME

Many simulations require large amounts of time, but simulations do vary widely in both length and complexity; some are quite brief. If time is a constraint, this should be considered when selecting or designing specific simulations. Often hidden in the "time" concern is doubt about the academic value of simulations. As more teachers gain experience and confidence in using simulations, this concern may be alleviated.

AVAILABILITY

This is a genuine concern, but it is one that can be addressed. Current textbooks virtually ignore simulations as a teaching strategy. This circumstance certainly makes simulations less available than traditional teaching materials; however, they can be obtained from sources such as those mentioned throughout this chapter. Moreover, school districts can provide a means for teachers to share their own teacher-made simulations with colleagues across the district as well as regionally.

LIMITED PARTICIPATION

Whereas most simulations are flexible enough to accommodate an entire class, others clearly cannot. In situations where some students will be unable to participate, teachers need to be resourceful in modifying the activity to make it more inclusive. Related tasks such as observing participating students' interactions, assessing progress and performance, or recording results could be assigned.

CONCLUSION

As teachers find themselves with longer blocks of instructional time, they now can take advantage of a variety of instructional strategies that will directly involve students in more active learning. Classroom simulations offer such an opportunity. Simulations can provide students with opportunities for proper social, emotional, and intellectual development, and teachers have found that students are highly motivated by educational simulations and enjoy learning while participating in them. As teachers find it more and more challenging to make learning relevant, interesting, and exciting for today's learner, simulations and simulation games can become an effective instructional strategy.

REFERENCES

Anderson, C.R. (1970). *Measuring behavioral learnings: A study in consumer credits.* Baltimore, MD: Center for the Study of Social Organization of Schools.

Birt, D., & Nichol, J. (1975). *Games and simulations in history.* London: Longman Group Limited.

Bloomer, J. (1973). What have simulation and gaming got to do with programmed learning and educational technology? *Programmed Learning & Educational Technology, 10(4), 224.*

Cruickshank, D.R. (1977). *A first book of games and simulations.* Belmont, CA: Wadsworth.

Cruickshank, D.R. (December 1968). Simulation. *Theory into Practice,* 190–191.

Cruickshank, D.R., & Telfer, R. (1980). Classroom games and simulations. *Theory into Practice, 19(1),* 76–77.

Ellington, H., Addinall, E., & Percival, F. (1981). *Games and simulations in science education.* New York: Nichols Publishing.

Goodsell, D.R. (1972). Simulation games for social studies. *The Independent School Bulletin, 31(3),* 44–48.

Jones, K. (1987). *Simulations: A sourcebook for teachers and trainers.* 2nd ed. London: Kogan Page.

Jones, K. (1991). *Icebreakers: a sourcebook of games, exercises and simulations.* San Diego, CA: Pfeiffer & Co.

Klietsch, R. (1972–1973). *Involvement learning . . . what's it all about?* ISI Product, 4.

Lewis, D.R., Wentworth, D., Reinke, R., & Becker, W.W. (1974). *Educational games and simulations in economics.* New York: Joint Council on Economic Education.

McKinney, P.T., & Dill, W.R. (1966). Influences on learning in simulation games. *The American Behavioral Scientist, 10,* 28–32.

Shay, C. (1980). Simulations in the classroom: An appraisal. *Educational Technology, 20(11),* 26–31.

Social studies curriculum program (1968). Cambridge, MA: Educational Development Center.

Stinson, J. (March/April 1993). Technology outlook on math and science: Conversations with experts. *Media & Methods,* 24–25.

Zuckerman, D.W., & Horn, R.E. (1970). *The guide to simulation games for education and training.* Cambridge, MA: Information Resources, Inc.

OTHER RESOURCES FOR SIMULATIONS

GENERAL

Collins, B.E., & Guetzkow, H. (1964). *A social psychology of group process for decision making.* New York: John Wiley and Sons.

Cruickshank, D.R., Clinger, J.L., & Peters, J. (1979). The state of the art of simulation in teacher education. *Simulations/Games for Learning, 9(2),* 72–82.

Devries, D.L. & Slavin, R.E. (1976). *Teams-games-tournaments: A final report and the research.* Baltimore, MD: Center for the Study of Social Organization of Schools.

Greenblatt, C.S., & Duke, R.D. (1975). *Gaming-simulations: Rationale, design, and applications.* New York: Wiley and Sons.

Heitzmann, W.R. (1972). *Educational games and simulations.* Washington, DC: National Education Association.

Jones, K. (1984). *Nine graded simulations.* Oxford: Basil Blackwell. Reprinted under license under the title *Graded simulations.* (1985) London: Lingual House/Filmscan.

Jones, K. (1987). *Simulations: A handbook for teachers and trainers.* 2nd ed. New York: Nichols Publishing.

Jones, K. (1987). *Six simulations.* Oxford, Basil Blackwell.

Lewin, K. (1935). *Dynamic theory of personality.* New York: McGraw-Hill.

Shirts, R.G. (1969). *Starpower.* (Available from McGuiver Shirts, 218 Twelfth Street, Del Mar, CA).

State Councils for Economic Education found at a major college or university in each state.

Wright, G.W. (1989). Teaching mathematics with technology: Probability simulations. *Arithmetic Teacher*, 16–18.

DIRECTORIES

Horn, R.E. (1977). *The guide to simulations/games for education and training.* 3rd ed. Cranford, NJ: Didactic Systems, Inc.

Horn, R.E., & Cleaves, A. (1980). *The guide to simulations/games for education and training.* 4th ed. Newbury Park, CA: Sage Publishing.

Stadsklev, R. (1974). *Handbook of simulation gaming in education, part 1.* University of Alabama Institute of Higher Education Research and Services.

Zuckerman, D.W., & Horn, R.E. (1973). *The guide to simulations/games.* Cambridge, MA: Information Resources, Inc.

6

LEARNING CENTERS[1]

The introduction of a block schedule requires high school teachers who have maintained the traditional one-dimensional role of lecturer to shift to a multidimensional perspective integrating a variety of teaching and learning models. Among the strategies long used by elementary school teachers and successfully adapted by middle and high school teachers is the learning center approach. Learning centers, also called learning stations, provide individual students or pairs of students with the opportunity to

◆ Practice skills already introduced to the whole group;

◆ Extend knowledge and skills beyond those gained by the typical classmate;

◆ Rehearse knowledge and skills before assessment;

◆ Practice knowledge and skills that were not mastered in an earlier unit.

Secondary teachers who establish learning centers can work with individuals and small groups with the assurance that other students remain actively engaged. Using the centers helps students to become independent, self-directed, responsible learners; the teacher shifts into a facilitative, coaching role. Finally, learning centers provide for the maximal use of people, time, and space resources in the classroom so that the needs of students with different learning styles, abilities, and interests can be addressed.

While the process of developing learning centers for use in secondary classrooms may parallel similar applications in

---

[1] This chapter was written by Pamela Ridge Moran, Principal, Stony Point Elementary School, Keswick, Virginia.

elementary school settings, the products of center use should reflect the greater complexity of content, and perhaps the availability of more sophisticated equipment, at the high school level. For example, a 6th grade teacher may set up a stereo microscope in a learning center. Students are taught to use the microscope in whole-group lessons, and then they have the opportunity to choose objects to magnify and draw in a science journal at the center. Because the teacher strongly believes that the correct use of a microscope is a skill worth maintaining over time, and quickly forgotten without practice, the microscope is available for the entire year.

A high school biology teacher choosing a similar approach would expect all students to master the use of a microscope, but also to become proficient at accurately recognizing cellular structures through ongoing practice. Providing microscope centers in the science lab or classroom extends the time available for students to refine the knowledge and skills necessary to demonstrate mastery.

CENTER PLANNING

Until it becomes an automatic component of planning for a new unit, the process of developing centers may seem cumbersome. A useful framework for planning ways to integrate centers into the block schedule in a meaningful and productive way is to ask the questions why, who, what, where, when and how.

WHY?

Identifying the purpose of a center is a critical first step. Will the center allow students who finish work quickly to move into an extension activity? Could it help a student gain a better understanding of how to develop research sources? Will it allow the teacher to create a workshop environment, so that individual conferences about writing can occur while other students are actively engaged at centers or in other projects? Will the center be ancillary to instruction, or an integral component of the unit? Will the center concentrate students' attention on higher-order or lower-order thinking skills?

Using centers to keep students busy with "drill-and-kill"

worksheets is a weak and inappropriate use of center-based instruction. On the other hand, centers that are constructed to enhance thinking and research skills, as well as to extend knowledge, can create intrinsic interest in a particular unit and increase students' motivation to learn.

For example, at one center in a middle school, students were to read several haiku pieces and answer recall-level questions, including counting syllables to ensure that the poet had used the correct meter. When asked to work at this center, students audibly groaned. Next door, in another language arts classroom, students were able to look through a portfolio of interesting photographs, select one, and create their own haiku response. They seemed eager to apply this approach. The teacher's comment, "I think the process of individually choosing the photograph is critical to the connection between poetic reflection and response," indicates that she had considered "why" before constructing the center.

A center may be targeted to address particular learning styles, achievement levels, or interest areas. Teachers often use manipulatives such as Lego bricks, art materials, story boards, listening centers, computers, or tradebooks to create specific center sites. The creative use of time, space, and recycled materials, such as old calendars (source of the haiku photographs) extends the range of possibilities of using centers during instructional periods.

In a recent summer institute, a high school teacher described how he used individual index cards listing a variety of data about countries to create a center at which pairs of students developed thematic groupings of countries (see Fig. 6.1). He described the many ways that students thematically grouped the laminated cards according to political perspectives, regions, economic development, etc. Students recorded the groupings, identified the theme, and justified their decisions based on the data they chose to use. Was he looking for one right answer? Actually, not. The intent of the project was to practice the use of inductive reasoning, as well as to develop a content base that would lead to intelligent discussions in the classroom. This approach allowed students to pair or be assigned in pairs to work at centers. Both students were held accountable for being able to describe and explain the information required as a result of using the center.

One teacher in the group suggested that in this day and age

of computer databases, a classroom equipped with multimedia technology certainly could capitalize on this center in a more "high tech" fashion than described above. Use of current CD encyclopedias, world or state atlases, or other multimedia sources of economic, geographic, demographic, and political data at a workstation center would provide students the opportunity to research and print out their own data for use in building thematic groupings.

FIGURE 6.1. SAMPLE INDEX CARD DATA SET

Country Name :

Political Organization:
Industrial Base:
Population:
Education:
Geographical Location:
Predominant Language:
Geographic Features:

The use of index cards allowed students to literally "shuffle" their thinking so as to develop and reinforce broad concepts associated with particular content. When center applications within a content area are developed by teachers, the process for organizing a particular center around thematic relationships more easily transfers to new units of study. Understanding thematic relationships is important to the study of literature, classification systems in science, mathematic formulas, and historical periods. The use of thematic centers provides an avenue to extend content learning among students.

The history teacher who wants to develop and reinforce the thematic origins of conflict among nations or the peoples of the world might use a similar approach, with task cards, to encourage independent processing and groupings of data that increase the student knowledge base about warring nations and peoples, past and present. Task card questions, such as found in Figure 6.2, prompt students to analyze data and shift students towards higher-order thinking processes.

FIGURE 6.2. TASK CARD EXAMPLE

How was the war in Bosnia similar to or different from the civil war fought in the United States? How does the Bosnian conflict compare and contrast to the revolutionary war fought between the colonies and Great Britain?

A teacher who has constructed multiple data sets may use such a learning center to differentiate inductive reasoning skill practice among students who, individually or in pairs, manipulate, categorize, and analyze data sets. This extra practice in applying or refining inductive thinking skills through a center approach provides students with skill rehearsal time that typically is not available during short instructional periods.

Why use learning centers? Learning centers allow individual students to enrich, extend, practice, refine, and remediate learning independently while the teacher engages other students in the learning community.

WHO?

Knowing your students is the key to the second planning step—deciding **who** will benefit from a particular learning center or how particular students can be grouped to put maximal collective intelligence to work at a center. Students representing various learning styles, intelligences, and interests can be paired purposefully for center activities such as the one with index cards. The student who engages in deep analytical thinking can model such thought processes for the student who tends to see superficial relationships—or none at all. Students who work best when physically active may be bored at a center involving a great deal of reading, so the opportunity to manipulate index cards may stimulate the "hands on" thinker who is paired with a student prone to reflective thinking.

Familiarity with how students in your classroom learn is an essential component in planning for centers to be used effectively. "Kidwatching" through direct observations of your students at work, interviews with individual students about their perceptions of how they learn best or activities that they prefer, open-ended questions on surveys, and standardized learning style inventories—all can provide the classroom teacher with information about the types of center and classroom activities that will meet the needs of individuals, small groups, and the whole group. In a block schedule, teachers have time to develop such learning profiles.

Who of your students would benefit from learning centers? Learning centers can be constructed to pitch content to students with different intelligences, learning styles, and achievement levels so that learners are motivated and interested in the content being taught.

WHAT?

Call it an objective, outcome, or expectation, but be sure you have identified **what** students are expected to accomplish in the learning center. A center that incorporates newspapers or current magazines and journals may be used to acquire knowledge of current events in one secondary class, or development of an expository writing style in another class. The teacher can and should make the purpose clear in three ways:

- State the purpose as a part of the center itself. Some teachers place the intended outcome or objective above the written directions as an immediate reminder to students.
- Introduce the center to the whole class before the students use it. Tell them what you expect them to be able to know and do when they have completed the center activity.
- Ask students to describe the center objective.

Establishing a clear focus helps students understand why they should complete the activity. Showing how a learning center contributes to the mastery of a particular skill or knowledge base increases the likelihood that students will view it as important. Remember that outcome or objective statements are written for the student, not the teacher; use language written for them. Here is an example of a written outcome for a Spanish learning center:

In this center you will listen to a tape of a series of sentences using active verbs. Please convert them to the past tense. Learning to convert verbs from active to passive voice will help you improve your Spanish conversational skills and improve your ability to comprehend reading passages. When finished, use the answer sheet to self-check and correct your work. Directions follow for use of the center and recording your work. Have fun!

What will be learned at the center drives the value of the center to the students and to the teacher. An effective center is inextricably linked to the intended outcomes, objectives, or expectations for learning associated with a particular unit or discipline.

WHERE?

A fourth dimension of planning for learning centers involves the creative assessment of usable classroom space. Many middle and high school classrooms are not constructed or furnished to support the use of learning centers. Often classroom spaces are shared with other teachers. Student desks, a file cabinet, a bookcase or two, and the teacher's desk and chair may constitute the only available resources. **Where** to locate centers may be as difficult a planning task as finding a way to display them in the classroom.

Many savvy teachers have discovered the value of making friends with the custodian. A trip to the storage area may turn up a table, movable blackboard, student desks, carts, or typing stands that can be used as a flat surface for equipment, book displays, project construction materials, or a center backdrop.

If, however, additional furniture is not available, try using bulletin boards (see Fig. 6.3) for center activities. An enterprising math teacher hung center folders from the ceiling along a back wall. Another teacher developed a series of centers in manila envelopes. They were easy to transport to another room, were contained in envelopes to deter mixups or losses of materials, and could be put away quickly. The teacher housed the envelopes in a vertical file folder holder on top of a file cabinet.

FIGURE 6.3. BULLETIN BOARD CENTER EXAMPLE

Human Diseases Center

Pictures of Effects of Some Diseases
(e.g., Ebola, Smallpox, etc.)

Folder Containing Newspaper and Journal Articles	Folder Containing Center Directions	Folder Containing Data Sets on Human Diseases
Folder Containing Recording Sheets		Folder for Completed Work

In thinking about where centers will be located, teachers have learned to assess student movement patterns in the classroom. Locating a listening center on a desk near the pencil sharpener probably will result in ongoing interruptions to the students using the center. At the same time, centers should be easily accessible. If the desks are in rows, students will need to move through or around the desks to reach centers. Leaving space for such movement is imperative. Teachers with available funds may want to consider purchasing round or rectangular tables to increase floor space for student movement as well as to enhance cooperative learning activities. Science teachers who work out of lab spaces often are blessed with enough counter space to set up centers more easily than colleagues in regular classrooms. They also tend to have access to more electrical outlets, which are necessary for media or technology based centers.

> Where a center is located is critical to its successful use. When planning a center, attention to the built environment is essential to center construction and placement. The creative use of three-dimensional space, analysis of movement patterns, and identification of electrical outlet sources is necessary to center planning and development.

WHEN?

This question relates to the timely use of a center in a particular unit, and to the timing of center use for a particular class. Experience has shown that centers are least effective when used to introduce new information or a skill, or when students have not been trained to use centers purposefully and appropriately.

In most cases, the use of centers is preceded by whole-group or small-group introduction to a particular concept, body of knowledge, or skill, and by opportunities for guided practice and early, immediate feedback. For example, a geometry teacher might introduce computational formulas for geometric solids, allow time for whole-group guided practice, and then direct students to begin using a center that promotes application of the formulas in activities that take into account whether the class is homogeneous or heterogeneous.

One math teacher used a center to present students with data about building materials necessary to construct a dog pen of a certain dimension. As they rotated in pairs through the center, students designed, computed, and evaluated their use of building materials to accomplish the project. The teacher had used this exercise as a cooperative learning activity, but she eventually chose to convert it to a center format to increase the range of activities available for students who finished seatwork early.

In addition to introducing centers at a timely point in a unit, it is also critical to "time" the use of centers to coincide with instruction that models how to use them. High school students work at much more complex cognitive levels than younger students, but they often have not had opportunities to develop the skills necessary to be self-directed, independent learners. Even students grouped as high achievers can be dependent learners, and may not demonstrate appropriate use of time, equipment, and center information without an introduction to the center and an opportunity to observe appropriate use.

The series of steps followed in this process can be used for a variety of instructional purposes, and are outlined here:

- Introduce the center to the students by describing the purpose, behavioral expectations associated with its use, directions for use, and how work at the center will be assessed.

- Discuss possible issues or concerns about center use with the class. Loud sound from a listening center, movement of students nearby the center, and improper care and use of materials are examples of issues that may affect appropriate center use.

- If possible, ask other classmates to observe a student or students modeling how to set up and use audio visual equipment, computers, microscopes, etc.

- When students begin to use the center, stop the whole group, when appropriate, and point out positive examples of specific expectations being demonstrated. Use of precise, descriptive language that doesn't praise but simply reinforces teacher expectations is critical.

- If problems occur, involve students in troubleshooting why a center is not working—academically or behaviorally. Ask students for feedback and use it. Communicate your regard and respect for their ideas. Acknowledge and make changes as needed.

Introducing one center and using it to debug problems before adding other centers will help you develop effective implementation strategies. Many teachers attempt too much when trying to implement a new strategy and end up abandoning the strategy before it has been debugged in their own situation. Don't create a system that is too complex relative to recordkeeping and supply maintenance.

Students function most effectively at centers when they have been instructed in appropriate procedures and behaviors for use. Time the use of centers to occur after your students have learned essential class routines, and after introduction to a unit and guided practice activities have occurred.

How?

Centers can be constructed around many types of equipment and materials available to classroom teachers. Materials may be as simple as index cards or folders, or as complex as microscopes; however, several key factors are essential, including your own classroom management style and expectations, organization of the center itself, motivation and interest of students, and development of self-directed, responsible behaviors when using centers, particularly those involving expensive equipment.

The most strategic use of centers occurs when teachers see a useful purpose for including them in their instructional "bag of tricks" and understand how to utilize centers with a variety of students. Centers can be as meaningful or meaningless as the teacher constructs them to be. Students are not fooled by the same old busy work, or attracted by work that is too simple to offer a challenge or too difficult to complete independently. Developing center tasks of moderate difficulty is important to maintaining student motivation and interest. Block scheduling allows the teacher to provide activities that meet the needs of the heterogeneous population usually represented in the classroom learning community, and strategic use of centers extends the learning potential of students scheduled in the block.

Creating center activities that can be differentiated to address varying abilities, interests, and talents is essential if a center is to be made available to all students. For example, a teacher of U.S. history constructed a learning center in which students examined a portfolio of political cartoons spanning a particular time period. Each student was asked to construct a political cartoon representing a major political event of the period. Each student extrapolated concepts of political humor from the cartoons and then personalized the project through creation of a cartoon designed and then drawn from his or her own individual perspective. Students with different learning styles brought different strengths to the project; their individual perspectives helped make sense of the political humor in the cartoons.

Incorporating centers into the classroom occurs most easily for people who can flex their teaching style and who set boundaries that are neither too permissive or rigid. The ability to create an environment in which students have a high degree of power and control over their learning and respect for the learning community allows teachers to use cooperative learning activities, seminars, and other instructional models that actively engage the learner. So how do teachers create active learning experiences, such as centers, that may be used simultaneously with other activities in the room? Clear, concise, and "user friendly" organization of the center itself is essential for students to work independently while the teacher works with other students. Teachers who have worked with centers over the years offer useful tips to the novice user. These components of a quality center are suggested:

♦   The purpose and directions are written in clear language. Audiotape directions are provided for auditory and learning disabled learners in addition to written directions.

♦   Equipment and materials are available or obtainable without attention from the teacher.

♦   A recording sheet or form is used by students to document their work at a center.

♦   Folders, envelopes, tubs (sink-sized or smaller), and index card boxes are used to store materials associated with the center.

♦   A specific location is defined at which students will place recording sheets, projects, or other documentation associated with center use.

Directions should be broken down into manageable steps for all readers. Asking another teacher or a student to make a trial run and give feedback to you about clarity and organization ahead of time increases the likelihood that centers you construct will be easy to process rather than requiring "on the job" revision. Assessing the abilities and skills represented among students in the class is also essential so that strategic and systematic pairing of partners can occur.

For example, pairing a fluent reader with a student who has difficulty processing written information will help prevent both passive and active off-task behaviors. If no fluent readers are in the classroom, you may want to consider using audiotaped instructions and content, particularly if a tape player with headphones is available. Linking visual and auditory information improves the chances of a student making sense out of what he or she needs to do without your assistance.

Teachers also may have access to technology that extends learning opportunities beyond text, paper, and pencil. Computers, particularly multimedia workstations, tape recorders or players, slide projectors, microscopes, laser disk players, and video players all can be used to create stations or centers where one or more students can work. Centers may involve the use of art materials for constructing projects related to a center task. Specialized equipment, such as graphing calculators, may not be available in enough quantity for whole group or cooperative learning instruction. Centers where students take turns using such equipment are an improvement over viewing demonstrations by the teacher. Science equipment may be set up in stations around a lab or classroom so that students can rotate through the centers over several blocks of time; however, remember that when students use equipment, accidents may occur.

Talking through expectations, rehearsing, and monitoring appropriate use are all strategies that effective teachers use to prevent accidental damage to expensive equipment. Assigning a student to check equipment before class ends also increases student accountability for appropriate use. Finally, modeling through your own behaviors the importance and value of classroom equipment and materials is essential to creating an environment in which students carefully utilize materials and equipment that do not belong to them. Effective teachers do this by maintaining a classroom that is neat and uncluttered. Equipment and materials have a designated location and are carefully stored after use to prevent damage.

Typically, in classrooms where students use equipment and materials safely and appropriately, they are regarded as competent to use equipment correctly. They are told how to use equipment rather than how not to use it. Some teachers have noted in past workshops that it seems that students only hear negative words such as "don't" or "stop." Instead of saying, "Don't forget to rewind the VCR when you finish," rephrase directions to say, "Remember to rewind the VCR when you finish." Using negatives is an easy habit to get into but a hard one to break. Tell students what you want them to do, not what you don't want them to do! Then model and rehearse what you expect.

> Thinking about how to use centers is essential to their success in your classroom. Your own classroom management style and expectations, organization of the center itself, motivation and interest of students, and development of self-directed, responsible behaviors when using centers are key factors affecting student use of centers.

CENTER USE MANAGEMENT

Using a recording sheet or form of some type also may help you to manage who has or has not completed a center. In some cases, students are completing projects that will be turned in for assessment purposes; in other cases the work may be oral, auditory, or "hands-on" in nature. When stations are used, teachers also may use a management sheet that directs students through stations in a logical order. Other teachers use contracts with students to define what work will be done over a period of time at centers.

The difficulty with most of these forms is that if systematic procedures for collecting and maintaining records do not exist, then records of work may be misplaced in the classroom or end up in the infamous "circular" file. The organized teacher will provide a manila envelope or folder for students that stays in one location and is accessible. Some teachers situate a clipboard at a center so that students can sign-up to work at, for example, a word processor and sign-off upon completion of their work. The teacher can tell at a glance how students are pacing themselves towards completion of a center. Another monitoring strategy involves development of anecdotal records of students' center work as shown in Figure 6.4. A different student's name is entered in each block; as the teacher circulates, anecdotal data about the

FIGURE 6.4. SPANISH CLASS ANECDOTAL RECORD EXAMPLES

Skip Henry 9/18–worked at listening center—took posttest on adjectives and scored 100% correct.	Meg Grasso 9/22–Meg seemed to work well with Skip at the center; she improved her recognition of the 20 common adjectives from 50–100% correct.	Jason Markham 9/24–Jason finished the listening center but did not feel he was ready for the test. He seems confused at times and gets off task.
John Morris 9/18–worked at listening center-appeared to have difficulty with translation of adjectives—may need a mini-lesson re: recent work.	Shanelle Jones 9/21–has made real progress in recalling and using specific adjectives recently introduced. She has used the listening center to practice—not talk with J.M.	Kate Jones 9/22–did not finish the center and complained about difficulty hearing the tape; will need to conference with her this week.

student are entered from teacher observation.

If recordkeeping software is available on a teacher-accessible workstation, tracking student progress towards completion of centers can facilitate integration of anecdotal and performance assessment data into the student record of progress. Another tool that has been used in some classrooms is the electronic message pad on which the teacher can write with light pens to build anecdotal records of student work in cooperative learning activities, seminar discussions, and at centers. These message pads can be used to store records as stand-alone tools, but also in some cases have data transfer and retrieval capability when integrated with a workstation database. Continuous research by department members to identify possible electronic tool applications that can be used to promote organizing and monitoring task activities is essential as more schools, particularly secondary schools, become networked, purchase high-powered multimedia stations, and move into block schedules where the use of multiple teaching models is expected. The increasing emphasis on performance assessment and use of portfolios to archive student work samples is another rationale for strategic use of available electronic productivity tools. An example of an electronic database constructed to track student project work associated with a center on 20th century conflict follows:

FIGURE 6.5. ELECTRONIC DATABASE ON 20TH CENTURY CONFLICT

Student Name	Date	Comments
Rico Emirez	finished 9/16	Project on Hiroshima in folder, worked w/Jim S. to write a diary entry from the different perspectives of a U.S. soldier and a Japanese mother
Sarah Cohen	finished 9/18	Project on the civil rights movement of the 1950's—written research on T. Marshall's role in Topeka school case—needs more detail added

Using such a database allows the teacher to develop a thumbnail sketch of what students are working on or have completed. When monitoring a class of students who may be working on independent thematic projects at centers, having a quick reference source allows the teacher to follow-up with students in the class who may need additional support that others do not need. Databases can be constructed around any parameters that the teacher feels are important to monitoring student progress on assignments. In the above example, the teacher chose to record both formative and summative anecdotes from observations of center use and completed work placed in the work folder. Without either a handwritten or electronic management system for tracking work, it is easy to lose touch with where students are in the process of using a center.

APPLICATIONS OF INSTRUCTIONAL MODELS

Activities illustrative of various instructional models can be constructed in learning centers in order to practice, reinforce, and extend what the student is expected to know and do. Inductive thinking, cooperative learning, synectics, concept attainment, and simulations are all models of learning that can be used in centers that serve individuals or small groups of students. However, centers are not designed to focus only on the process of learning. The overlap of content and process within the centers is critical for the student to develop meaningful knowledge and skills and produce quality products.

INDUCTIVE THINKING

A center designed to develop or enhance inductive thinking skills often is best used by students working in pairs. While an individual student can engage in inductive thinking in isolation, working collaboratively with a peer supports developing ideas from different points of view. The cooperative learning strategy think/pair/share can be linked to inductive thinking and used at a center where students each "draft" their own reasoning before working together to interpret and analyze a data set. However, students must understand both the language of a strategy and its use before working at a center where the strategy is employed. In think/pair/share center activities, students would move through these steps:

♦ Individually read through the center activity.

♦ Record an individual response to the questions associated with the activity (think).

♦ Get together to share responses with each other (pair).

♦ Once all groups have completed the center, responses are shared through teacher questioning using numbered-heads together or circle of knowledge (share).

A secondary art teacher uses a center-based approach to extend students' inductive thinking about architectural styles. A number of folders of photographs are available for students to use throughout the unit. For example, pairs of students or individuals will examine a photographic portfolio of buildings with different Grecian column styles. Students then group the columns according to structural elements that eventually lead to labeling the columns as Ionic, Doric, and Corinthian. In doing so, the students develop the capability to extend their "definition" of architectural column from broader to more specific knowledge of how columns are similar and different.

Centers that promote inductive thinking can be set up visually through the use of photographs, slides, paintings, or even CD-ROM and laser disk technology. Centers also can utilize written lists, index cards, and sentence strips of items or information that constitute data sets. However, it is important for students to be able to group data set items with common attributes and to label the items in ways that make sense. Students who benefit from opportunities to manipulate data visually or kinesthetically in order to make sense of the information may understand and apply inductive thinking skills better at a center than in whole-group discussion or cooperative learning activities.

COOPERATIVE LEARNING

While cooperative learning activities typically are visualized as occurring with the whole group or even a split group, they may be applied equally well to task work at learning centers. Assigning roles to students is important to build accountability for group participation when more than two students are working together at the center. Students can be assigned to:

♦ Record information;

♦ Facilitate the center's group;

♦ Manage equipment and use of materials;

♦ Act as a teacher-student liaison.

However, students should understand and have practiced assigned roles before participation at a center in order to reduce confusion among group members. Directions should include background about roles. Role cards may be included at the center so that students can draw cards to determine who is assigned what role. If students usually work in assigned teams, then classroom strategies may already be predetermined for assigning roles when starting an activity.

The role of teacher-student liaison in a cooperative group is particularly critical to ensure that you do not have four students from the same center all simultaneously asking you for the same information. Students can be taught to consult with at least three other students or written sources ("the three before me" rule) before asking the teacher for assistance. Students still depend on the teacher to explain directions, answer equipment questions, and resolve confusions. If the teacher's role shifts from lecturer to learning facilitator, supervision of other activities, individual conferences with students, and minilessons with a small group will become focal for teacher attention while students work independently at centers.

Many of the same strategies used in cooperative learning groups are applicable to centers. Students can think/pair/share with ease, as exemplified in the inductive reasoning center approach already described. Another strategy that lends itself to center-based instruction is that of roundtable. Students can practice the strategy while recalling information associated with a particular unit. Rather than the teacher posing the starting question, one student might draw the question from a folder or index card box and pose it to the small group. After reflection time, students at the center silently circulate a response sheet. For example, chemistry students might list on the response sheet characteristics associated with families of elements on the Periodic Chart. In mathematics, pairs of students might work individually at a center to solve application-level enrichment problems, but also work cooperatively in a pairs check model to analyze and correct errors. In pairs check, four students can work with a set of problems. In center-based pairs,

♦ A group of four students forms two pairs;

♦ Within each pair, one student solves the problem while the other partner coaches and encourages;

♦ Partners change roles and solve a second problem; the "new" coach provides encouragement;

♦   After working through two problems, the two pairs check work together, record correct answers for the team, reinforce the team, and move on to the next set of problems.

SYNECTICS

The synectics model encourages students to use their imagination, insight, and intuition to develop metaphorical images that can be expressed through unique, descriptive language. While synectics (described in detail in Chapter 4) is by nature a group activity, students who have learned to use the synectics approach can work through some of the steps of a guided synectics activity in a learning center individually or in cooperative groups as well. Using the synectics strategy of developing language associations in the learning center allows students to practice the skills that lead them to become more creative writers, thinkers, and problem solvers who process and remember through metaphorical visualization.

CONCEPT ATTAINMENT

Another instructional model described in detail in Chapter 4 and readily adapted to the learning center situation is the model of concept attainment. Students are first introduced to the model through whole-group activities. Afterwards, centers can be used to reinforce and rehearse understanding of specific concepts being taught in a unit.

It is critical that the first phase of the model (steps one through six as described Chapter 4) be completed as a whole-group activity before students are directed to work independently at a center. Without this base, the student may be confused, lost, and uncertain of why the activity is important to learning. An example of an effective lesson sequence is:

♦   In French class the teacher introduces students to a set of masculine and feminine nouns by presenting the nouns and labeling them as examples or nonexamples. In whole group, the students compare the examples in the two attribute pools, and identify the essential attributes and a concept definition.

- ◆ A center is constructed so that students have the opportunity to critique either written or recorded phrases in order to identify whether the presented examples represent either masculine or feminine nouns.
- ◆ Students in pairs or individually record their responses on a response sheet and justify the answers based on previously determined attributes from the introductory lesson.

Any concept for which the teacher can generate examples and nonexamples lends itself to development of centers that support and reinforce the learning of the concept. Wave theory in physics, genre in English, and art periods in humanities studies are all examples of content applicable to the concept attainment model.

Centers also can be constructed around index cards, photographs, audiotapes, or hypercard stacks that are accessible to the "techno" literates. Students can work in pairs to provide collaborative thinking in the construction of the concept. One student may act as the prompter or coach to assist others in applying the model at a center. The concept attainment model provides a concrete way to build or scaffold conceptual thinking among students regardless of prior experience or ability and lends itself to easy planning and construction by the teacher beginning to initiate center use.

ASSESSMENT OF STUDENT PROGRESS AT CENTERS

Centers will be valued and used effectively by students if they find them interesting, helpful to the learning process, and valued by the teacher. The teacher is responsible for creating centers that students value and for sending the message that center time is worthwhile. One way to send this message is to pay attention to students working at a center and to the products that emerge as a result of center use. Centers are one place where the formative assessment process can be used primarily to inform instruction and extend what the teacher knows about how individual students learn. Assessment at centers can occur in several ways, including:

- ◆ Teacher observation of students at work;
- ◆ Teacher examination of response record forms;

- ◆ Teacher conferences with students during and after center completion;
- ◆ Teacher **and** student assessment of final projects associated with center work.

Centers typically are used when students are engaged in small group or individual activities. The teacher's role at this time may range from high supervision and involvement with specific students to circulating for brief conferences with all students. When in the circulation or "management by walking around" mode, the teacher has the opportunity to observe students and make anecdotal records about their successes, difficulties, and work habits. The traditional gradebook does not lend itself to recording much other than numerical grades. Consequently, teachers who utilize observations as an integral assessment component often use notebooks or binders to maintain anecdotal records. Teachers with access to laptop computers or notepads also may use technological tools to collect and update observational records. The use of standardized rubrics allows the teacher to assess student behavior or achievement both formatively and summatively within the context of performance (see Fig. 6.6).

FIGURE 6.6. RUBRIC FOR CENTER LEARNING BEHAVIORS

The student . . .

Consistent Behavior
- ◆ Is always on task and works until task is completed
- ◆ Shows initiative and helps others as needed
- ◆ Always gains attention through appropriate means
- ◆ Completes work as directed without prompting

Consistent Behavior, With Support
- ◆ Is usually on task and works until task is completed
- ◆ Works appropriately and helps others with some guidance
- ◆ Usually gains attention through appropriate means
- ◆ Completes work with little prompting

Inconsistent Behavior
- ◆ Is usually on task but needs prompting to complete tasks

- Works appropriately with others with little prompting
- Gains attention through appropriate means but sometimes needs prompts to do so
- Completes work with regular prompting

Unacceptable Behavior
- Is often off task and needs prompting to work on tasks
- Works appropriately with others only with prompting
- Often gains attention through inappropriate means
- Seldom completes work

When observing students at a center, the teacher may want to ascertain work habits as unobtrusively as possible, and from a distance. At the same time, interaction with the students about their work leads to insights into how students are thinking and approaching the assigned work, as well as what works or doesn't work about the center. These qualitative data look and feel differently than traditional assessment. Rather than being a high-stakes evaluation, center observational data can provide information relevant to the need for further instruction and development of future centers.

Teachers who use observational data report that it is most helpful when precise, specific language has been recorded in written records. Writing that Bill has done a "good job" at a center becomes meaningless hours after it was recorded, describing Bill's attention to the task, including details about his written responses and documenting his capability to work independently, all are important to developing a learning profile for Bill. This information also can be used when in conference with students or parents to elaborate upon strengths and areas that need attention.

TYPES OF CENTER MATERIALS AND EQUIPMENT

Centers can be constructed so that students use a variety of media and equipment as learning tools. Centers are as simple or complex as the instructional materials and equipment that are available to the teacher for use. Centers can be organized in different sizes of boxes, displayed on bulletin boards, or kept in folders for use at tables or counters. Centers can be used to support an activity in which the materials change throughout the year.

For example, a current events center could be an ongoing learning activity in almost any content area, with reading materials updated on a daily or weekly basis.

READING-RELATED CENTERS

Newspapers, magazines, journals, articles, computer software, and selected books all can be used to support development of knowledge and skills through center work. Center goals should align with unit objectives to support students to practice and extend research skills, apply study skills, perform critical thinking, and use writing skills. In a World Geography center, students used *National Geographic* and other nonfiction sources to develop research projects related to topics such as the impact of humans upon tropical rain forest environments. Students were able to opt to do individual or small group oral reports with illustrative posters, written reports, skits, or panel discussions as final projects. The opportunity to work at the reading centers provided students who, for different reasons, had difficulty accessing school and local library resources with the background knowledge needed to complete the projects.

LISTENING CENTERS

Almost every classroom can use a listening center at some point in the year. Foreign language classes may use listening centers as an ongoing activity that is integral to the development of listening and conversational skills. Listening centers can be used within other content areas as well. Audiotapes that integrate news broadcasts, music, and speeches by world leaders of the 20th century bring historical events and time periods alive for students. Books on tape can be used in English classes to add verbal color to classic literature without the confusions often associated with the use of movie versions of the classics. Students with learning disabilities may benefit particularly from the availability of such listening centers. The physics student listening to excerpts from Stephen Hawking's book, *A Brief History of Time,* may be drawn into reading the whole book and ultimately gain a philosophical perspective upon scientific thinking often not presented in the classroom.

Listening centers typically allow three to four students access to the audiotapes through the use of headphones. Most secondary media centers can provide listening center equipment or can purchase such equipment. The use of headphones is essential to reducing noise stimulation of other students in the classroom. Hookups also are available for multimedia work stations so that multiple headphones can be used.

TASK CARDS

Task cards can be used for practice of a specific skill, rehearsal for a test, or extension or enrichment of the content being studied. Task cards can be used by individuals or small groups of students. Some teachers construct task cards from index cards that can be kept in an index file box. Other teachers may use 8" x 11" card stock that can be stored in a manila envelope or file folder. Lamination increases durability. Lamination also allows cards to be designed so that students can mark responses on them with water-based markers.

Task cards can be used to promote development of concepts through the use of the concept attainment model or to promote inductive reasoning through the inductive thinking model. These models can be used with all disciplines at the secondary level. In home economics, for example, task cards could be used by students at a center to develop a conceptual rationale for grouping particular foods or recipe types together. In a vocational class, students could focus on grouping wood types based upon characteristics listed on task cards.

Another use of task cards applies to students who need additional support to master a particular skill or who have the capability to move more quickly through the content. Task cards can be used to break down a particular skill, such as report writing, into steps that students can follow. Including samples of quality work representing each step of the process provides students with an accurate picture of the target skill. One step in developing report writing could be to develop the prewriting strategy of webbing. Students would develop a content web using sample models available at the center. This use of visual examples, along with verbal descriptors of the steps, provides visual learners with prompts or cues for what their work should look like when completed.

CASE STUDY ACTIVITIES

Students often enjoy and become absorbed in case study analysis. The use of case studies promotes higher-order thinking through the application of course content. Case studies present students with a scenario in which they must think through the situation and make choices that appropriately address or explain the problem. For example, students in an automotive class may be presented with a case study of a vehicle that is experiencing braking difficulty. The students are expected to figure out the source of the difficulty and make decisions about how to best correct the problem based on the data presented. This case study also could be presented through a center or as a cooperative learning project for the whole class.

Case studies can be used to study historical conflict, scientific dilemmas, character development, geographic exploration, and author studies. In earth science, the presentation of rock and mineral samples with test equipment at a center allows students to work to identify unknown specimens.

A presentation of background information on Ernest Hemingway would support students to explore sources of conflict and characterization presented in his fiction writing. Cultural, socioeconomic, and geographical information related to third world countries could be presented at a center so that students might develop a futuristic perspective on the potential of the country to thrive internationally.

Using case studies at a center provides students with the opportunity to apply what they have learned in past activities and to use research skills to find other needed information. Students may be assigned to work in case study teams or individually. Case studies can be presented through activity packets with supporting information or task cards. A final oral or written report detailing student responses is essential.

TOOL APPLICATIONS

Each discipline has tools associated with its work. In math

and science classes, students may use measuring tools, microscopes, experimental equipment, graphing calculators, and computers to complete center activities. When a particular tool is not available in sufficient quantity for large or small group activities, the teacher can place such equipment at centers for individual use. Use of tools associated with a particular discipline engages students in real-time applications that are critical to understanding the discipline. Passive learning through viewing teacher demonstration of equipment use or demonstrations on a videotape does not provide the important kinesthetic engagement associated with hands-on use.

When students use equipment at a center, it is essential that they know proper procedures for use. Some teachers "license" a few students to assist at centers so that the teacher does not have to interface with each group or student using the center. If materials such as chemicals, recipe ingredients, or art supplies are needed, these licensed students can assist with monitoring center use and needs. Expecting students to work independently and responsibly is predicated upon their knowing how to use centers, where to find necessary supplies, and what to do to seek help before asking the teacher for assistance.

ART-RELATED PROJECTS

The use of art materials at centers can enhance student interest in content and also contribute to increased quality in final projects. Integration of visual and performing arts into projects can be supported at centers and extended into other activity times within the block. For example, students using task cards to practice comparing and contrasting animals representing the five classes of vertebrates might turn their knowledge into a rap song that could be presented to the class. Other students might work on a mural for display outside the door representing a particular historical period, an ecosystem, mathematical or scientific formulas, or a scene from literature. For example, the formula for computing force ($F = MA$) could be represented pictorially and mathematically in a mural.

Providing students with alternatives to written projects allows students to use strengths from areas other than verbal-linguistic or mathematical-analytical intelligence. When given the opportunity, students may extend themselves creatively through projects in ways that the teacher may never observe in the traditional classroom. One teacher allowed students to create photodocumentaries to accompany poetry pieces being analyzed through a seminar approach. The use of inexpensive, disposable 35mm flash cameras opens up possibilities for creation of student projects and portfolios extending from center activities. The list of possible projects associated with center outcomes is endless—skits, plays, poetry, graphics, panel discussions, simulations, role plays, murals, songs, audiotapes, slide shows, and technological presentations.

WORKSTATIONS

The inclusion of computer workstations in the block-scheduled classroom allows teachers to use technology in both traditional and innovative ways. Students may use the work station to draft, revise, peer edit, and publish personal writing assignments. Other uses include application of databases in case study analysis, experimentation in science classes, software applications in mathematics, and CD-ROM applications to everything from building knowledge about fabled Shakespearean productions to musical instrumentation and composition.

Some teachers are exploring how to keep the computer in use throughout the class period regardless of the group activity. If used in this way, the computer becomes an integral component of the instructional program rather than an "add-on" to class activities. Connecting multiple headphones to the system increases the likelihood that students will work cooperatively in taking on different roles during the completion of work station tasks.

Even though widespread technological applications are beyond the funding ability of most schools, the costs of high-speed, multimedia workstations are decreasing rapidly enough to make state-of-the-art technology more available to the educational market. The innovative teacher needs to be ready to integrate such technology into classroom centers as soon as it is available.

CONCLUSION

Successful integration of centers into the secondary classroom can extend learning experiences available to students working in longer blocks of time. Centers provide teachers who want to individualize learning activities with the time to engage students in meaningful and challenging assignments, maximize use of equipment and materials, provide instruction that meets the needs of students with different intelligences and learning styles, formatively assess progress, and develop profiles of learners that will inform instructional decision making. The strategic use of centers frees students and teachers to work independently during activity times.

Teachers who are willing to change professional practice in order to address instructional needs will find centers among the many viable alternatives to lecture-based instruction. Teachers must remember, however, that for a center to be used successfully, it must:

♦   Be purposeful, meaningful, and interesting;

♦   Be clear and organized for independent use;

♦   Be preceded by introductory instruction;

♦   Engage students in activities of moderate difficulty;

♦   Allow learning to be assessed;

♦   Create linkages to content, themes, and skills.

The teacher who wants to use centers effectively must specify clear expectations that centers or stations are part of the work of the student and that centers are important to learning. Multiple opportunities for students to describe, practice, rehearse, and critique center use must be provided. Finally, the teacher's role must shift from director of learning to facilitator of learning, so that students can develop the self-directed, independent learning skills necessary to maximize their learning potential.

REFERENCES

Butler, K.A. (1988). How kids learn: What theorists say about learning styles. *Learning88, 17(4),* 30–34.

Caine, R.N., & Caine, G. (1990). Understanding a brain-based approach to learning and teaching. *Educational Leadership, 48(2),* 66–70.

7

INTEGRATED TECHNOLOGY[1]

A block schedule provides teachers with the time necessary to incorporate technological tools into the curriculum and facilitate active student participation in the learning process. This chapter provides suggestions for integrating computer and video technologies in the block schedule, using instructional strategies discussed in other chapters.

Integration of technology into existing curricula is challenging and time consuming. Why should teachers go to the trouble of integrating video and computer media into their lessons? What is the advantage in adopting methods of instructional design that encourage or require the use of technology tools to improve student learning?

POSITIVE BENEFITS FOR LEARNERS

Research on educational use of technological tools developed and implemented since the late 1980s shows similar findings on some basic issues. Integrating current technologies into the curriculum:

- ◆ Makes complex tasks feasible;
- ◆ Increases teachers' expectations of students;
- ◆ Provides students with opportunities to work at a higher order of cognition;

---

[1] This chapter was written by Jean Friend Condrey, a former mathematics and physics teacher and currently a doctoral student in instructional technology at the University of Virginia.

- ◆ Shifts the locus of control in the classroom from teacher-centered to student-centered instruction;
- ◆ Accommodates the individual needs, intelligence, and styles of learning of students.

(Means & Olson, 1994; Wilson, et al., 1993; Sheingold & Hadley, 1990; Braun, 1990.)

Technology tools can extend students' ability to construct knowledge for themselves. The use of instructional media is appropriate for every subject area at every grade level. (More sources on the impact of technology on student-centered learning are listed at the end of this chapter.)

Exploring software programs and learning to use camcorders is time consuming in the classroom. A positive benefit of this expenditure of time is the modeling of problem-solving and troubleshooting techniques. Modeling methods to find acceptable solutions to problems encountered when using technology is highly instructive. Teachers and students can find answers together and develop alternate methods when necessary. Chris Dede, an expert in information technology and education, sees the transferability in this skill:

> In today's workplace, by the time you fully understand something, conditions have already changed. So what people are mastering in work is the ability to make decisions given incomplete information, inconsistent objectives, and uncertain consequences. And that's what we need to be teaching in education—not so much what we know and how we know it, but what to do when you don't know something, and how to act when you don't know exactly how to get where you want to be. (O'Neil, 1995, p. 9)

A cooperative approach that models problem-solving will encourage student-to-teacher, student-to-student, and teacher-to-teacher interactions. These interactions are crucial for the development of a nonthreatening learning environment that encourages discovery and inquiry.

It is important to avoid the trap of unrealistic expectations. Using technological tools in instruction will not simplify teaching; it will provide teachers with greater opportunity to adopt the role of facilitator. Effective integration into the curriculum creates the potential for teachers and students to work as a team toward cooperative and authentic learning.

The indirect benefits of integrating computers and video technology into instruction are numerous. Accommodations for individual strengths, weaknesses, and disabilities are more manageable for teachers when they use tools that can direct learning or promote creative construction of knowledge. Students can benefit from the refinement of communication skills and the cultivation of problem solving and higher order reasoning skills. The specific technology provides opportunities for them to take an active role in their own learning. Teachers and students can discover new motivation to expand learning and create real-life applications and products if a genuine commitment is made to utilize the media equipment as an integral part of instruction.

HOW DO I INTEGRATE TECHNOLOGY INTO MY INSTRUCTION?

Instructional strategies using technological tools can be guided by the teacher or by the student. Teacher-guided instructional strategies incorporate video and computer technology to support instruction when the goal is a standardized outcome—knowledge of factual information, or base-level concept development, that is important for each member of the class to develop at a comparable level. For example, world studies students using tutorial software to study the location of foreign countries will increase their base knowledge and expand their concepts of global proximity. A chemistry class studying gas laws might watch a video recording about cloud formation to increase their comprehension of the behavior of gases and the relationship between pressure, temperature, and volume. Inquiry, synectics, and concept attainment instructional strategies provide teachers with opportunities to guide the use of video recordings and computer-programmed instruction as support for content information and concept development.

Student-guided use of technology is appropriate when the learning objectives are broad and abstract. Outcomes will be variable depending on individual student experiences and generally should involve a greater degree of higher-order reasoning

FIGURE 7.1. INSTRUCTIONAL STRATEGIES USING TECHNOLOGICAL TOOLS

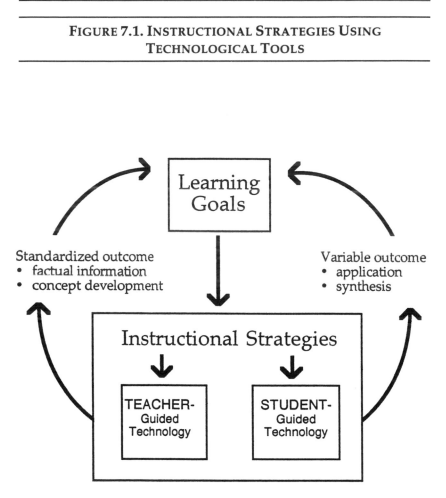

than standardized outcomes. Cooperative learning and simulation instructional strategies accommodate this student centered use of technology by placing it in the hands of the learners to create their own products.

Teacher-guided and student-guided use of technology should support an instructional strategy that is defined by an established learning goal. Both standardized and variable outcomes should lead to new objectives for learning, beginning the cycle again.

Computers and video equipment are the focus of this chapter because they are the most common tools found in schools. These tools are discussed in both teacher-guided and student-guided approaches. This is not meant to be a complete summary of the technology available for instruction or the methods for integration. A list of suggested resources for further investigation into these and other technologies can be found at the end of this chapter.

Teachers are encouraged to begin with a tool that is comfortable to them. If the camcorder is a familiar medium, begin with the integration of teacher-guided instructional strategies using video technology. Teachers more comfortable with computers should integrate teacher-guided instructional strategies using familiar software as a beginning point. Once a base level proficiency with the camcorder or software is achieved, teachers should progress to computer and video strategies that are student-guided. These require the teacher to serve as a technical assistant as well as facilitator of learning.

COMPUTERS AND SOFTWARE TECHNOLOGY

Computers provide the means for teachers to extend students beyond the limits of traditional resources. Teachers can access databases around the world in a few seconds and acquire information that normally would take weeks to receive in the mail. Students can write papers, work on self-paced tutorials, produce creative documents, generate artwork, create music, take data measurements—the possibilities are almost endless. It isn't necessary to have a lab full of state-of-the-art equipment. One computer can do the same job as 20 computers. Fewer computers will simply limit the number of students who can work concurrently. Careful management and organization can make even a few Apple IIe's valuable for instructional purposes.

Why would a teacher switch from paper-and-pencil exercises to the use of unfamiliar equipment and software? The answer lies in a simple four-letter word that is the bane of many an educator's existence—**time**. New programs and vast quantities of information are being added continuously to already full curricula with very little being removed. The time crunch to cover factual material is a vexatious problem that leaves less and less time for abstract reasoning and higher-order thinking skills in the classroom. Computer software and hardware can manage drill-and-practice instructional tasks in a fraction of the time required for paper-and-pencil activities.

This reduction in time to complete an assignment provides teachers with the opportunity to extend students' comprehension beyond the mechanics of a skill. Education is more than memorization of facts and comprehension of basic concepts. Students must be able to apply information to produce a product, solve a problem, create a system, generate concepts from facts, and infer applications from concepts—reasoning skills that go beyond the concrete. They grow as learners by doing.

INTEGRATION OF COMPUTERS

Computers are only machines. The capabilities of these machines are determined by the software, hardware accessories, and the user. The limits of the instructional power of the machine will be determined by the vision of the user.

The initial point for selecting an instructional strategy involving any technological equipment is always the establishment of the learning goals. Establish these goals first to avoid placing too great an emphasis on the equipment. Make the tools fit the instruction and not the instruction fit the tools. Frustration and wasted time can be limited by using the right tool to accomplish a task. Software is designed and marketed to do a certain job well. Determine the software capabilities needed and select a product that can do the job. The school system's technical coordinator is a good resource for determining what is available and for making purchasing decisions.

It requires time to know how to use a software program or an accessory tool, but the benefits from using computers in instruction greatly outweigh the challenge and time involved.

Most newer software programs have user-friendly formats with drop-down menus. This feature greatly reduces the old need to memorize commands, so students can concentrate their efforts on the task and not the software. Time spent to achieve a comfort level with computer tools will be rewarded with greater instructional capabilities and benefits.

COMPUTER PRODUCTS

Computer products are available for a multitude of educational uses. Software for programmed instruction, spreadsheet and data management, utilities programs, and word processing is readily available. These programs usually do not require additional equipment, although a printer is extremely beneficial. A wide selection of desktop publishing software, graphics packages, reference materials, communications software, presentation programs, and multimedia packages is also available for the most popular computer platforms. These usually require various types of accessory hardware. A brief general description of the capabilities of each of these varieties is given in this section.

Educational suppliers offer an abundant selection of courseware for programmed instruction. Courseware is software intended for instructional use. The programmed instruction can take the form of self-paced tutorials, games, and informational presentations. Many of these provide some form of self-evaluation as a check for information comprehension. The software is used as a medium for the introduction of a topic, the development of a basic concept, or remediation through repetitive applications. Examples of programmed instruction include software for vocabulary comprehension, historical facts, location of states and capitals, or mathematics computations. These programs can furnish factual information and application exercises in an interactive drill and practice format. Tutorial software can decrease the classroom instructional time needed for development of certain basic skills because of the rapid generation and feedback of repetitive examples. Programmed instruction has positive application in the block schedule, particularly when regrouping students for practice on specific skills or content deficiencies. Students can work in small, temporary, homogeneous break-out groups using software appropriate for different levels of comprehension. All students can be actively engaged in the same topic at the same time in small groups so that teachers can monitor and adjust instruction without having to teach one group while policing another group. (For more information on the "Concept-Progress" model of scheduling see Canady & Rettig, 1995.) Drill and practice are needed in small measure and programmed instruction software can meet that need.

Multimedia programs are a more recent addition to educational software. These programs combine text, graphics, sound, video, and animation in interactive and hypermedia formats (Vaughan, 1994). Some provide a self-check of comprehension and others do not. This type of program requires a computer with fast speeds, high memory availability, and a sound system. These programs typically are available only on CD-ROM.

Spreadsheet and data management programs allow the user to manipulate numerical and written information easily. This would be beneficial when assessing results from a survey where the responses need to be sorted for analysis. Most typical spreadsheet and data management programs will have graphing and list sort capabilities. Graphs can be used for analysis and in presentations. List sorts can be used to organize information according to a particular category. For example, data recorded from a survey can be sorted to produce an alphabetic listing of all respondents who answered a specific question with a specific answer. Most word processing packages include a basic spreadsheet program.

Utility software programs enhance the capabilities of the computer. These can be used to compress files, detect viruses, diagnose system problems, enhance memory, increase speed, and for other useful housekeeping functions. Compression and decompression programs are useful for large files with big memory requirements. Movies and multimedia files are examples of documents large enough to require compression. More often than not, school systems with networked computers usually have a technology coordinator who tends to the utilities needs of the system.

Word processing is the most common use of software. Students and teachers alike can use word processing programs to produce papers with a professional touch. The real value of these programs is the ease of word manipulation. Most programs include spelling and grammar correction features and a thesaurus. The spelling correction feature advises the user of possible mistakes and offers suggestions for change. The grammar correction feature also points out possible mistakes and follows up with a suggestion and statement of the rule that applies. The user must read and make choices in a simple programmed instructional format. These features are a nonthreatening form of remediation that is seen by students as helpful rather than punitive.

Many word processing programs also have spreadsheet and desktop publishing capabilities. Graphics can be imported for illustration from clip art, scanned pictures, or video, and placed anywhere in the document. These features are useful for small projects with basic demands. Larger projects with specific requirements should use software programs designed to do the desired task. Using the appropriate software will save hours of unnecessary frustration and enable the user to generate a high-quality product.

Desktop publishing software has the capability to generate, manipulate, and import graphics and text easily within a document. This allows the user to arrange text and illustrations at angles, in shapes, in columns, or with text wrapped around pictures. Creativity is easily accommodated in these programs. Students can create flyers, brochures, and catalogs or simply liven up a report. Desktop publishing programs range from fairly simple features to professional quality programs. The computer memory requirements increase as the flexibility of the features increases. A printer is needed with desktop publishing to make a hard copy of the final product. Additional hardware that would be beneficial includes a scanner to import existing graphics and a CD-ROM to import from commercial stock illustrations.

There are two varieties of graphics software packages: stock illustrations and production. Stock graphics software packages are archives of drawings, photographs, or pictures that can be used to illustrate documents produced in word processing or desktop publishing. These can vary from simple line drawings to color photographs. Graphics production software is used to create original artwork. Drawing tools can be used to produce graphics or pictures can be imported and manipulated for a desired effect. Graphics production programs place few limits on visual creativity, but they tend to have very high memory requirements.

Most stock illustration software requires the substantial storage capacity and read-only format of CD-ROM, although some clip art is available on disk. Additional beneficial accessories for importing graphics include a scanner, digital camera, video capture card, and drawing tablet. The memory capacity of the computer will determine the hardware requirements for graphics production. Graphics typically require a high memory capacity. Professional graphics production programs and some desktop publishing tools may require the use of an external hard drive or optical disk storage system to accommodate the large memory demands.

Many word processing packages have graphics capabilities as added features. The capabilities are limited but beneficial for importing graphics created with other programs and for creating drawings within the document. Desktop publishing programs also feature import and drawing capabilities.

Reference software refers to information archives and databases. Encyclopedias, dictionaries, phone books, and atlases are examples of reference software. These typically are available only on CD-ROM because of the quantity of information they contain. Most schools install CD-ROM stacks for reference software in the media center or library for maximum student access.

Communications programs are used for telecommunications. Many museums, private corporations, and libraries have databanks and professionals available for research and inquiry. Text, pictures, video clips, and live telebroadcasting can be transferred through the telephone lines. This allows the user to send and receive information through a commercial service provider. Many service providers offer access to the Internet and World Wide Web (WWW). This access allows the user to communicate with remote computers across the world. The cost of telecommunications involves the monthly fee to the service provider and the cost of the call to the service provider, which may be local or long distance. A computer, telecommunications software, and a modem also are required.

Presentation programs are designed to make generation and delivery of presentations easy and professional. The software enables the user to create slides of information that work in the same way as transparencies for the overhead projector. These slides can be controlled by the keyboard, a timer, or a remote control device. Most presentation software has the capacity to import graphics, audio clips, and video clips into the slides. These programs require the use of an overhead projector and an LCD (liquid crystal display) panel when used for group presentations.

TEACHER-GUIDED COMPUTER APPLICATION

Teacher-guided instruction using computers and software involves students completing a task where the outcomes are fairly standardized. Teacher-guided computer activities can be used either for programmed instruction, remediation, or as a follow-up to check comprehension. For example, art students may show understanding of shading and shadows by producing a shadowed drawing using graphics software. World studies students can create a fact sheet on the demographics and climate of Hawaii using a word processing package and information gathered from an encyclopedia database. Driver education classes can study the mechanics of a car collision using programmed instruction.

SAMPLE TEACHER-GUIDED COMPUTER APPLICATION

One example of a teacher-guided computer activity is the use of tutorial software as part of an inductive reasoning exercise (similar to the concept development model discussed in Chapter 4). The class should generate a list on the board of things they know about the tutorial topic. This list will be the basis for the development of categories to be used for gathering information

Students should make data sheets with a column for each category. Teams or individuals can work through the computer tutorial, moving at their own pace and taking notes using these sheets. The learner must decide on the category column that is the best fit for the information.

The follow-up activity involves a peer check in small groups. Students sit in groups of three or four, but not with members of their own team. They compare notes and make any additions or changes necessary. Each student should have the same information at the end of the exercise, but it isn't imperative for that information to be in the same category or worded the same way.

The concluding activity is a comprehension check. The class should return to the list of statements generated in the first step of the process, and decide which are true. "Why" and "How do you know" questions are beneficial at this point to make connections between the content and the concept. This is an additional opportunity for students to discuss the information as a class and make changes in their notes. Some statements might not have been addressed by the tutorial. The teacher can address these directly or assign them for research as an extension process.

This lesson should take approximately one instructional block, or 2½ traditional class periods. While each student has the same basic information at the end of the instruction, use of the computer tutorial allows students to work at their own pace and to be actively engaged in the process of gathering information and concept development.

STUDENT-GUIDED COMPUTER APPLICATION

The learning goals in student-guided computer applications should be broad and emerging. Student teams can create products that are variable and individualized to meet the established goals through application and synthesis of concepts and content topics. Groups should have one to three students and the timeframe should fit the scope of the project. The team plan will determine the equipment requirements. Although it is important for the tools to fit the task, in some cases, the team plan may have to be modified to fit the hardware available. Many times a local business or university will have the equipment that is needed and an arrangement can be negotiated. Students frequently will need additional time to learn new software programs in order to accomplish the desired task. Effective use of computer technology for these projects requires student access to the software and hardware during nonclass time.

TEACHER RESPONSIBILITIES

The teacher is responsible for establishing cooperative teams, setting a realistic timeframe for the project, stating learning goals, and establishing the grading criteria. The expected date of completion, learning goals, and criteria for grading should be shared with students at the beginning of the assignment to establish expectations. Many times a project may require more time than can be accommodated within the instructional block. This should not discourage the teacher if the project has value. The curriculum and students' personal schedules should be taken into account when establishing a reasonable timeframe for the project. Students need to have a certain amount of control over the demands on their time. It is always necessary to consult with them to establish a realistic timeframe if the project is to be successful in achieving the desired goal. Major problems can be avoided with planning around those events that traditionally drain a student's noninstructional time, like homecoming or prom week.

Broad goals allow for a large measure of variability in the final products. Students usually need guidance to develop plans that are reasonable and meet the established goals. Large projects should be segmented into smaller units or narrowed to a smaller scope. Tasks that are too ambitious become unmanageable and create a negative impact on the team.

An additional teacher responsibility is technical assistance. Teams will need help manipulating the software throughout the entire project, especially if the students are unfamiliar with the program or hardware. It will be helpful to keep software instruction manuals and pertinent technical resources in the same room with the computers. Students frequently are the best resource for solutions to technical problems. New discoveries about software and hardware can be written on a sheet for Frequently Asked Questions (FAQ) and posted on a bulletin board for everyone to use as a reference. This gives students the opportunity to share their findings and establishes a collaborative resource for troubleshooting technical problems.

FIGURE 7.2. TEACHER RESPONSIBILITIES

- Establish cooperative teams.
- Generate a realistic timeframe.
- State broad, abstract learning goals.
- Establish the grading criteria.
- Provide technical assistance.

TEACHER RESPONSIBILITIES FOR STUDENT-GUIDED COMPUTER AND VIDEO ACTIVITY

Project expectations and objectives should be a reliable reference point for teachers and students. Expectations for the quality and quantity of work, research requirements, means of technical support, and final product objectives should be established and modified with student input from the beginning of the project. Learning objectives should be broad and allow a wide-range of possibilities. Consistency from group to group is not a desirable attribute of this method of student-centered instruction. The common goal is an application and synthesis of knowledge constructed through experience in a team-coordinated process. The class can learn from each other and gain an appreciation for their differences when sharing the final products.

Teams should organize and keep track of time spent on their project. This can be accommodated through the use of a project timeline and a team time tally. The project timeline is an organized work schedule. A sample timeline is given in Figure 7.3. It allows the team to project target dates for completion of each of the stages of the assignment. Diverse personal schedules and possible changes in the instructional block must be taken into consideration when planning a realistic timeline.

Team members also are responsible for keeping a running tally of their actual time spent on the project. A sample team time tally is given in Figure 7.4. Each student is responsible for accounting for the amount of time spent on the project and the specific task accomplished. These should be cumulated onto a single form and submitted with the final project.

Grading this type of work requires qualitative and quantitative approaches to assessment. Teams should turn in the plan proposal, project timeline, team time tally, research bibliography, first draft of the product, the final product, and individual and team evaluations, if they are used. Small projects may not require all of these. The team grade will be determined from these items with a variable individual evaluation component to allow for the irregularities of unequal participation and disruptive behavior. A sample point system for computer and video projects is given in Figure 7.5. Percentage of the grade should be established for each component of the project and agreed to before the student planning stage. At times it may be necessary to modify the point system for individual groups to accommodate for individual

(Text continues on page 211.)

FIGURE 7.3. PROJECT TIMELINE

Sample Project Timeline

Project Title:		
_____ Block:_____		
_____ Date_____		
Team Name:		
_____		
Project Managers:	1.	
	2.	
Content Managers:	1.	
	2.	
Technical Managers:	1.	
	2.	
By the end of the block on:	we plan to finish:	
Wed, Oct 5	Planning	
Wed, Oct 5	Researching	
Fri, Oct 7	First draft production	
Tues, Oct 11	Final draft production	

FIGURE 7.4. TEAM TIME TALLY

Sample Team Time Tally

Date	Day	Hours	Names	Task
12/7	Mon	1.5	John, Jerry	research
12/8	Wed	2	Kim, John, Jerry, Jane	planning
12/9	Fri	1.5	Kim, John, Jane	word processing
12/13	Mon	1.5	Jerry, Jane	graphics
12/15	Wed	1.5	Jerry, Jane, Kim	desktop publishing
12/15	Wed	1.0	John	product clean-up

Accumulated Time Totals:	
Name	**Total Time in hours**
John	4.5
Kim	5.0
Jerry	5.0
Jane	6.5
Total Group Time	21 hours

Comments:

FIGURE 7.5. INDIVIDUAL PROJECT ASSESSMENT

Individual Project Assessment

These percentages are only recommendations. The actual percentage will vary depending on the emphasis placed on the various stages of the process.

Name: _____   Block: _____

Team Name: _____

Stage	Description	Point percentage
Plan proposal	• Is it comprehensive? • Does it provide details? • Does it include the talents of the whole team? • Is there group agreement on the plan?	5 %
Time line	• Is it realistic? • Does it meet the established time frame requirements?	5 %
Research bibliography	• Does it show variety? • Is it comprehensive? • Is it written in the appropriate format?	5 %
Computer: First draft of the product	• Is there evidence of organization? • Does the work follow a sequence? • Is there evidence of troubleshooting? • Do team members have a plan for determining what may need modification? • Is there evidence of acceptable quality work?	15 %

Video:Storyboard	• Is it a useful guide for filming? • Does the work follow a sequence? • Does it show organization prior to filming?	15 %
Final product	• Does it meet the learning goal? • Does it follow a logical sequence? • Is there an introduction, main body, and conclusion? • Has extra effort been put into the product to establish a point? • Does it stand alone or need further explanation?	25 %- 40%
Presentation	• Does it follow the introduction, viewing of visual, explanation, questions format? • Do all members of the team have the same level of understanding? • Do the members have a clear understanding of the learning goal?	5 % - 10%
Team Time Tally	• Is it complete? • Is it accurate? • Is it realistic?	5 %
Individual evaluation	• Does it state specific personal contributions, including cooperative efforts, time spent, and descriptions of specific tasks? • Does it suggest the grade earned?	15 % - 30%
Team evaluation (optional)	• Do each of the evaluations from other members of the team support the self evaluation? • Are specific contributions listed by other team members similar to those listed in the self evaluation?	0% -15 %
Individual Total		

education plans or team imbalance, at the teacher's discretion. Team members who are unable to make adequate contributions to the team effort should be given other independent opportunities to synthesize content information and to meet the objectives of the project. An extension of the group's timeline may be a possible solution, but decreasing expectations should not be a consideration. Quantity requirements are determined by the team plan, which may be modified to make the load reasonable for team members who must cope with the project in the absence of other members. Project expectations and objectives are the reference point team members must use to determine if their modifications are acceptable.

STUDENT RESPONSIBILITIES

Students are responsible for plan development, research, production, modification, presentation, and evaluation in student-guided computer activities. The small size of the team eliminates the need for clearly defined roles in these projects. Members can split assignments equally or as they see fit. Teams may choose to adopt the roles of project manager, content manager, and technical manager as a means to organize the group. The role of each of these managers is defined in detail in the student-guided video technology section of this chapter.

FIGURE 7.6. TEAM RESPONSIBILITIES FOR STUDENT-GUIDED COMPUTER ACTIVITY

- ◆ Plan a product that meets the target objective.
- ◆ Research the topic.
- ◆ Produce the product using the tools available.
- ◆ Modify the product according to feedback.
- ◆ Present the finished product.
- ◆ Evaluate individual efforts and the final product.

The planning stage of the project is crucial. Brainstorming techniques work well to help team members isolate and organize their ideas. The group should generate a list of any and all ideas that come to mind for the project. These can be pared down to two or three possibilities. A final decision is not necessary until the research is complete. Individual time tallies should begin in this stage.

Students should be encouraged to develop creative and unique products. For example, a team may decide to produce a futuristic newsletter written in the year 2060 with articles describing "current" environmental problems stemming from the pollution generated in the 20th century. The learning goal in this case is for students to demonstrate comprehension of the impact of pollution on the environment.

Research of the topic under study extends the students' knowledge base, serves to verify examples or applications used in their product, and sparks ideas that may require modification of the plan. A research bibliography and the project timeline should be submitted at the end of this stage.

The team should develop a first draft of the product in the production stage and submit it on the day noted on their project timeline. This stage requires close adherence to the proposed schedule. The content of this draft should be complete and ready for final adjustments into a finished product. Teachers should provide content and esthetics feedback on the first draft. The grade should be based only on the content and not the use of the technology in this stage of the project. Providing students with an opportunity to modify the esthetics of the first draft without a reduction in the grade encourages them to try new computer skills and risk learning new processes that do not have guarantees for success.

The modification stage provides the chance to polish the product. This is the time for students to pay close attention to the esthetics of the product and use the full potential of the software and hardware available. The final product should be submitted at this phase of the project. As with the production stage, teams must be held to scheduled timelines.

Completed projects should be presented to the class by team members. This provides closure and provides the students the opportunity to share what they have learned. A question and answer period should follow each presentation. Each student should submit an individual evaluation of his or her participation in the project. These should be confidential. The evaluation should state specific contributions to the team effort. These contributions should include cooperative efforts, time spent on the project, and an assessment of the quality of their work. Students should also suggest the number of points they feel they have earned for their part in the team effort. The point value for this evaluation should be established from the beginning of the project. The Individual Computer Project Assessment offers recommendations for point percentages. These are only suggestions and should be adjusted to the goals and purposes for the project. Teams should submit the cumulative team time tally and individual evaluations on the day the project is presented.

Teachers may wish to include a team evaluation in the grading structure. Each member would write a confidential evaluation of the others in the team from a positive viewpoint. This evaluation approach is not always productive and may be eliminated from the grading criteria at the beginning of the project at the teacher's discretion.

SAMPLE LEARNING GOALS AND PRODUCTS FOR STUDENT-GUIDED USE OF COMPUTERS

An example of a learning goal for a social studies class may be for students to gain an appreciation for the diversity of people in China. A team may decide to search computer databases for information and graphics. These could be used to produce a map of China with pictures and written descriptions of the various cultures placed in the appropriate location on the map. Another team may choose to correspond with individuals in China on the World Wide Web. Their product may be a comparison chart showing the responses to specific questions asked of individuals living in different provinces of China.

For a chemistry class, the learning goal may be for students to apply knowledge of organic compounds to everyday life. One team may elect to create a marketing brochure targeted at selling petroleum products to a rapidly developing third world country. The brochure might expand on specific petroleum products used to manufacture everyday household goods. Another team may wish to pursue the effects of synthetic organic compounds on women's apparel. They can produce a catalog using desktop publishing tools to show the evolution of clothing material in the United States and its effect on fashion.

Video Camera and VCR Technology

The videocassette recorder (VCR) and video camera, or smaller camcorder, are perhaps the most easily accessible media equipment available for classroom instruction. The equipment tends to be low cost and low maintenance and is easily adapted for use with computers. Video equipment has not changed as rapidly as other technologies in the past decade, so many students are familiar with the equipment and its use.

Teacher-Guided Video Application

Teachers can develop and reinforce constructs using commercially produced videotapes as part of their instructional strategy. Many types of audio and visual media can be used in place of written materials and handouts, including compact discs (CD), videodiscs, reel-to-reel film, cassette audiotapes, and phonograph records. For the sake of simplicity, only videotape is discussed here, but the same methods apply for all the audio and visual media mentioned. Videocassette tapes can be purchased from educational suppliers or developed by students and integrated into the lesson to introduce a topic or to reinforce and refine a concept. Video should not be used as a stand-alone lesson outside of the context of an instructional strategy if its intent is to instruct. Students are most familiar with video equipment as a means of entertainment. **Showing a video in the classroom outside of the confines of a directed instructional purpose transfers the activity to entertainment status.**

The steps for integrating video are determined by the specific instructional strategy. The basic format when video is used to introduce a topic is to view some or all of a tape and manipulate the information to generate a concept or pattern. When video is used to reinforce and refine a concept, the material should be viewed after specific information is manipulated or categorized using cooperative groups or whole class discussion.

FIGURE 7.7. TEACHER-GUIDED VIDEO EQUIPMENT NEEDS

Teacher-Guided Video Equipment Needs:	
• Videocassette tape:	Preview the tape to determine compatibility of the content with the learning objectives. It is not necessary to show students the entire tape to achieve maximum benefit.
• Videocassette Recorder (VCR) and Television:	The VCR should be hooked up to the television to view the recorded videocassette tape. It may be necessary to link two televisions together if the group is large or spread out across the room. This would allow students to view the material within their cooperative groups without rearranging the furniture.

Teacher-guided video applications are those where the teacher determines the materials to be used and the direction of their use. Physics and physical science classes can use video in the analysis of motion, for example. Students can drop or throw a bright colored object, say a basketball, from a second or third story window while others videotape the event from the ground. Analysis can be used to determine the value for the acceleration due to gravity with the effects of air resistance or the approximate vertical distance the object fell.

Another example of a teacher-guided video application is the analysis of a story in an English class using a directed reading-thinking activity (DRTA) (see Chapter 8 for a more detailed explanation of this strategy). The teacher can show the first few minutes of a commercially produced video appropriate for a literature lesson. The class can be asked to make predictions about the plot of the story and these should be posted on the board. Students should be encouraged to share the reasons behind their thoughts. After all predictions have been written, the viewing of the video story is continued until the plot reaches a turning point. The class should be asked to evaluate the posted predictions and eliminate those that do not match the new information gained from the latest viewing. This cycle should continue to the end of the video, with follow-up analysis.

Other uses for teacher-guided video applications involve having students record events using a camcorder. These recordings can be used later in instruction. Biology students can record dissections; drama students can record performances; athletes can record practice activities; all of these can be used for analysis and evaluation in the classroom. The concept to be derived is specific for each of these examples, but each student will have the same basic comprehension from the activity.

The medium of video is a tool which allows the teacher to guide every student to the same fundamental concepts. Students are actively engaged in the process of acquiring the concept by seeing it happen and hearing input from their peers that explains it in terms of individual experiences. Comprehension of content materials and the ability to generalize will be increased by involving as many senses as possible. This is the true value of the use of both video and computer equipment. The student is the center of a learning process that stimulates the visual and auditory senses beyond the capabilities of a printed page. This process is facilitated by the increased length of instructional time in a block schedule.

SAMPLE TEACHER-GUIDED VIDEO APPLICATION

One example of a teacher-guided video application is the cooperative learning strategy, jigsaw. The purpose of this lesson is to introduce students to information about Spain, but the strategy is equally effective for other topics and disciplines. Students work in cooperative groups on specific categories of information about Spain, specifically about its culture, geography and climate, history, education, and government. Each member becomes an expert for one of the categories and is responsible for ensuring that every member of the group understands the content information. Students should be familiar with the responsibilities of working in cooperative groups. The chapter on cooperative learning can provide more detailed information. This lesson is intended for use in a Spanish language or geography class.

Equipment needs include a VCR, television set, and a commercially produced instructional video of Spain that is appropriate for the learning objectives. In this case, the objective is to develop a basic understanding of the culture and people of Spain. The video should be previewed to decide what portion is germane to this lesson.

Initial discussion of the assignment should center on the expectations and timeframe involved in each step of the process. Furniture should be arranged for group work so that each individual gets a clear view of the television. This process should take approximately three blocks in an alternate-day block schedule. Traditional class schedules will require six to eight class periods.

Day 1: Discuss the assignment. Assign groups and tasks. View the video in expert groups. Generate and submit one conceptual statement describing the expert group category.

State the learning goal and separate the students into cooperative groups. Each team member will be responsible for becoming an expert in one specific category within the topic. Categories can be assigned randomly or selected by members of the team. The suggested categories are Culture, Geography and Climate, History, Education, and Government. Group size is determined by the number of categories. In this case there are five categories, so each group will have five members. The Geography and Climate content area can be separated into two categories if it is necessary to have six members per group. Every member of the group must have a category and every category must be represented in each cooperative group.

The activity involves viewing the video as a resource for information about Spain. Students are to take notes only about their assigned category while watching the video. They are to become experts about their topic. During the next block class, they will develop a teaching strategy to introduce the information to the other members of their cooperative groups. To facilitate this, experts, one from each cooperative group, will sit together in their expert groups during the video and share information among themselves. While students are still in their cooperative groups, answer any questions they may have about the lesson and their responsibilities. Ask them to break up into expert groups once everyone understands the assignment.

Expert groups should be given 5–10 minutes to discuss the types of things they will listen for in the video. For example, the government group may decide that information on government-supported programs is significant to their category, but any information on government- supported public universities is not. This discussion process is important to direct each member's attention to specific aspects of the video information provided by the video. Groups will have the opportunity to refine their decisions about "gray areas" of their category after they view the video. Sometimes the information is complex and expert groups may need time to reflect. Groups may request a 3-minute timeout if needed for purposeful discussion. In that case, the video is stopped while the expert group sorts out the information. The teacher should instruct the students not to make their topics too restrictive.

Show the portions of the video that meet the learning objectives. Expert groups occasionally will wish to talk softly among themselves, but this should be held to a minimum. Emphasize that the groups will have the opportunity to compare notes after the video.

The remaining class time should be spent in expert groups to accomplish two goals. First, members of the group should compare notes and make sure their information is consistent. They may need to refer back to the video to check their facts. Second, after they are satisfied that their information is accurate and complete, group members must decide on the most important concept or idea that emerges from their data. This concept is to be submitted by the group at the end of the block. Students typically need guided practice in the development of a concept the first few times this process is used. For example, the Culture group might establish the concept that religion plays a substantial role in every part of life in Spain. Note this is a concept the students derived from facts: the percentage of Catholics in the country, the Jesuit schools, the religious events and holidays, the involvement of religion in history and culture.

Day 2: Develop teaching methods and aids in expert groups.

Students should work in expert groups to develop a strategy to teach their category information to the members of their cooperative groups. They may choose to develop a crossword puzzle with a word bank or create a game that matches questions with answers. They may decide to provide a few paragraphs of information with keywords written in a code that must be deciphered. Any strategy they create must require the knowledge of the subject to complete. A final copy is submitted at the end of the block along with an answer key. Copies of the teaching aid and answer key will be needed for every student in the class.

Day 3: Return to cooperative teams and share information. Take notes on each category.

Students should work in their cooperative teams to develop a full concept of the culture and people of Spain. Each expert is responsible for teaching the others about his/her specific category.

Experts should begin with the main concept and explain the reasons it was selected. Cooperative team members should take notes. The introduction of the content information using the teaching aid is second. The expert can assist team members and share the answer key.

Every student in the class is responsible for the same material in this instructional strategy. Provide them with the opportunity to copy notes in their notebooks and check their comprehension of facts as a wrap-up activity.

Extensions of this activity can shift the technology to student-guided strategies. Expert groups might choose to search online databases and libraries for additional information or to post questions to electronic newsgroups. The resultant information could be presented to the teams in a printed format or as a Web document.

This example of a teacher-guided video application can be easily transformed into a lesson in another discipline. For example, a health class could use this procedure with a video on communicable diseases. The learning objective might be to understand how diseases are transferred. An extension assignment could be the production of an informational flyer to be distributed to other students in the school. A biology class could produce recycling informational posters from a video on waste management. The objective could be to state methods of reducing waste products in landfills. Products will vary from team to team, but the outcome will be standardized because the same base knowledge is used for the entire class and the learning goals are specific. These products give students the chance to creatively restate information given from a video and to give the information meaning beyond the classroom.

STUDENT-GUIDED VIDEO APPLICATION

Effective use of video equipment in student-guided applications requires teachers and students to have at least brief training. Practice using the camera, being filmed, and seeing themselves "on television" also is useful in developing a comfort level with video. Students will become proficient in using the equipment with repetition and peer coaching in cooperative groups.

Groups can range from three to six students depending on the size needed for the specific task. More than six per group becomes a management problem for the team and is not recommended. A basic introduction to the camcorder and filming techniques will be beneficial. It is a good idea to have students begin using the camcorder with small assignments filmed in the classroom; this will allow every student to have the opportunity to become familiar with using the camera and being filmed. As with any technology, some students will have expertise with video cameras. These students are a good source of technical support in the classroom and frequently are eager to share. Peer coaching is a constructive method for students to develop a healthy admiration for each other's capabilities and differences.

Video products can range from illustrations of concrete facts to visual development of abstract concepts. Initially, products should be developed as an extension of the strategies used for content learning. For example, geometry students can film real life examples of parallel lines or a chemistry student can film examples of metal corrosion. Once the filming process has been modeled successfully in class, students can plunge into a more constructivist approach for generating abstracts from concrete information with a product that visually illustrates the concepts. These products allow others to see things through the learners' eyes.

Student-guided video applications can be used in every discipline. Such applications are especially useful in integrating content from various subject areas. Students in English classes can create and record news reports of events that take place in a specific reading assignment. For example, Edgar Allan Poe's "The Pit and the Pendulum" could become a media event with live broadcasting of a hostage situation. Reporters can switch between the action at the scene and the background information provided by the newscaster in the studio. Outcomes will vary depending on the team perspectives and analysis of the Poe work. The learning goal for this project might be the development of a construct for the emotion of terror.

An example of cross-subject integration is the topic of Columbus. The learning goal might be the development of the concept of the logistics of exploration in the 15th Century. The social studies class may study Columbus' adventure across the ocean using computer programmed instruction on ocean currents. This information can be used to create maps of possible routes that could get the ships to the New World before the sailors ran out of food and fresh water. The English class can research the costumes of the day using on-line databases and correspond with experts in the field by e-mail, creating a catalogue of clothing merchandise as a final product. This catalog can be generated with software publishing tools and printed. The biology class can research the problems sailors encountered with food storage and preparation, disease, and medical practices during Columbus' time, using on-line databases. A final product might be a "copy" of Columbus' cook's diary or a letter home from the ship's doctor, produced using a word processing program. The math classes can generate a spreadsheet of the cook's food supply needs for the crew. The cost of those supplies in the currency of the day could be calculated and determinations of storage in the limited space of Columbus' small ships could be proposed using the principles of geometry. Putting these activities together would not require the student in the math class to also be in the same social studies and biology classes. The information generated by one class can be developed into a video presentation and shown as expert content information. The process involves active participation in a project that connects several disciplines in a fashion similar to the themes approach used in elementary schools. Videotaping the class conclusions to share with all the classes involved provides closure and purpose for the assignment. It also generates the excitement that comes from knowing that the work being done is needed by another group and part of a larger effort.

Additional suggestions for learning goals using student-guided video technology might be to generate a theory of the culture of Americans of the Midwest for history class; develop an appreciation of the art of the Dutch Masters for art class; create a visual expose' of the writings of Robert Frost for a literature class.

PREPARATION

Putting technology in the students' hands provides a means for the learner to synthesize content information in a manner that extends comprehension of the concepts. An added bonus is the accommodation of the strengths of each student and the opportunity to expand personal experiences. Advance preparation is a critical component of the effective use of video. In student-guided video use, the learners are in charge of a large portion of the task. For a list of video equipment needs, see Figure 7.8.

TEACHER RESPONSIBILITIES

The teacher needs to establish balanced cooperative teams, a reasonable timeframe, project expectations and objectives, and the criteria for grading (see Fig. 7.2). Ideally, a cooperative team will be composed of three to six students with a blend of capabilities and experiences. Student groups typically will be strong in some areas and weak in others. Asking for assistance outside of the team should be encouraged to help counteract deficiencies and accommodate the social needs of students within the confines of the task at hand.

Producing a professional quality video is not necessarily an objective in this process. Content knowledge and its accurate application are the basis for establishing objectives and grading criteria. Student groups typically are self-motivated to produce a quality product to the best of their abilities, especially when supported and encouraged by the teacher and their peers. Practice and opportunity will go a long way to smooth the rough edges.

FIGURE 7.8. STUDENT-GUIDED ACTIVITY VIDEO EQUIPMENT NEEDS

Student-Guided Activity Video Equipment Needs:	
• Camcorder or video camera:	Camcorders are smaller and easier to take on site than video cameras but both will do the job. Check to be sure the tripod attachment is on the camera or in the case.
• Tripod:	A sturdy one will protect the equipment from falling over if accidentally bumped.
• Batteries:	At least two charged batteries will be needed. Improperly charged batteries will not have much power and it's always safer to have a spare.
• Power pack:	The camera can run from direct current (DC) with batteries or alternating current (AC) with a power pack that connects to the camera and plugs into a wall socket. Connecting the camera to the power pack is more reliable than battery power and increases the time available for filming.
• Videocassette tape:	Good quality professional tape will last longer than inexpensive tape. It also will cause less wear and tear on the camera and editing equipment. There are different sizes of videocassette tapes. The tape you use to record must also be the size needed for the camcorder and the VCR. Most schools use U-matic, VHS, or 8 mm tape.
• Videocassette Recorder (VCR) and Television:	The VCR should be hooked up to the television to view the recorded videocassette tape.
• Editor (optional):	Tapes can be edited by using a video editor or by connecting two VCRs together so that one copies from the other.
• Extension cord (optional):	This will give you greater mobility using the power pack.

Grading student video projects requires qualitative and quantitative approaches to assessment similar to the evaluation of student-guided computer applications. Teams should turn in the plan proposal, timeline, team time tally, storyboards, research bibliographies, final products, and evaluations. Each of these is discussed in the previous section on computer integration except for the storyboard. A storyboard is a method of organizing the visual and audio components of a filming project. Small video projects may not require all of the elements listed. The team grade will be determined from these items with a variable individual evaluation component to allow for unequal participation and disruptive behavior in a similar fashion to the student-guided computer activity assessment. A sample point system is given in Figure 7.5 that can be used for either computer or video projects. The grading criteria should be established at the beginning of the assignment with student input, and modification for individual education plans may be necessary.

Student Responsibilities

Students are responsible for the direction and completion of a majority of the tasks in student directed use of video. Team-shared responsibilities help in the development of conceptual schema that are influenced by the background experiences and strengths of individual team members. These responsibilities include planning, researching, script and storyboard writing, filming, editing (optional), presenting, and evaluating. The scope of the objectives will determine which of these responsibilities apply to the particular project and to what extent. Group members should choose or be assigned the role of project manager, content manager, or technical manager. The number of team members to work in each role will be determined by the size of the group and the scope of the project. Every team member should have an assigned role. The project managers are responsible for the planning and evaluation stages of the process, organization of the presentation, and accumulation of data for the team time sheet. Content managers are responsible for coordinating research efforts, ensuring every member of the group understands the content information, coordinating script writing, and working with the technical manager to develop the storyboard. Technical managers are responsible for equipment, filming schedules, and coordinating efforts in filming and editing. The technical manager works with the content manager on the storyboard and with the project manager on the presentation.

FIGURE 7.9. TEAM RESPONSIBILITIES FOR STUDENT-GUIDED VIDEO ACTIVITY

♦ Plan the project.

♦ Research the topic.

♦ Write the script and storyboard.

♦ Produce the videotape.

♦ Edit the film if applicable.

♦ Present the finished product.

♦ Evaluate individual efforts and the work of the team.

Planning is always the first team step, regardless of the size of the project. Team members must make decisions on their plans for the project, roles of team members, and equipment needs. "What," "when," and "how long" questions must be answered for each of these areas. This stage puts the mechanics of organization into gear. Teams will submit project proposals that include detailed plans and a list of necessary equipment. Proposals must be approved by the teacher before students begin to work on the project. This step allows the team to develop an internal organization. It also provides the teacher with a means of keeping track of equipment needs and helping students to mold plans of a manageable size.

The project managers are in charge of this part of the project. They are responsible for submitting completed team proposals and a cumulative team time tally on the day of the presentation.

Teams must strive to adhere to their schedules as closely as possible to avoid time crunches and equipment shortages. It is almost certain that the plans will change throughout the process, but teams must be made aware of the importance of careful design. The original plans have a locking effect that teams must take into account when changes are made, especially if quantities of camcorders and VCRs are limited. After the team plan is approved, the team manager can sign up for equipment. Equipment may not be available at the most desirable times when changes are made. Occasionally another team can trade times, but usually the original plan must be adhered to with only slight modification.

Research typically spreads itself out over the duration of the project, but the main body of the work should be done before the script and storyboard are written. It is not unusual for plans to be modified at this point in light of new information gathered in research. The team plan to meet the objectives will determine the depth of research necessary. Small projects may not require any information beyond the basics acquired in teacher-guided instruction. Content managers organize this process. Their responsibility is to insure the accuracy and reliability of the scripts. Teachers can require the content manager to submit a team bibliography to illustrate the quantity and variety of materials used.

Writing a script and developing the storyboard is the third stage of the process. Once team members have modified their plan, the content manager makes sure every member of the team is familiar with all of the information gathered in the research and coordinates the writing of the script. Large projects may require a complete script before working on the storyboard. Both can be written at the same time for smaller projects or more experienced teams.

The storyboard is a plan to incorporate visual and narrative information for filming in a frame-by-frame format. The easiest storyboard method is to use 5" x 7" index cards. Each card shows the video and audio components for a specific camera shot. Students should sketch a drawing of the camera shot on the left side of the card. Beneath the sketch, the technical manager can write filming notes on lighting, background, sound, closeup views, and other technical cues necessary for good filming. The script should be written on the right side of the card. Every camera shot requires a different card. These cards can be reordered until the team is satisfied with the sequence. The order of the cards indicates the filming sequence (Bunch, 1990).

Filming is under the supervision of the technical manager. Small projects are easily filmed during a single block period, but larger ones may require additional time outside of the instructional block. This is not possible when teams change plans and the equipment is not available. Changing the date or time equipment is needed typically requires students to film after school hours or on weekends.

Technical managers can save a great deal of time by checking equipment before they are ready to film. Advance planning for extension cords, extra battery packs, and videotapes will reduce frustration levels and decrease filming time. Other team members can assist in the process by setting up any props for the taping location and rehearsing before filming.

Editing the tape is a nice feature that makes the final product look polished and connected. This stage helps students outside the team get an organized concept of the teams' interpretation of the learning goal. Film can be "cut" using an editor if one is available.

Schools that do not have editing capabilities may have to record the tape in sequence with only one take per scene. Any retakes are recorded over the original taped segment. This requires very careful planning, organization, and attention to detail. A second possibility is connecting two VCRs together so one can copy from the other. The new tape would be a copy of the selected segments from the original tape. This method allows the team to film a particular segment several times, not necessarily in sequence.

The technical manager is responsible for the editing phase with input from the entire team. Members should make recommendations for the selection of the best choice of a particular filming sequence.

Presentation of the final product is the culminating event. The project and technical managers work together to organize this opportunity to teach the rest of the class. The presentation should include a verbal explanation of the project, a viewing of the product, and a discussion or explanation justifying the product's ability to meet the initial learning objective. This phase is very important for the other members of the class. It is the team's chance to have others view conceptual development and application as they themselves envision it. Students are encouraged to ask questions and make comments. The diversity and talents of individuals are readily apparent at this point. The learning goes well beyond the stated learning objective. Teachers need to establish expectations at the beginning of the presentation phase of the project. The products are highly personalized and all criticism must be constructive to be beneficial. Students should be encouraged to embrace the differences and multiple intelligences of others and make an effort to see ideas through the team's eyes. Diversity is a beneficial and desirable component of life.

Evaluation of team efforts is necessary for constructive modification and improvement of the process. It is also a necessary component of grading. Team members should submit a written evaluation of their own participation in the project. This should include a statement of the grade they feel has been earned and a detailed justification of contributions to the team effort. It is important for the students to see the grade as a reflection of the work that was completed and the cooperative efforts employed. The students' efforts and their roles in the whole process are critical factors in the success of the project. These evaluations are to be confidential and represent the variable component in the team grade (see Fig. 7.5). Each person also might be asked to submit a confidential evaluation of the other team members. This step is optional and not always a valid check of contributions within the group.

THE NEED FOR ADVANCE PLANNING

Advance planning traditionally has been one of the hallmarks of a good teacher. This does not change with the inclusion of media equipment in the design of instruction. Objectives for the instruction must be stated clearly from the beginning to avoid confusion about the role of the equipment being used. This is doubly true in the initial phases of technology integration. It is important to use the media tools as an integral part of the instruction to allow the students to increase the depth of their learning. The learning goals are the primary objective, with the media used as a means to an end.

Grading procedures also should be established in advance of the instruction. These procedures and the instruments for qualitative and quantitative assessment should be developed and shared with students at the introduction of the assignment. The intent is twofold: First, the purpose is to establish the learning expectations for the lesson. The second purpose is to provide students with a signal of closure—an answer for the "How do we know when we're finished?" question that is typical in student-guided learning assignments. Assessment instruments may need to be modified once students dig into the challenge. Student-centered learning is not as predictable as teacher-centered instruction and flexibility is important. Change is a normal part of any process and should be expected, especially while teachers and students work to become more accustomed to the integration of media equipment in instruction. Unforeseen circumstances may arise, necessitating a change in objectives, grading, or use of equipment. Careful preparation will ensure that when events take a turn, adaptations can be swift and effective.

CONCLUSIONS

Block scheduling offers teachers the chance to delve deeply into their bag of teaching strategies to improve student learning. It provides the instructional time necessary to effectively shift the role of the teacher to facilitator in a student centered instructional environment. Technology provides the tools to accommodate this shift and expand learning into the higher order realms of application, analysis, synthesis, and evaluation. The integration of technological tools into instruction creates an opportunity for teachers to develop new methods, new strategies, and a vision of change. Block scheduling presents educators with the freedom to put that vision into practice.

REFERENCES

Braun, L. (1990). *Vision TEST (Technically enriched schools of tomorrow). Final report: Recommendations for American educational decisionmakers.* Eugene, OR: International Society for Technology in Education. (ERIC Document Reproduction Service No. ED 327 173)

Bunch, J. (1990). The storyboard strategy: Planning effective training by translating instructional design principles into practice. *Training and Development Journal, 45,* 69–71.

Canady, R.L., & Rettig, M.D. (1995). The power of innovative scheduling. *Educational Leadership, 53(3),* 4–10.

Means, B., & Olson, K. (1994). The link between technology and authentic learning. *Educational Leadership, 51(7),* 15–18.

O'Neil, J. (1995). On technology schools: A conversation with Chris Dede. *Educational Leadership, 53(2),* 6–12.

Sheingold, K., & Hadley, M. (1990). *Accomplished teachers: Integrating computers into classroom practice.* New York: Center for Technology in Education, Bank Street College of Education.

Vaughan, Tay. (1994). *Multimedia: Making it work.* Berkeley: McGraw-Hill.

Wilson, Brent G., et al. (January 1993). *Evaluating the impact of technology at Peakview Elementary School.* In: Selected Research and Development. Symposium conducted at the conference of the Association for Educational Communications and Technology, New Orleans, LA.

TECHNOLOGY RESOURCES

NOTE: The following resources can provide additional information about the role of technology in the shift from teacher-centered to student-centered instruction.

Dwyer, D. (1994). Apple classrooms of tomorrow: What we've learned. *Educational Leadership, 51(7),* 4–10.

Hancock, V., & Betts, F. (1994). From the lagging to the leading edge. *Educational Leadership, 51(7),* 24–29.

Laszlo, A., & Castro, K. (1995). Technology and values: Interactive learning environments for future generations. *Educational Technology, 35(2),* 7–13.

Van Dusen, L.M., & Worthen, B.R. (1995). Can integrated instructional technology transform the classroom? *Educational Leadership, 53(2),* 28–33.

ADDITIONAL TECHNOLOGY RESOURCES

Brown, P. (1990). Steps toward the evolution of a new medium: Computer-aided art and design. *Leonardo, 23(2/3),* 197–200.

Froman, A.D. (1992). Electronic baby steps. *The Computing Teacher, 20(2),* 24–26.

Geiger, K. (1993). Hearts and minds: Technology and the personalized classroom. *Electronic Learning, 12(5),* 50.

Heinich R., Molenda M., & Russell J.D. (1993). *Instructional media and the new technologies of instruction.* New York: Macmillian.

Marshall, G. (1993). Zen and the art of evaluation. *The Computing Teacher, 20(8)*, 48–49.

McCormick, T.L. (1995). Problem-solving projects. *The Science Teacher, 62(3)*, 27–29.

Smith, J. (1992). Goin' wild in Hypercard. *The Computing Teacher, 20(4)*, 24–27.

Smith, R.J. & Gibbs, M. (1994). *Navigating the Internet*. Indianapolis: Sams.

Vaughan, T. (1994). *Multimedia: Making it work*. Berkeley: McGraw-Hill.

Wigley, H.S. (1993). Ways of using technology in language and literacy teaching. *TESOL Quarterly, 27(2)*, 319–322.

Zollman, D., Noble, M.L., & Curtin, R. (1986). Modeling the motion of an athlete: An Interactive video lesson for teaching physics. *Journal of Educational Technology Systems, 15(3)*, 249–258.

8

CONTENT AREA LITERACY INSTRUCTION: READING AND WRITING STRATEGIES[1]

The worker of the 21st century, whether blue collar or professional, must be a life-long learner who is able to adapt to ever-changing demands. This means that our job is changing from helping students become content area informed to helping them become content area literate. In this chapter, we define this critical difference, tell specifically how our teaching needs to change, and present a blueprint for planning content area literacy instruction within the block schedule.

To be content area literate is to be able

♦ to read and understand the standard written materials of the content area;

♦ to write clearly and knowledgeably about the subject; and

♦ to converse with others who are within the circle of the content area community.

[1] This chapter was written by Tom Gill, Associate Professor, West Chester University, West Chester, Pennsylvania, and Laurie Nelson-Gill, Educational Consultant, Kennett Square, Pennsylvania.

CONTENT AREA LITERACY KNOWLEDGE AND SKILLS

To be content area literate, one must acquire specific knowledge and skills:

♦ The reader/writer must be able to recognize and spell printed words with fluency and automaticity.

♦ The reader/writer must possess the content knowledge that is assumed by the authors of content area exposition in order to understand the ideas presented in a discipline's texts.

♦ The reader/writer must be familiar with the specific vocabulary of the field which becomes more obscure and occurs less frequently as the text becomes more sophisticated.

♦ The reader/writer must have internalized the language and structure of content area text, which differ substantially from oral language and narrative text and are even particular to each discipline.

The question, of course, is **how** to plan instruction that promotes optimal growth in these competencies. Effective content literacy teaching must adhere to a few basic principles:

♦ Students only get better in reading and writing in the content areas by spending much time reading and writing in the content areas.

♦ Students only become skillful readers of content area texts by plentiful reading in materials that they can read fluently and truly comprehend.

♦ Students learn how to converse with others in the circle of the content area community by taking part in content area discussions on a regular basis.

♦ Content area vocabulary increases not by memorizing definitions of words but by hearing or reading new terms as they occur in contexts that are understood and by making associations between new and known words according to their related prefixes, suffixes, and roots.

Adhering to these principles means real changes in the use of materials and time management in content area classrooms.

The questions to be answered in this chapter are, first, how content area teachers can match students of wide-ranging literacy abilities with the appropriate materials and, second, how they can organize instructional time to include sufficient work in the activities that result in content area literacy.

DIAGNOSIS-BASED, PRINCIPLE-BASED, SANITY-BASED ORGANIZATION

Our teaching plan is first diagnosis-based, because what texts we use with whom depends on the highest level each student can read with relative ease, or can understand when read to. It is principle-based, because our allocation of time for classroom activities is guided by their congruence with the content literacy principles put forth above. Finally, it is sanity-based, because we are determined not to embark on a plan that is good in theory, but stressful or even impossible to implement.

What follows is a guide for **diagnosing, teaching,** and **organizing** in this framework.

DIAGNOSING

Our first order of business is to determine the highest level of material in our content area that each pupil can read with understanding, or listen to if need be. We establish our point of reference by seeing how well each student can handle the grade-level material. From our textbook (or a grade-level trade book in our content area if our school has embraced the use of multiple trade books rather than textbooks), we select a section from one of the early chapters that does not depend upon preceding material but is rich in content. We want this selection to be long enough to have content cohesion, but not so long that one who is a slower or poorer reader takes too long or is overwhelmed by the task. We have found that about a 3–5 page selection that hangs together from heading to heading works well. The students then are asked to silently read this selection, put away their texts, and write as complete a retelling of what they read as possible. Some teachers feel more comfortable with accompanying the retelling with 10 good comprehension questions, and we have no problem with this effort to quantify the results.

While some of the students are taking this test of silent reading comprehension, the teacher can begin to assess the students' word recognition ability and fluency. To accomplish this, we select a chapter from the midsection of the book. On your copy of the chapter, bracket off every 50-word segment. Gather the students in groups of eight to ten and call on each one individually to read orally in round robin fashion. When you call on a student to read, write his or her name in the margin of your copy where the reading begins. As the student reads orally, make a mark on each word that the student miscalls or omits, as well as a mark at any place the student adds a word that is not there. When you have enough of a reading sample (in 50-word segments) that you think represents that student's word recognition and reading fluency, call on the next student to read the next segment. We have found about 150–200 words to be a reliable sample of one's oral reading of a particular text, but in cases where the text is clearly too difficult, feel free to cut off the reading at 50 words or less. After the reading, determine each student's **word recognition in context score**. Just count each word as if it were a question on a test. Therefore, for a student who read just 50 words, each error would count 2 points. For the student who read 200 words, each error would count 0.5 points. Multiply the number of errors times each error's value and subtract from 100. Therefore, the student who read 50 words making four errors would get a 92% word recognition in context score, while the student who read 200 words making eight errors would get a 96% word recognition in context score. We also judge fluency at the time of the oral reading by placing in the margin of our copy a check-plus for "very fluent reading," a check for "fluent enough," or a check-minus for "disfluent," word-by-word oral reading.

Similarly, we choose chapters from other textbooks in the same subject written at other grade levels. For the sake of efficiency and honoring the fact that reading ability at the secondary level is more accurately defined by range rather than level, we select chapters from books in the particular content area written at every other level rather than at each grade level. The school librarian can help find publishers from whom samples of these textbooks can be acquired. Used schoolbook depositories, both within school systems and privately owned, are also good sources. Remember, we are not trying to purchase sets of these for instruction, but single copies are needed only for diagnostic purposes. Those students who read the grade-level text making more than five errors per 100 words and/or disfluently are asked to read from the lower level selections until the highest level is determined where the student can read with 95% accuracy and with moderate fluency. By traditional criteria, two or fewer errors in word recognition per 100 words denotes one's **independent reading level**. High-achieving students, who gain far more in literacy each year than their poorer-reading classmates, are given material at this level to read in school (Shannon, 1988). Three to five errors per 100 words, with 75% comprehension, has withstood the test of time in denoting one's **instructional level**, the level of difficulty of text that can be used beneficially with a teacher's help (Betts, 1946). For content area exposition, we believe that word recognition needs to be even more accurate than this, as any struggle with word recognition takes cognitive energy away from attention to the content to be learned (Perfetti, 1986). More than five errors per 100 words indicates that the material is on one's **frustration level**.

Over the years, many techniques have been developed for helping students better understand content area texts. Recently, the emphasis has been on helping students become more strategic in their content area reading. However, as Kletzien (1991) found, students are not able to fully apply comprehension strategies they have learned to material that is at their frustration level.

Students who make four or fewer errors per 100 words while getting a check-plus fluency rating are asked to read from progressively higher-level texts. We recommend audiotaping these oral readings so that teachers can refer to them to check or to justify to others why they placed students in the materials finally chosen.

Once the highest level that one can read with word recognition accuracy and a modicum of fluency has been determined for a student, we give him or her a three to five page selection from the beginning of that text to assess whether or not it can be read silently with acceptable comprehension. It is quite possible, of course, for one to be able to read the words accurately but not have sufficient prior knowledge of the concepts and/or be familiar enough with that level of text language to understand it. Imagine if someone were to change 10% of the words in a text to nonsense words as below:

> The modern septudinal is a highly effective device for combining large amounts of applositories for productive activity under unified condugination. Its many advantages over other forms of dilatifies, as we shall see later in the chapter, have attracted the bulk of climoran funds and assets available to havorital.

> [The modern corporation is a highly effective device for combining large amounts of resources for productive activity under unified management. Its many advantages over other forms of ownership, as we shall see later in the chapter, have attracted the bulk of capital funds and assets available to business.]

This would put us in an empathetic position with one who has word recognition ability but not the specific vocabulary arsenal to readily achieve comprehension. For students to improve their content area literacy optimally, they must do much reading where word recognition, fluency, and comprehension are all adequate.

Reading the following puts us in the position of those who are poor spellers to the point of not being able to trust their knowledge of vowels in reading:

> 1t 2s p3ss4bl5 f6r 7s t8 st9ll r1cr23t4 5h6 78th9r's m12n4ng b6t n5t w7th89t 1 str3ggl2. 5f, th4n, w2 f3nd th5t 6 st8d7nt 6s 5bl6 t7 r92d s4l3ntly 2nd 4nd1rst5nd th3 gr2d1–l3v4l t6xt b3t r62ds 7r4lly 7n8cc8r4t3ly 2nd d4sfl74ntly 2t th2t l6v3l, w4 w5ll c7rt24nly n7t h6d3 th6 t9xt fr4m th8t st3d5nt
>
> . . .
>
> It is possible for us to still recreate the author's meaning but not without a struggle. If, then, we find that a student is able to read silently and understand the grade-level text but reads orally inaccurately and disfluently at that level, we certainly will not hide the text from that student . . .

. . . but we do know that the student stands a greater chance of being able to attend to the meaning if he or she is given audiotaped recordings of the grade-level text to ease the cognitive load of word recognition at that level. If a student is to make gains in independent content area literacy, he or she must be given much reading at an appropriate challenge level so that the conscious mind can fully attend to the meaning of the text while the mind's eye subconsciously readily recognizes the words.

How wide a range can one expect in a heterogeneous class? A time-tested rule of thumb to determine the expected reading levels in any one grade has been to take ⅔ of a student's age (Bond, Tinker, & Wasson, 1979). A heterogeneous class of 14-year-old 9th grade students, therefore, will range in their reading levels from below 5th grade to above 12th grade, with one-third reading below and one-third reading above grade level (⅔ of 14 is about 9 years range; 4½ years above 9th grade and 4½ years below 9th grade).

After everyone has completed the oral and silent reading assessment, we read to the whole class exactly the same three- to five-page selection and retest comprehension in exactly the same way. In this way, we can determine which students can listen to and comprehend the textbook even though they cannot read and comprehend it. When we suggest to teachers that these students be provided books on tape, we understandably are met with incredulous looks. But think about it! Grade-level content area textbooks are on the frustration level of approximately one-third of the students. No matter how hard they try, they cannot grasp the author's message. Would we dare deny this access to information if these students were blind? We recall a community college student who was discovered to be unable to read aloud an upper-level text accurately but who proved he could understand it when read to him. He was taken to a storeroom of textbooks and trade books on tape. After sampling the audiotapes, he began to weep at the overwhelming realization that he was going to be able to "read" whatever his mind could grasp.

There is another advantage that all can gain from listening to material being read aloud (whether in person or on tape) that is on a level that they cannot read with ease themselves. At the beginning of this chapter, we argued that full content area literacy required text language awareness—an internalized sense of the grammar and diction of content area writing on a sentence, paragraph, and text structure level. Being read to at the highest level one can understand, and being encouraged and given feedback in one's attempts to write in that genre, yields improvement in vocabulary and a feel for the subtleties of sophisticated text. We have witnessed students who have accomplished real and expedient improvement in their writing by coupling copious amounts of writing with hours of listening to tape recordings of short stories, essays, compositions, novels, and textbooks. Awkward expressions in writing are nothing more than oral language written down, and the hours that these students spent listening formed an internalized sense of the dialect of written language.

Once these levels of effective reading and listening are found, textbooks, trade books, magazine articles, essays—any material—can be compared quickly by the teacher to the different level text selections chosen for the diagnosis. This subjective, but direct, comparison allows the material to be "accurately enough" categorized by instructional range and matched with the reading and listening abilities of students (Singer, 1975). We have found that the typical heterogeneously-grouped middle or high school content classroom yields three main clusters of instructional ranges at a grade level, with a few students functioning at exceptionally higher and lower levels. The match of difficulty of material to the reading competence of the student is "good enough" when it falls within the range of plus or minus one grade level. We try to keep in mind that it is more instructionally sound to have a student start in relatively easier material and then move in and out of more difficult materials on that same topic.

Units then can be formed around the basic areas of study for a course, and materials appropriate for all students can be readily gathered. This gathering of materials is, of course, a considerable task, but it can be accomplished over time when the task is shared with colleagues and a collective file is organized by theme and level.

TEACHING

The next step in planning is to dedicate blocks of instructional time for those instructional activities that truly result in content area literacy improvement.

READING

Our first area of instructional concentration is:

Lots of reading for meaning, with concomitant discussions before, during, and after reading in material at a level where students can recognize 95% of the words and read with fluency and understanding.

We are assuming at this point in our plans that the instructional levels of the students have been determined and that the material to be used with each cluster of students honors the requirements both for listening and reading. Our attention now turns to the "concomitant discussion before, during, and after reading."

Much has been written about techniques that foster comprehension. However, all of the techniques that we have used and found effective share certain specific commonalities in procedure, which we try to follow in our teaching. First, the cluster of students with whom we are working gives the text a cursory examination and identifies its relationship to its context. Is it a chapter within a unit? A unit within a textbook? A textbook within a field? From this examination, the students hypothesize about what information and ideas the author might intend to convey. Next, each reader is to state not only what is known about these things presently, but also what can be conjectured to be true. For instance, if a chapter is thought to be about how plants produce the energy to grow, the readers are to declare before reading, in writing and then in discussion, how they think plants do accomplish this. It makes no difference at this point whether the students are correct or not—only if they are being sincere. The teacher now knows the cusp of their knowledge—where they are correct, where they aren't and their levels of content sophistication—and can assist their performance as they read to find out. The text has already been selected to fit their present levels of content literacy, and the teacher knows what degree of support to provide. The teacher determines how many pages the students are to read silently. We always tell the students to ask for help on any words that they question, so that we can help them and make note of what words are new for each student. No teacher's guide can tell you what is truly new vocabulary for each student; only each student can do that.

After reading the first section, the teacher assists the students in refining their knowledge by asking "What do you think now?" and "Read to me the part that made you think so." Within this general guideline, a true discussion—a conversation—can take place. This is quite different from traditional question and answer banter, in that we try not to ask questions to which we already know the answers. That's testing, not teaching! What do you think? Why do you think so? What do you think will be addressed next? What do you know or think about how that works? We don't mind being resources ourselves, but only after the students have hypothesized and tried to glean the answers themselves through reading and discussion with each other.

This approach is obviously Socratic in nature and as old as teaching itself. However, the form we have described is our rendition of Russell Stauffer's Directed Reading/Thinking Activity (Stauffer, 1969). The more we read about, think about, and practice techniques in teaching comprehension, the more we find ourselves drawn back to this basic approach. A wonderful byproduct of this approach is the attention students give to their reading. There is nothing as cognitively motivating as the guess. A car company spent a fortune a few years back on a two-page ad that simply asked on the front side of the page, "Guess what car company makes more front-wheel-drive vehicles than any other in the world?" The Madison Avenue ad writers knew that if you made a guess, there was no force that could keep you from turning the page to find out.

Further, this approach leads to the long-term remembering that comes from understanding rather than from memorizing. It has been suggested with some strong evidence that what is understood is not forgotten (Bolles, 1988). Sometimes we forget that we remember it, and it may take something like an old song or even hypnosis to jog our memory, but it is there. "Understood" simply means that our mind embraced it within the framework of our prior knowledge, either by its fit with our present hypothesis (what Piaget called assimilation) or within a frame created anew as we changed our minds to fit the new information (what Piaget called accommodation). However, if the new information is outside our cognitive reach (what Vygotsky (1978) called our "zone of proximal development"), we are at a loss, and the information goes "over our heads" regardless of instructional efforts. If students do not understand, they can only memorize to pass the test on Friday and "seem to be rather than be." Good teaching has been defined not as simply presenting information within students' zone of proximal development, but as assisting performance in this zone (Tharp & Gallimore, 1988). In teaching content area literacy, this "performance" is reading, discussing, and writing within and across the content areas.

As you might imagine, teaching in this vein takes time. One cannot quickly "cover" the information in a chapter in this way. And certainly not every chapter, every article, every trade book can be gone through in this careful, interactive manner. But block scheduling does allow us the time to conduct these careful intellectual scrimmages of unbroken concentration with students, as long as the students who are not participating in this particular guided conversation are engaged in projects that they can do independently or with each other that truly exercise their content area literacy. Meaningful independent projects that truly engage students traditionally have been omitted from the list of possible in-class activities because they take too much time. From the primary through the secondary school years, they have been assigned to be done at home, where their success has depended on the amount of encouragement, supervision, and support that home could provide. Block scheduling, then, not only allows the intensive, teacher-guided intellectual scrimmages, but also the extensive intellectual exercise of in-class projects. The organizing section details these activities and the distribution of time that allows them.

WRITING

Our second area of instructional concentration is:

Lots of writing in which students try to express their ideas as they pertain to the content area while being encouraged to rewrite to extend their use of written language structures and content area vocabulary.

Writing can be utilized through a content area course in a multitude of ways. As a reminder to ourselves to get in as much exercise of content literacy as possible, we try to make it a rule in our content area teaching to read to students or have students read to gain information rather than our giving it to them orally. Likewise, we try to have students write before, during, and after discussions. As previously mentioned, before students read we have them write their divergent hypotheses about how plants grow, how fractions are divided, the stopping distance of an automobile on wet pavement, how an idea becomes a law, or where they think Melville will take Ishmael in the next chapter. Then we interrupt them as they read to ask them to write and share what they have learned and to monitor their thinking processes. After they read and discuss, we ask them to write new position papers explicating their reconsidered concepts in organized formats (similar to Listen/Think/Pair/Share described in Chapter 3).

We also believe that a moratorium should be declared on all true/false, multiple-choice, and fill-in-the-blank questions on tests and assignments. We should take every opportunity to require our students to think, to analyze, to synthesize—in short, to write. As content area teachers, we all know that we never learned as much about our content area through study as we did through teaching it. That's what writing does; it calls on us to give considered explanations of what we think. While reading, listening, and experimenting give us information, writing helps us reflect so that we know what we know and what we don't. As Francis Bacon said, "Writing maketh the exact man."

Block scheduling gives the uninterrupted time in our content area classrooms for our students to engage in the more intensive and extensive effort of constructing expository compositions. Much has been written about the value of teaching the process of writing. Whereas our generation was required to produce a final product for evaluation, students now in elementary, middle, and high school language arts classrooms are being helped with each stage of the construction of a composition, from brainstorming for ideas to the final editing of the final draft. However, just as enough reading cannot be done in reading class for one to become fully literate, English class should not be the only place where composition is exercised. The realization that most of literacy is gained through its exercise has changed the old focus of reading and writing in the content area from "every teacher a teacher of reading and writing" to "every teacher a requirer of reading and writing." Just as blocks of content area class time need to be dedicated to reading, so must blocks of class time be dedicated to writing. Block scheduling allows such topics as, "If it hadn't been for the belief in Manifest Destiny, what difference would it make today?" or, "Investigate, compute the effect, and defend a plan for reducing acid rain." We embrace the basic steps of the writing process shown in Figure 8.1 (p. 247).

HELPING RELUCTANT WRITERS

In helping students along in this process who may be reluctant to leave the safety of fill-in-the-blank and short answers, we have found two approaches helpful.

HONORING THE QUINTILIAN PROGRESSION

First, we try to honor what has come to be known as the Quintilian progression. Quintilian was a teacher of rhetoric in second century Rome. His advice was to foster the following stages of confidence and competence in writing, both across a student's progression and across each composition that a student attempts:

- **Freedom of expression.** In short, students have nothing to mold if they aren't freely putting ideas down on the page. Any emphasis on correctness prior to this only leads to stilted writing. With students who are particularly reluctant to write, we even design activities which reward simply the number of words written on a content area subject during set lengths of class time.

- **Sincerity of thought.** Once a student feels comfortable putting thoughts freely on paper, attention then can be drawn to the predraft step of organizing in accord with a plan.

- **Clarity.** The first rough but complete draft should be written and self-, peer-, and teacher-critiqued only in terms of how clearly the ideas have been expressed. "What does this mean?," "Tell me more about this," and "For example?" should be the guiding comments and questions.

- **Correctness.** Tread carefully in this stage as a content area teacher. Any heavy emphasis here, especially in an area where the student does not have the prerequisite knowledge to realize the correct construction, be it grammar, punctuation, or spelling, will force the student to write more primitively or to mistrust your invitation to share sincerely in the content area conversation. Partnerships with English teachers work wonders here. Expository compositions can be judged and responded to for their content by the appropriate subject area teacher, while the English teacher can help the student focus in on the appropriate areas and levels of sophistication in the art and science of language composition that the English teacher has the training and experience to glean.

- **Eloquence.** As our students grow in their exposure to and awareness of content area texts, vocabulary, and concepts, they can revisit their compositions and try on new words, ideas, and written language constructs.

SERVING AS A WRITING MODEL

The second source of help for the content area writer is the content area teacher who serves as a writing model. By this we mean more than the good advice to have your students see you writing and to share your writing with them. Rather, in addition, we urge you to share your tussle with the 10 steps in the writing process as described in Figure 8.1. Take a topic that is similar to, but not the same as, the ones that your students are assigned. Then, on an overhead, go through the 10 steps with them. First, you complete the writing for a step in the process as you think aloud, and then you help them as they look to your model while concatenating to that step with their own topic. The idea is that your writing will be on a topic close enough to the students' writing that they can use your writing and thinking as a scaffold, but different enough from theirs that they are called on to shape their own particular ideas, linguistic constructions, and diction. All that is required on your part to be effective in this is the nerve to be intellectually honest—not great skill as a writer. We must extend an honest invitation to this next generation in our charge to join the larger community and conversation of content area thinkers. There is no more sincere invitation than your willingness to take part in this process as a mentor.

FIGURE 8.1. STEPS IN THE WRITING PROCESS

- ◆ Define and specify the topic.
- ◆ Brainstorm; write down everything you can think of that might be in a paper on this topic.
- ◆ As you brainstorm, try to arrange your ideas in their relationship to each other. This may be done as simply as making separate lists, or by chaining the ideas as they coordinate and are subordinate and superordinate to one another in a web.
- ◆ Form an outline from your web that reflects the number and arrangement of the paragraphs in your composition.
- ◆ Write an introductory paragraph that includes your thesis statement and the supporting ideas in the order that they will appear in the body of the composition or paragraph.
- ◆ Write the first draft of the composition from start to finish.
- ◆ Write a concluding paragraph.
- ◆ Reread, and get peer and teacher feedback on your draft, concentrating on organization and clarity.
- ◆ Revise according to self- and other recommendations, concentrating on clarity of the major points, the defending rationale, and the specificity of supporting evidence.
- ◆ Get feedback again, and revise in terms of reaching out to use more sophisticated content area vocabulary and writing constructions.

THE RESEARCH PAPER

We would like to add one last note on the subject of writing as it pertains to that infamous assignment, the research paper. We actually like and encourage this assignment for students at all levels. We have two suggestions. First, encourage your students to include more direct sources of information than those available in the library. In particular, teachers have found that interviews with area "experts" and lay people lend an authenticity to the work. Interviews with grandparents who lived through the Depression or with the local waste water manager are valid resources that bring fresh approach and depth to research for the middle and secondary school student.

Second, while we embrace the tried-and-true process of using note cards to systematically record information gathered from texts and other sources, we urge students to take these notes with the book closed after reading, writing the summary information and source on the front side of the index card. An asterisk on the front of the card would denote that a particularly poignant or illustrative direct quote had been recorded on the flip side of the card. The student arranges these cards according to the emerging outline. When the student is writing the paper, we have him or her first read the appropriate cards for a section, and then write the paper without reference to them. After the writing is done, the student then goes back to the cards to insert any specifics and direct quotes. This procedure gives some assurance that the student writes in his or her own voice from his or her new-found knowledge and uses direct references appropriately—as a means of supporting and substantiating one's own point of view. The activity described above will be more successful when students have access to word processing (Chapter 7).

LISTENING

Our third area of instructional concentration for content literacy instruction is:

> **Reading to students at the highest level that they can understand, to ensure that any problem with word recognition does not deny them access to information, and to ensure exposure to more sophisticated expository syntax, text structures, and vocabulary.**

We encourage teachers to use the same critical questioning technique in reading to students that is used when they have students read the texts themselves. Thus, the Directed Reading/Thinking Activity becomes the Directed Listening/Thinking Activity. One instructional advantage in reading to students is that you often can have larger groups or even the whole class listening and responding as you read the same selection to them all. Last semester, we taught a lesson on the Declaration of Independence to a group of "basic level" homogeneously grouped twelfth grade government students. The classroom teacher had assessed these students in the manner described in the diagnostic section of this chapter and found their government text reading levels to range from 5th to 10th grades. First, we found texts written on the Declaration of Independence that ranged appropriately in difficulty. Then we met with the students in whole-group, where they wrote and shared their present states of knowledge on "The Declaration," and they conjectured as to the matters of which they were unsure. A summary of all of this was recorded for the group. They then were given materials in accord with their content literacy, and they skimmed and discussed what information it seemed the first section of text would hold. The teacher made the rounds, stopping at each of the three groups to get them to predict what they would be told in that section. They then were charged to read the section and, with the book closed, write down what they had learned. Coming around again, the teacher listened in on their discussions of what they had verified or changed their minds about, calling on them to give substantiation from the text. They then made predictions and hypotheses regarding the next section, and read and wrote as the teacher continued to conference group by group. On completion, they all met together and, making reference to the original group-written summation of their prior knowledge, recorded what they now knew and now questioned. The teacher then read to the students the corresponding section from the grade-level government textbook that was assigned to every student. This reading to the students was conducted using the same interruptions for predictions, summaries, and substantiations used when they were reading for themselves. Afterwards, the group consensus was revised again.

By adding the step of reading to them from the higher-level text after their own investigations in lower-level texts, the students were exposed to much of the same core information written in more sophisticated form and diction. Also, it was a shared community conversation time during which their multileveled explorations could be gauged against a higher source.

VOCABULARY

Our fourth area of instructional concentration is:

Vocabulary study that concentrates on the relationship between prefix, suffix, and root across a word's derivatives and across other words that share common morphemic units.

Vocabulary knowledge has been shown to be a strong predictor of reading comprehension (Nagy, 1988). It has been found that the average high school graduate can read and spell approximately 40,000 words. When every distinct string of letters is counted as a different word (e.g., word, worded, wordy, words), one analysis of the vocabulary load up to 8th grade in school books revealed the use of over 85,000 different words in the over 5,000,000 printed words examined in textbooks (Adams, 1990). A very high percentage of the vocabulary that appears in print consists of words called, appropriately, high-frequency words. In fact, 75% of the over 5,000,000 words sampled in the above study represented only 1,000 different words. Ninety percent were the repetitions of 5,000 words. The frequency of occurrence of these words gives insight into the long-term memory task at hand. For instance, whereas the most frequent word (**the**) occurs over 73,000 times per million words of reading, the five-thousandth most common word (**vibrate**) occurs only 10 times per million words (Adams, 1990). Words that are particular to the written language of middle and secondary school level content area texts, then, decrease in frequency of appearance as the text becomes more sophisticated. However, these low-frequency words carry much of the significant meaning in higher-level text. How can the mind hold onto something that occurs so infrequently and respond to its rare occurrence with automatic recognition and comprehension? The answer may well be in one's knowledge of the spelling patterns of these low-frequency words (Templeton, 1983).

Most of oral language vocabulary consists of one- and two-syllable words of Anglo-Saxon origin. These are the same words that occur so frequently in written text at all levels. The association between their oral language pronunciation and their spelling is bound by sound-to-spelling pattern regularities (Henry, 1990). These spelling/sound pattern categorizations, together with these words' extremely high frequency of occurrence, permit the mind to amalgamate the spelling of each with its sound and meaning, leading to automatized word recognition and spelling. However, written language has additional vocabulary that is seldom used in speech and even occurs infrequently in writing. The sounds of these words, when spoken, reveal little of the relationship among them, both across derivations (say, "derive," "derivative," and "derivation" and listen to the shifts in sound) and across words (the words "amnesia" and "mnemonic" both share the same root). But as we can readily see by these same examples, while the sound shifts, spelling honors the saliency of the morphemes—the meaning units in words. Why does "sign" have a "g"? Because a sign is a signal. Why isn't "health" spelled "helth"? Because it has to do with "healing." Similarly, when our voice goes down on an unaccented syllable, the vowel sound is usually a schwa regardless of the spelling. Therefore, the second syllable in **competition** is pronounced the same as the second syllable in **composition**. Competition has an **e** after the **p** not because of sound, but because it comes from **compete**; and **composition** comes from **compose**. Good spellers understand this relationship even though they do not consciously realize that they do. These spellers who have tacitly realized the morphophonemic (sound and meaning) nature of English spelling have a way of cognitively categorizing and mentally filing words of low frequency by their roots. In fact, all the words that occur in textbooks share just 2,000 roots. While it is certainly true that words only become part of one's vocabulary by first being noticed and analyzed for meaning through their occurrence in texts that are understood, the remembrance of their orthographic forms is aided by an understanding of their spelling connections.

While most middle and high school students have mastered the basic spelling patterns of the Anglo-Saxon-based standard vocabulary, many have not realized these sound-to-meaning spelling connections. Their phonetic spellings of **competition** as **compatition** and **derivation** as **duravation** reveal this to be so. We have found that content area teachers can sensitize students to these meaning connections in the following way:

First, show your students directly the sound-to-meaning connection in known words (sign–signal; health–heal; compete–competition; compose–composition; inspire–inspiration). Next, have them examine content area words that they know to determine their roots and compare them to other known words that share the same roots. We have found it helpful for the student to follow these steps:

♦ Divide the word into syllables: **con sti tu tion**.

♦ Divide the word into prefix, suffix, and root: **con stitu tion**.

These first two steps bring to the students' attention the difference between dividing a word into its sound clusters (syllables) and its meaning clusters (prefixes, suffixes, and roots).

♦ What do the prefix and root of this word mean?

Here students need a good secondary-level dictionary. We like Houghton Mifflin's *American Heritage Dictionary*, the high school hardback edition, because it has etymological information at the bottom of the definition and an appendix of Indo-European roots. For example, after the definition of **constitute** it says:

[Middle English constituten, from Latin constituere, to cause to stand, set, fix: com-(intensive) + statuere, to set up (see stā- in the Appendix of Indo-European roots in the dictionary).] (1982, p. 280)

By this we see that the prefix means "intensive" and the root means "to set up." It is interesting that most teachers and students alike will first think before looking in the dictionary that constitution does not have a prefix since taking off "con" leaves "stitution"—obviously not a word. But to have a root, a word does not have to have a root word that can stand alone, as in "unable." A test can be to ask oneself if a new word can be made by the substitution of another prefix. In fact, that is our next step:

♦ What other words share this same root where the root is spelled the same as in the key word?

Here we have the students guess all they can and then look up stā- in the appendix of Indo-European roots in the dictionary to find the others. There we find **substitute** (to stand in place of), **restitution** (to set up again), and **institution** (to set up in, or establish).

Over the centuries, as words passed from Indo-European

through Latin, Greek, German, and French to English, the spellings of the common roots changed their surface forms but still share orthographic commonalities. These more abstract signs of sharing are important to vocabulary connections and memory, so our next step is:

♦ List other words you know that share the same root but in which the root is not spelled exactly the same as it is in the key word.

Further search under **stā-** in the appendix reveals **statue, statute, staunch, stable, steed,** and even **rest** [re-(again) + st (to stand)] (pp. 1542–1543), from the military term to come to rest, or to stand again after marching! All share a common heritage.

Then we ask the student to take off and add other suffixes to examine the sound, meaning, and syntactical shifts across derivatives:

♦ Take off and add other suffixes to this word.

"Constitute" and "constituted," "constitutional" and "constitutionality" are rather straightforward, but it is "constituent" with its accent on the second syllable that gives the sound cue for the correct spelling of the "sti" in constitution.

It is not the goal to use this process to learn new words directly, although the process certainly can be used to examine new words in relation to known words. New vocabulary must be picked up in meaningful contexts that are read and listened to. What we are doing with these orthographic gymnastics is to sensitize the students to the relationship between spelling and meaning, so that their minds can cognitively store the new infrequent words when they come upon them in context. This kind of examination can be great fun and provoke wonder. A class studying transportation was amazed to find the connection between **pterodactyl** and **helicopter** [heli (twist) + co (with) + pt (wing)].

Note that if you were to divide **helicopter** into syllables, you would make a division that splits the root. The same would be true for **recognize** [re (again) + co (with) + gn (to know)]. Students are helped greatly in their vocabulary growth by seeing the difference between dividing words into syllables and into morphemes. Once they have done a bit of this successfully, we find that they no longer are able to look at words unilaterally and that an improvement in spelling and a comfort with a more sophisticated vocabulary is actualized. If you, as a content area teacher, make a list of those words particular to your field and used in your texts, you will quickly find many morphemic connections among those words and between each word and the body of words that most of your students already know.

ORGANIZING

Exercising content literacy requires concentrated work with clusters of students matched with material both by their content knowledge and their ability to deal meaningfully with expository texts. It takes a block of concentrated time to work effectively with middle and high school students as they try to comprehend written information on the cutting edge of their content area knowledge. Questioning and urging hypothesis-making before reading; interrupting the reading act to call on the students to assess their progress and process; refining new knowledge after reading by referring back to specifics in the text; writing during each stage of this process; focusing on sharing one's thoughts in a composition of some length and detail; examining new vocabulary in relation to its context and in relation to the morphemic units of known words—all of this process paints a picture where material gets pulled apart rather than "covered."

All of these processes also take time. But students need time to build and maintain momentum, and students need time to read, write, and revise. As we write this chapter, we try to imagine walking into a classroom, receiving an assignment, reviewing expectations, and then starting to write only to be told after 45 minutes or so to pack up and go to another class and to take up a different project with the same intensity. Real projects, real thinking, real language realization takes more concentrated time. Conversely, but from the same cognitive thrust, activities that are not meaningful cannot be tolerated for longer periods. Block scheduling, therefore, has the ironic effect of not only allowing but requiring tasks that one can sink one's teeth into—and as learners and as students of the learning process, we know this type of task to be that which yields real educational gains.

In the real world of teaching, even given block scheduling, there are two main things that often keep teachers from making such lessons a reality. First, teachers feel the awesome press of the amount that they are expected to cover. Second, teaching on instructional level means much small-group work with the teacher rather than whole-class instruction. We think that block scheduling, when looked at through the lens of what we know to be true about literacy and learning, provides the opportunity to meet the challenge of these two concerns. We use the planning format shown in Figure 8.2 as our guide.

We address the first concern, that of covering enough material, by embracing the "less is more" philosophy. The amount of material that will be addressed and remembered by a student is directly related to how involved that student becomes in the topic and how hooked he or she gets on the rush of finding out things through extensive and intensive reading and writing in the content areas.

Our first step, then, in what we call sanity-based organizing, is to ask what are the main topics or themes that we want to cover across the school year in a course. We use as a parameter the number of divisions in our school schedule. Many school systems operate on a six, 6-week schedule or a four, 9-week schedule; we find that either allows adequate periods for the study of major content area concepts. We are heartened that the national associations of teachers of social studies, math, and science have recommended that each school year a handful of major concepts be studied in depth rather than so much material and so many details be covered.

As teachers in a discipline select the concepts and plan for instruction, we urge them to communicate with their fellow teachers across the curriculum to find natural points of congruence. We know that many secondary schools have embraced the cross-discipline team approach and do much planning in concert. Certainly block scheduling facilitates this by providing extended time blocks for planning and cross-discipline endeavors with students.

Next, we diagnose and cluster the students based on their reading and content area sophistication, as revealed by the oral and silent reading and the listening assessments described earlier. While our activities will mingle students of different literacy levels, we make note of which students cluster around the various instructional levels to be sure that we do not ask students to read

FIGURE 8.2. DIAGNOSIS-BASED, PRINCIPLE-BASED, SANITY-BASED ORGANIZATION

Step 1   **Determine the main topics and themes to be covered.**

<u>Theme 1</u>   <u>Theme 2</u>   <u>Theme 3</u>

Step 2   **Cluster students according to their level of content area reading and listening competencies.**

<u>Textbook Reading Comprehension Clusters</u>

<u>Cluster 1</u>	<u>Cluster 2</u>	<u>Cluster 3</u>
Donna L.	Marjorie H.	Robert W.
Sarah C.	Danny R.	Anne K.
Alison L.	Billy T.	Paul L.
etc.	etc.	etc.

<u>Textbook Listening Comprehension Clusters</u>

<u>Cluster 1</u>	<u>Cluster 2</u>
(Can comprehend grade level texts through listening, but not by reading.)	(Cannot comprehend grade level texts through reading or through listening.)
	Artie S.
John K.	Billy B.
Rebbeca D.	Sarah S.
Jenny G.	etc.
etc.	

Step 3   **Determine the proportion of class time to be spent in each area of instructional concentration.**

	<u>Reading</u>	<u>Writing</u>	<u>Listening to texts</u>	<u>Word Study</u>
Recommended:	40%	30%	20%	10%

Step 4   **Determine the class activities in each of the areas of instructional concentration that can be conducted with or without the teacher and which involve the whole class, groups, or individuals.**

material on their frustration level. These clusters also serve as a reminder to make listening accommodations for those who can gain by listening to the grade-level material that they cannot comfortably read themselves.

Using this diagnostic information, and the samples of text written at the various levels which we selected to conduct our reading diagnosis, we now can collect all sorts of materials, estimate their levels, and identify what to use with whom.

The next thing we determine is how we want our students to spend their class time. Because our goal is for our students to become content area literate and independent of us, we try to translate our belief in the content literacy principles into time and tasks. We have found a good rule of thumb to be a **4–3–2–1 rule**—40% reading for meaning at instructional level, 30% writing for authentic content area purposes, 20% being read to at the highest content level the student can understand, and 10% direct work in vocabulary study.

We embrace the basic tenets of readers' and writers' workshop. We believe that students do become content area literate primarily by reading and writing in that content area. We think the classroom should be a workshop or academic laboratory rather than a lecture hall. The tone should be more of a newsroom with groups forming and reforming to work collaboratively. The teacher's role is to work with groups at times, conference with individuals at other times, and only occasionally address the whole class. The terms "coach," "mentor," "intellectual agitator," and "resource" are more appropriate than "lecturer." Again, we like Tharp and Gallimore's definition of teaching as assisting performance (1988).

The question raised earlier, "How do I teach all when I am trying to teach each at his or her instructional level?," is answered by the variety of activities for reading, writing, being read to, and vocabulary study. We separate activities in each of these areas into two main categories—those that require the teacher and those that don't. Then we further divide each of these categories into activities that can or should be done with the whole class, with groups, or with individuals.

READING

WHOLE-CLASS AND SMALL-GROUP WORK WITH TEACHER

In reading content area material our main technique is the critical questioning **before, during,** and **after** reading, as described earlier. This intensive reading is done with relatively short pieces of content text, such as chapters or sections of longer chapters. Because we are responding to our students' hypotheses and because we must put the student in materials at their instructional level, this activity calls for small groups working with the teacher. There are variations on this theme, however, that can involve the whole class at once. Earlier, when discussing the work with the 12th grade government class and the Declaration of Independence, we told of the whole class pooling their prior-knowledge hypotheses as a group; breaking into instructional-level clusters to read and discuss a piece of text written on the cluster's level while the teacher moved from group to group; then gathering together for postreading summary, reflection, and listening at a higher level.

GROUP, COOPERATIVE PAIR, AND INDEPENDENT WORK WITHOUT THE TEACHER

Work in texts around a common theme can be done independently if the teacher sets up study guides that call on students to write their predictions and hypotheses to a teacher-written prompt. After reading, students then respond in writing, giving substantiation from the text for their postreading declarations (Vaughan & Estes, 1986). The key to this and other reading activities done without the teacher is that they should be attempted in texts in which the student makes no more than one or two errors per 100 words, since the teacher is not there to help. Obviously, students could do this in cooperative pairs, and we encourage this, as sharing helps to authenticate, elucidate, and motivate; however, we give one strong caution. Growth in literacy is made only through reading materials that students can negotiate on their own. When a weak reader is paired with a better reader in material that is on the instructional level of the better reader, the poorer reader may get access to the information, but he or she does not gain in content area literacy. Therefore, this arrangement would count in our plans under the heading of "listening to texts" for the poorer reading member of the pair and "reading" for the better reader.

There are forms of extensive reading that we want every content area student to be taking part in, too. One is reading books in common with a small group of other classmates. In this activity, the teacher meets with the group to get them started and collectively the students set a goal as to when the group members will get to a certain page. We like to furnish students with yellow stickies so as they read they can make notes and respond to teacher designed guides or to more generic prompts such as, "This part surprised me"; "I found this part particularly informative;" and, "This directly applies to a current event." When the group meets back together, the idea is to converse about what was read and its relation to the larger theme being studied, to assess one's new knowledge, and to make conjectures and page goals for the next section to be read. This procedure and group discussion, popularized under the name of Grand Conversations (Peterson & Eeds, 1990) or Socratic seminars (Chapter 2 of this book), can be handled by students without the teacher (after several times with teacher guidance and modeling) as the students' maturity and sophistication allow. Teachers have found it best that students read these books in common during class time, with the rule that no one is to read ahead of the designated stopping point. This, of course, requires that blocks of class time be given to this reading. If faster-reading students complete the section in less than the allotted time, they can read independently in their self-selected books as described below.

INDEPENDENT WORK

In addition to the books read in common, all students read books independently. In social studies, it may be a book such as Gore Vidal's *Burr*; in science, Nigel Calder's *Einstein's Universe*; in math, John Allen Paulos' *Innumeracy*. The criteria are that it connect with the theme and that it be on the appropriate level for the student or on audiotape. Within these bounds, students each select their own books. Again, blocks of class time are allowed for in-class reading, but goals can be established that also depend on out-of-class reading. Dialogue journals are kept, in which each student corresponds with the teacher and fellow students. These journals are most effective if they take the form of personal letters in which students share how the reading has affected their attitudes as well as their minds. The teacher and fellow students respond in kind, sharing thoughts and feelings rather than judgments or criticisms. Periodically, the whole class can gather together to share what they have learned as it pertains to the particular aspect of the content area that is being concentrated on in the 6 weeks' theme.

MATERIALS

Whereas textbooks still can be one source of information, we find teachers depending more and more on other sources, such as articles and essays, for their small-group critical reading activities. These teachers reserve the textbook for critical thinking/listening activities with the whole class, reading the textbook aloud after students have studied the subject using material on their various levels. Used this way, the textbook provides a common frame of reference. But it is the more authentic texts that the world traditionally uses after going to school that are used in these classrooms as the main sources of information. Textbook publishing companies plan their next textbooks up to 10 years in advance. Many companies are putting resources into the development of alternatives to the textbook for instruction after the turn of the century. They are designing separate, smaller volumes and anthologies that can be used to build a compendium of sources based on the themes to be studied and the expected range of content literacy. Bill Gates of Microsoft recently affirmed his corporation's number one goal: to make the Internet an educational resource available to all schools and to every pupil. The age of the dependence on one content area textbook as the primary source of written information in a course is, thankfully, coming to an end.

In reading and listening, students get information simultaneously from four major sources: articles, essays, chapters from various textbooks or chapters from primary sources, used in teacher-guided reading activities; trade books, read in common with classmates; a book chosen by each student for independent reading; and the class textbook, read or listened to by each student as a common reference. The degree of the teacher's involvement varies with the activities. While the content area Directed Reading/Thinking lessons need to be done with the teacher, Grand Conversations, dialogue journals, and the reading required for both can be conducted or worked on without the teacher, individually, in cooperative pairs, or in small groups. Directed Listening/Thinking activities can be conducted with the whole class or at least larger groups by the teacher; and they should be, periodically, to ensure discussions and debate among students of differing reading levels. But much listening can be done independently of the teacher through audio- and videotapes, CD-ROMs, and interactive videodiscs. To promote content area literacy, whenever the instructional objective is for students to gain information, we try to have them do this by reading or being read to; the result is to increase their attentional exposure to content area written language.

WRITING

WORK WITH THE TEACHER

In writing, three main activities require the teacher's direct engagement. The first is the guided writing process; the teacher shares his or her writing, step by step, and the students follow the model while writing on a topic of their own. The second is individual conferences with students as they are working on their content area compositions. These are very short (3–5 minutes) and are a way for the teacher to touch base with each student to troubleshoot, to prod for more detail, example, and explanation, and simply to do whatever it takes to keep the ball rolling. In conferencing with students as they write personal narratives, stories, and expositions, teachers of the writing process first ask, "How can I help you?" When questions then are asked, these teachers refine them and turn them back on the student. They read or listen to sections of the student's composition and keep responding, "Tell me more." "What do you mean here?" "Write that down." For the content area teacher, an additional role is to see when students are getting off track in terms of accurate information and to direct them to resources or give direct explanation.

The third writing activity that requires the teacher's direct classroom time is the writing-sharing sessions. In this small-group activity, students read aloud from their writing-in-progress on common topics or themes, so that they can discuss the ideas and press each other for clarity, completeness, and eloquence. The teacher's role is to model helpful responses, much in the way that he or she conducts the individual conferences. With practice, students assume the role of peer facilitators providing constructive feedback during this sharing session.

WORK WITHOUT THE TEACHER

Many writing activities and aspects of the writing process can be done, or even should be done, in the absence of teacher intervention. More writing-sharing sessions are done without the teacher than with, often at the end of each step in the writing process and in preparation for the next step. These are effectively accomplished both in cooperative pairs and small groups.

Another content area group writing project that has been found effective is textbook writing. After students have completed a unit of study and have a feel for its scope and components, they outline a chapter on that topic for the student-authored textbook. They then assign responsibilities for writing the sections, peer editing, and publishing. This gives all students a chance to incorporate all of their knowledge gained through the various sources into a cohesive piece, and can even stand as the final cooperative assessment for that unit.

ASSESSMENT

Writing also is used as a major source of teacher-assessment and self-assessment. At the beginning of any unit or section of study, students are asked to write to reveal their prior knowledge and state their present hypotheses. This can be as straightforward as, "What led up to World War II?" or, "How might plants be categorized?" or, "How do you think the acidity of rain might be measured?" or, "Explain the purpose and process of determining fractions of fractions." At the end of the unit, the same questions are responded to and students and the teacher can evaluate growth.

Of course, too, shorter forms of writing are constantly interwoven in all the learning activities—writing hypotheses for the next section of text, writing summaries after reading a section, making and revising informational lists, and the like. Again, just as we try to have students read rather than listen to us, we try to have them write rather than tell us.

VOCABULARY

WORK WITH THE TEACHER

In vocabulary study, two activities require the teacher's direct time—dealing with the vocabulary specific to the selection read in a teacher-led critical thinking activity, and teaching students how to examine words by their morphemic units. Because real vocabulary acquisition depends on abstracting the definition from a meaningful context rather than memorizing definitions, we do not advocate preteaching vocabulary. However, the teacher may want to simply list pertinent content words that will appear during the study of a particular selection of a 6-week's unit, and have students first hypothesize as to their meaning and use, then revise their responses after reading and study. For the most part, however, we depend upon the students' response to our charge that any words they question during their reading must be pointed out to us, so that we can make note of them for postreading study. We lead this study by asking the students to go to the text first to glean the meaning from the context. Only then do we turn to references for formal definitions (but only for clarification; not for memorization) and to conduct the structural analysis of a word's morphemes in comparison to known words.

WORK WITHOUT THE TEACHER

Once we have demonstrated and practiced together the morphemic word analysis described earlier, we leave most of the work with words to independent work. We ask students as they read to mark those words they question. We also require them to list from their texts content area terms that they do know. Students then are required to analyze morphemically a set number per week. Remember, however, that it is not the number of words analyzed that will bring vocabulary growth, but the depth of understanding of the morphophonemic principle, gleaned by the intensive analysis and comparison of a relatively small number of words and the attentional exposure to great numbers of words through extensive content reading, writing, and being read to. We encourage students to extend their vocabulary reach as they write and rewrite expository pieces and as they converse with us and their peers.

On our planning sheet, we can list and categorize all of these content area literacy activities as outlined in Step 4 of Figure 8.2. Then we schedule 2- to 6-week segments of block-scheduled time that result in each student spending class time in accord with our 4–3–2–1 proportion guide. We distribute teacher time evenly across the students and proportionally across the tasks.

GRADING

The question of grading is always a difficult one, but we believe that content literacy instruction's focus on process and product lends itself well to the two major areas of student measurement, effort and achievement. In the past, effort and achievement have influenced students' grades without clear demarcation of the weighting of each. When too much weight has been placed on effort, teachers have been charged with having no standards. When too much weight has been placed on achievement, teachers have been charged with not encouraging and rewarding effort. Our recommendation is that the two be kept separate and that students be graded on each.

Criteria for effort can be made in terms of amounts produced and the teacher's evaluation of the good faith of the effort. For instance, it can be required that a certain number of pages be read and a certain number of responses be prepared for sharing in a group's conversation. In writing, the students could be required to take their compositions through several stages of development, each with predetermined amounts of work and peer and teacher feedback. A set number of vocabulary words can be assigned to be investigated in the manner described above. Teachers may ask for the students' self-evaluations of the qualitative effort given to each of these assignments before exercising their authority as the final arbiters. It can be argued that it is only effort over which the student has any direct control. We well know that all of our students will not be at the level of achievement that we hope for them by Friday, or the end of the semester, or the end of the year. However, we know that progress can only be made through persistent effort, and it is this effort that we must encourage and reward if achievement is to result. Students often ask, "Does this count?" or, more precisely, "Is this for a grade?" Until the coin of the realm in school is changed, our answer to both questions is always, "Yes." And the main thing that does count, and therefore is graded, is effort. We are not editors for *The Atlantic Monthly;* we are teachers. If our students put forth genuine effort and respond honestly, our job is to see that our response encourages them to keep the ball rolling.

We are, of course, also given the charge to evaluate achievement, and we think that this can be done better than in the past. Typically, we have judged achievement as the extent to which performance met our criteria. Can the student state the four major causes of The Depression? Can the student explain how sugar dissolves? Can the student apply the Pythagorean theorem to solve a word problem? The difficulty of the questions and the expected number correct for each grade assigned have been based on our experience with students. We could decide whether to curve the grades or not, but ultimately the test was set to fit our standard of expectation. The problem, of course, is in the wide range of prior knowledge and skills that students bring to any grade level. We suggest instead that the formative and summative assessments talked about in the section on writing be used as a measure of one's achievement in relation to him- or herself and in relation to one's peers. At the beginning of a unit, the answers to the formative questions (such as those given as examples in the writing for assessment section above: "What led up to World War II?" "How might plants be categorized?" "How do you think the acidity of rain might be measured?" "Explain the purpose and process of determining fractions of fractions.") could be placed in piles according to their holistically judged level of sophistication. The percentage of students' papers in each pile represents the real distribution of prior knowledge in relation to the topics to be studied. For example, a science teacher might find that hypotheses as to how plants produce the energy to grow fall into four easily distinguishable levels. (The English teacher might categorize the same essays into four different piles based on how well they are written.) This teacher might find that 15% of the students fall into level 1, 25% into level 2, 40% into level 3, and 20% into level 4. As mentioned earlier, this initial assessment gives information which also can be used in selecting appropriate materials and activities.

At the end of the unit, the summative essays can be categorized by the same process. In this way, students, parents, and schools can learn where a student's progress stands in relation to him- or herself as well as in relation to fellow classmates. If these kinds of data are collected across class sections and across years, the expected distribution can be determined; the realistic and admirable goal is that the complete distribution improve in quality of summative response. Parents then get the kinds of information they need—answers to, "How hard is my child trying? What does he know? How much has she learned? How much does he know as compared to his peers?" Students get the kind of feedback they need—encouragement for their honest efforts and direct evidence of their own conceptual growth within the content area community. In fact, we suggest that notebooks be kept containing samples of response essays from past semesters so that parents can see the rationale of their child's achievement evaluation and students can peruse models of more sophisticated responses that are within reach. Students may well not be able to understand explicitly how their writing needs to be extended to the caliber of Gore Vidal's description of the struggle between Aaron Burr and Alexander Hamilton, but they well may be able to glean the significant difference between their own performance and that of past and present fellow high schoolers whose answers were placed in the category just one above their own.

What this ultimately looks like on a report card will have to be decided by each school district. And there will be much debate and resistance in letting go of the familiar, no matter how unsatisfactory it is. But one thing is clear. Students do not go from not knowing to knowing. Rather, they have hypotheses about how things work, some correct and some not, which they are constantly changing as they learn more and as they use and interpret information. Certainly, there are facts, and what is true is of primary importance; but it is understanding that provides not only the glue for facts, but the vehicle for their use. Whether we embrace the acquisition of facts or development as the aim of education, we must press for and evaluate growth in understanding. And growth in understanding can only result from sincere effort in thought-provoking activities using materials within one's conceptual grasp.

CONCLUSION

The heart and soul of this plan is obviously the blocks of time that are dedicated to reading at an appropriate level and concentrated writing for genuine purposes. A too-fragmented day does not allow for this differentiation of instruction nor for this degree of concentration on the process. Unnatural, smaller time blocks have subtly, but forcibly, moved us into a frame of whole-group, product-driven instruction. The student's response has been to find the shortest distance between the two points and resort to memorization for the purpose of passing our tests. Ironically, it is process-oriented content area instruction that yields the most understanding—and it is understanding that is memory's glue. Further, by emphasizing the process we bring validity to the phrase "lifelong learners." As our intensive, differentiated instruction requires, and our block scheduling allows, extended student class time in reading, writing, and listening and the cooperative sharing of learning will yield more extensive exposure than our lectures ever could.

REFERENCES

Adams, M.J. (1990). *Beginning to read: Thinking and learning about print.* Cambridge: MIT Press.

The American heritage dictionary of the English language, high school edition. (1982, rev. 1993). Boston: Houghton Mifflin.

Betts, E.A. (1946). *Foundations of reading instruction, with emphasis on differentiated guidance.* New York: American Book Company.

Bolles, E.B. (1988). *Remembering and forgetting: An inquiry into the nature of memory.* New York: Walker and Co.

Bond, G.L., Tinker, M.A., & Wasson, B.B. (1979). *Reading difficulties: Their diagnosis and correction.* 4th ed. Englewood Cliffs, NJ: Prentice Hall.

Henry, M.W. (1990). *Words: Integrated decoding and spelling instruction based on word origin and word structure.* Los Gatos, CA: Lex Press.

Kletzien, S.B. (1991). Strategy use by good and poor compre-henders reading expository text of differing levels. *Reading Research Quarterly, 26,* 67–86.

Nagy, W.E. (1988). *Teaching vocabulary to improve reading comprehension.* Urbana, IL: NCTE; Newark, DE: IRA.

Perfetti, C.A. (1986). Continuities in reading acquisition, reading skill, and reading disability. *Remedial and Special Education, 7,* 11–21.

Peterson, R.L. & Eeds, J. (1990). *Grand conversations.* Portsmouth, NH: Heinemann.

Shannon, P. (1988). *Broken promises: Reading instruction in twentieth century America.* Glenview, IL: Greenwood.

Singer, H. (1975). The SEER technique: a noncomputational estimate of readability. *Journal of Reading Behavior, 7,* 244–267.

Stauffer, R.G. (1969). *Directing reading maturity as a cognitive process.* New York, NY: Harper and Row.

Templeton, S. (1983). Using the spelling/meaning connection to develop word knowledge in older students. *Journal of Reading, 27,* 8–15.

Tharp, R.G., & Gallimore, R. (1988/1991). *Rousing minds to life.* Cambridge, England: Cambridge University Press.

Vaughan, J.L., & Estes, T.H. (1986). *Reading and reasoning beyond the primary grades.* Boston: Allyn and Bacon.

Vygotsky, L.S. (1978). *Mind in society: The development of higher psychological processes* (M. Cole, V. John-Steiner, S. Scribner, & E. Souberman, Eds. & Trans.). Cambridge, MA: Harvard University Press.

9

DIRECT TEACHING, LECTURING, AND PLANNING[1]

"Whatever will we do for 90 minutes?" was the first thought that raced through our minds when our principal gave us the opportunity to change our daily schedule from short 55-minute periods to the 90-minute periods found in most block schedules. We exploded in curiosity and conversation over the ensuing weeks and had many questions. Our search for information uncovered the fact that we were not the newest kids on the block and that other schools were attempting this new schedule. After a year of visits and investigation, the faculty decided to change the daily single-period schedule to the 4/4 semester block schedule.

After all the evidence gathering, our question still remained: "Whatever will we do for 90 minutes?" This chapter helps answer the question of effective use of longer scheduled classes by examining how to use the Direct Instruction model in three ways:

+ As a method of instruction;

+ As an organizational structure for lectures; and

+ As a way to plan a lesson in longer class periods.

These three ways to use the Direct Instruction model are small adjustments to what many teachers already do. Most teachers discover that after they have been "around the block" a few times

---

[1] This chapter was written by David H. Vawter, a former social studies teacher and currently a doctoral student at the University of Virginia.

they feel more comfortable with the schedule and do not wish to return to the old system.

THE DIRECT INSTRUCTION MODEL

The Direct Instruction approach is the foundation for most instructional models because many different kinds of strategies may be incorporated in the design of the lesson. Lessons may be inductive, cooperative, learning-centered, or interactive, but lectures and written lesson plans should follow the steps in the Direct Instruction approach. The advantage of the Direct Instruction approach in a block schedule is that the teacher has more time to develop each of the six steps in the model, while varying the tactics of instruction within each step. The six steps of the Direct Instruction approach, as listed by Gunter, et al. (1995), are:

1. Review previously learned material.
2. State objectives for the lesson.
3. Present the new material.
4. Provide guided practice with corrective feedback.
5. Assign independent practice with corrective feedback.
6. Review both during and at the end of the lesson.

STEP 1: REVIEW PREVIOUSLY LEARNED MATERIAL

Linking new learning to previous learning is a powerful way to increase comprehension and retention. Conducting a review also supplies information on how well the students learned and whether reteaching is necessary. This review should take the first five to ten minutes of every lesson.

Block scheduling provides the extra time to include many different review strategies. One day, students could check homework in pairs or in cooperative learning groups. The next day, the teacher could ask review questions or play a review game. Another day, potential quiz questions could be written on the board or overhead for the students to work on as they enter the room. On a fourth day, the major ideas from the previous lesson could be in a puzzle or on a handout. Any small warmup activity will reorient students to the content of the class and provide a quality transition between different teachers, different classrooms, and different lessons.

STEP 2: STATE OBJECTIVES FOR THE LESSON

Depending on the strategy, the teacher may state the objectives at the beginning or the end of the lesson. Sharing objectives at the beginning of the lesson provides students with an organizational aid to help categorize and store the information. Stating the objectives at the conclusion of the lesson, often used in the inductive method, provides an ending organization to help review and retain the presented material.

There are many ways to state objectives; but remember, objectives are to delineate what students are **to learn**, not what they are **to do**. There are three parts to each objective. One component describes the skill or behavior that will be observed; the second component describes the conditions under which the objective will be met; and the third part states how the students' success will be evaluated (Dick and Carey, 1990).

EXAMPLES OF OBJECTIVES

♦ Students will list from memory six different reasons for the Civil War.

♦ Given 10 algebra problems, students will correctly answer eight while showing all work.

♦ Given a short story, students will discuss how the author developed the theme in the story and provide at least three examples to support their position.

STEP 3: PRESENT NEW MATERIAL

When presenting new material, the teacher has the flexibility to choose from many different strategies. For example, the teacher may choose to lecture, do a cooperative reading assignment, present a strange or puzzling story for an inquiry lesson, or provide the information for a class discussion.

STEPS IN PRESENTING NEW MATERIAL

♦ Analyze the content to be presented according to the needs of the learners.

♦   Chart the content from the most general to the most specific.

♦   Break all skills into small segments to be presented in logical order.

♦   Develop an advance organizer for the lesson that will provide a reference point for the material.

♦   Select the main points or steps to be presented and limit these to a reasonable number, depending on the learners.

♦   Select examples to illustrate each main point and connect each point or step to the preceding point and to the advance organizer.

♦   Ask questions to check for understanding and watch for signals from the class that indicate lack of attention.

♦   Summarize the main points and connect them to the next phase.

(Gunter, et al., 1995.)

STEP 4: PROVIDE GUIDED PRACTICE

The key to guided practice is for the teacher to demonstrate the correct procedures of the necessary skills for the students. This is accomplished by the teacher working through the first four or five problems in each section of a practice sheet and then having students attempt similar examples. Demonstrating the correct procedures for each set of questions provides enough guidance and direction for students to experience success on each assignment and relieves the anxiety of some students.

Next, it is important to give students three to five problems to complete on their own, while the teacher monitors the class, then pause to correct these first few problems. The old saying "practice makes perfect" is incorrect; the truth is that practice makes permanent! Assigning a few problems or tasks, then checking for understanding, allows the teacher full control of the pace by either continuing with the lesson or pausing to reteach and practice a difficult concept. During guided practice, the teacher maintains the choice of instructional method by deciding whether students work alone or in groups to complete the problems or when they check their answers. It is important that teachers consistently check for student understanding throughout the lesson. Asking questions is one of the most common ways for instructors to determine whether students have learned the content of the lesson; with longer class times there is the opportunity to conduct internal reviews more often. Questions can be class oriented or aimed at a particular student; however, making a habit of asking only one student to answer a question robs the rest of the class of a chance to participate. Using pairs check, round robin, numbered heads, think/pair/share, or other cooperative learning strategies ameliorates this problem (Kagan, 1990). In cooperative groups, individual responsibility for each student's answer to a problem is maintained by having students hold up their own solution or by giving their partner's answer. These ideas and more are discussed in the cooperative learning strategies suggested in this book and in other readings listed in the references.

How do teachers ensure that all students have a chance to answer the questions, and that questions have not been asked of only brighter students, female students, or minority students? Some teachers have a management system that tracks the students who have answered a question. One idea is to create a seating chart, place it in a clear plastic cover, and make tally marks (with an erasable pen) to keep an account of the students who answer questions, ask questions, or participate in some way.

The most sensitive part of this step is helping students learn from their mistakes. Because the teacher has planned extra time for guided practice, learners who do not understand or who need help can get the necessary assistance. Asking students who have just learned the process to provide examples of how they accomplished the task is a possible way to reteach or to correct a student's mistake. When students work in small groups, they provide a dozen or more tutors in the classroom.

STEP 5: ASSIGN INDEPENDENT PRACTICE

Independent practice sounds better than seatwork, but it is akin to the same idea—the students are to continue to work without the guidance of the instructor. If the teacher follows the suggestions for guided practice, then assigning the rest of the practice should not be a cause of stress for anyone. This is the time for the teacher to circulate and assess each student's progress.

With the longer timeframes inherent in a block schedule, teachers may plan for a couple of mini-assignments or different working arrangements during the same class. The students need not work alone, and group independent practice ideas, such as a Jigsaw II strategy (Slavin, 1986), are appropriate in this step. Some teachers dispute the value of having students work in groups or pairs in the classroom, but these same instructors might be surprised how often students decide to work cooperatively outside class.

STEP 6: REVIEW

There are two major kinds of reviews: formative and summative (Scriven, 1967; Ornstein, 1990). Formative reviews take place throughout the lesson, while summative reviews occur at the end of the lesson.

It is important to stop often throughout each lesson and conduct reviews designed to assess students' understanding. To accomplish a short formative review, students may be given a few quick questions or sample problems to complete. Using hand signals to check understanding is another effective review technique. An example of a hand signal review strategy is the "hand at the chest" technique; students make a fist at the bottom of their neck, and on a designated signal from the teacher, students put up one finger if they think the answer is true and two fingers if the answer is false. If there were a, b, c, and d choices, one finger could be choice a, two fingers could be choice b, and so on. The fist is placed at the top of the chest, just below the neck, so students cannot look around, take a majority count and be politically correct with their answer. With a quick glance around the room the teacher can ascertain student responses.

Depending on the ages and skill levels of students, internal reviews, conducted throughout the lesson, should take place every 5–7 minutes. Because a hand check only takes 10–15 seconds, almost no time is lost. In fact, the reinforcement will improve retention and save time; it is much more difficult to fix a bad habit than to make sure learning is done right the first time. Teachers will save time and effort by having short spot checks during the lesson.

A summative review occurs at the end of the lesson. This is a longer summary, with more questions for the students and concluding remarks by the teacher. As a lawyer attempts to sway a jury with his concluding remarks, this is the last chance for a teacher to leave students with the important information. Summarizing the main points by tying them back to the stated objectives is an excellent way to help students categorize the lesson and bring closure to the class.

The Direct Instruction method often works best when the purpose is to transfer information from the teacher to the student in a very efficient manner. An example from an Economics class may serve as demonstration of a Direct Instruction lesson. The lesson, called "The Sign of the Econ," is an explanation of an important but often a new concept for high school economic students: the equilibrium point.

We started with a review of the last 3 days of teaching. The definitions of supply and demand were reviewed by having students quiz each other and then share with the class. Once we had refreshed our memories, I went to the next step.

I said that before they left today they were to learn three things: how to draw a supply curve, how to draw a demand curve, and how to identify on those curves the most important point in all economics. If they understood what this point was, then I said they not only would do well in my class, but they also would understand how our entire economic system worked, and maybe make some money for it too. I did not tell them the exact definition of the point; my goal was to create a little suspense over a rather dry topic.

To present the new material, a worksheet with review information was provided and another review was conducted to make sure everyone understood the definitions of supply and demand. I gave the rules for drawing a supply curve, and students practiced on a chart that was partially filled out for them. The same process was repeated for the demand curve. More data were given to the students for them to draw a curve. They checked with a partner to see if their curves matched; then we looked at the correct answer as a whole class. They then had to organize new information and drew supply and demand curves on their own. After reviewing the process, a student draw his supply curve on the board. Another student drew a demand curve on the same graph on the board. This was the first time any of the students had seen both a supply curve and a demand curve on the same graph. A student would observe that the lines cross at the middle and I would say that this was **the point** and, as the class bell was about to ring, that the first five students to write down what the name of that point was from our textbook and give it to me tomorrow would get five points.

The next day, we reviewed the definitions and rules for supply and demand curves, and I gave an explanation of the equilibrium point and its importance.

There is an old saying in the business world, "Plan your work and work your plan." The Direct Instruction approach is a way to plan and deliver a lesson. The six steps outlined here have been tested over many years and found effective.

By reviewing at the beginning, during, and at the end of class, teachers help students learn the material while providing transitions into and out of the lesson. By stating objectives, teachers provide order to the lesson and have planned how to measure its success. When presenting the new material, teachers should check for understanding, have internal reviews, and then provide both guided and independent practice for the students.

Even though the class may be 90–100 minutes long, the teacher maintains full control of pace and style, because he or she may choose the teaching technique (for example, lecture, group work, discussion, pairs, or inquiry). Any teaching style or instructional method can fit into this plan.

The Direct Instruction approach is not only a strategy for effective teaching, but also an effective way to organize a lecture. Next, we will look at how to improve lectures in a block schedule.

USING THE DIRECT INSTRUCTION APPROACH IN THE LECTURE

Building more effective lectures is a process that includes clear organization, student involvement, and enhanced delivery style. This section will examine ways to use the six steps of the Direct Instruction approach to plan a lecture, and ways to include more student interaction to improve lectures. Delivery tactics are so important that they are reserved for the following section.

Can you list the top 10 fears of most Americans? According to the *Book of Lists* (Wallechinsky & Wallace, 1977), what Americans fear most is public speaking. This fear is five levels above the fear of death! If teachers overcome this fear every day, shouldn't we get more respect and a larger salary?

Did these questions get your attention? If so, they were a good introduction to a discussion on better lectures. Asking questions is one of the best ways to capture the minds of students. The questions can pique their curiosity; better yet, if the students must respond by making a statement or raising their hands, they now share ownership of the lesson. There is an old saying, "People defend that which they help create." Any way a teacher can involve students will be advantageous, because the success of the lesson is a combination of both teacher and student input (Clark, 1987).

Telling an interesting or funny story is another effective way to draw students into a lecture. A story will do more than set up a lesson. Because the learners must engage their imaginations to complete what the story tells but does not show, they become part owners of the story, and of the lesson as well.

A puzzle, interesting fact, joke, or quotation can be a good opener, especially if the age and experience of the students are considered when selecting material. To gain students' attention, make the topic, examples, and information relevant to their lives. The best way to learn about students is to converse with them, either individually or in small groups, and honestly listen to what they have to say. The longer class time in block schedules provides an opportunity to include interpersonal relationship exercises that can help you know your students.

Where can strong "grabbers" be found? Experienced teachers and the library are good sources of interesting facts and appropriate quotes. Taking time to know students and understand their culture will prepare a teacher's mind to listen for appropriate stories. When you hear a catchy joke or story, write it down, for such anecdotes are quickly forgotten. Build your repertoire of openings!

Finally, do not underestimate the power of your voice or body language to capture students' attention. Raising or lowering your voice, moving to a position that signals the start of the lesson, or making a startling noise, like clapping, are useful tactics.

REVIEW PREVIOUSLY LEARNED MATERIAL

Reviewing information in a quick question-and-answer session is an effective introduction to a lecture, accomplishing three purposes. First, the review questions will tell the teacher how much information must be retaught. Reviewing too much will bore the students, while reviewing too little may hinder some students in finding success in the lesson. Second, a review will determine how much of the teacher's topic is new, and what depth the teacher may achieve. Third, the teacher may ask the students what they want to know about the topic, and these student responses could help design the presentation (Palmer, 1983).

STATE OBJECTIVES FOR THE LESSON

If in the process of planning a lesson the teacher writes objectives, then the lecture already has an effective organizational structure. Telling students the objectives serves as a good transition from the attention getter to the body of the presentation. A teacher may say, "These are the three things that you should learn today." If students are expected to learn by taking notes, having the material organized in advance will assist them. There are many creative techniques to inform students about the organization of the teacher's talk. One of my favorites is to walk to my door and say, "Before you walk out this door you should know. . . . " However done, telling an audience what is coming will aid them in their retention and then provide closure for the lesson. Best of all, revealing the organization provides a smooth transition between points of the presentation, for teachers and students alike.

INSTRUCTIONAL GOALS FOR THE LECTURE

♦ To provide students with specific information not readily available in other formats.

♦ To create interest in specific subject matter, a real or imagined problem, or an issue of historical or contemporary importance.

♦ To introduce a new instructional unit or topic of study.

♦ To assist students in organizing facts, ideas, and relationships so that they must be brought into sharper focus and understood more clearly.

♦ To summarize key concepts, important facts or procedures, that need to be reviewed at the end of a unit or assignment.

♦ To present a set of facts or important ideas quickly.

(Cooper, 1994.)

PRESENT NEW MATERIAL

What do teacher educators, English teachers, speech teachers, and business teachers all have in common when it comes to teaching communication? They teach the same organizational framework for any message:

Tell them what you are going to tell them.
Then tell them.
Then tell them what you told them.

The first part of this formula, "Tell them what you are going to tell them," might be classified as a topic sentence by an English teacher, a salutation by a business instructor, an introduction by a speech instructor, or an objective by a teacher education professor. It provides the audience the structure that will enable them to follow the presentation more easily.

The second part of the formula: "Tell them," is the body of the letter, speech, essay or lesson. It is often organized into three parts because that is about the maximum the human mind can remember. For example, a past-present-future or a first- second-third structure is a good organization that enhances student comprehension.

The last component of the formula, "Tell them what you told them," is the conclusion. In this section a teacher reviews the major points and organization of the presentation.

Because this simple organization almost guarantees success, it is surprising how many communicators do not follow this format while writing, giving speeches, or doing lessons. A good example of this format often is found in places of worship. The speakers are forced to speak to large groups and only have one chance to get their two or three points across. They employ many strategies discussed in this chapter.

When presenting new information to students, the teacher can plan for more interaction with students by using the Lecture-Recitation technique. The process is circular and repeated every 5–10 minutes, depending on the age of the audience. The Lecture-

Recitation cycle consists of information presentation, comprehension, monitoring, and integration (Kauchak & Eggen, 1993).

LECTURE-RECITATION CYCLE

♦ Present new information.

♦ Check for comprehension.

♦ Monitor student progress.

♦ Integrate information with previously learned material.

In the first phase of the cycle, the teacher presents part of the new information. In the second phase, the teacher conducts a small internal review. The teacher may ask summary or review questions, ask students to provide examples, or paraphrase the information. The final phase of this process is to ask students to explore relationships in the information. In this last phase, students attempt to relate the information to already learned material by comparing and contrasting or by looking for causes and effects (Kauchak & Eggen, 1993).

One way to increase student interaction in lectures is by allowing the students to participate in the design of the lesson. Students can participate in the building of the lecture by providing examples to make the presentation more relevant to their lives. Another way to increase participation is to stop and conduct a mini-class discussion after an important point.

The most fundamental concept in lecturing in the block is to keep it short. Having more time in class does not mean using more time to lecture. More than one small lecture is possible in 90 minutes, but these should be separated by student activities or other teaching techniques.

The length of the teacher talk will vary with age and skill level. Middle school teachers estimate that their students can maintain attention for about 10 to 15 minutes, while high school students are in tune for 15 to 20 minutes. After these brief sessions, the teacher should take a moment to change the activity. For example, the "5-minute pause that refreshes the memory" includes students' working individually or in groups going over notes, listing important points, or developing questions (Canady & Rettig, 1995, p. 238). Even if a teacher adopts all the tips and ideas presented in these sections, the teacher should keep the lectures concentrated on one or two important points, then change the pace. The instructor can return to a prior point to conduct a quick review before continuing to the next two or three points.

PROVIDE GUIDED PRACTICE

How will the teacher know if the students are keeping pace with the lecture? All students do not listen at the same speed as speakers talk (Svinicki, 1990). In a lecture-based lesson, guided practice means the teacher actively assists students as they follow the presentation. One example of guided practice is a note-taking guide, which is useful for both teacher and students. The teacher provides the guide, which could be an outline of the lecture or full notes with blanks for the students to fill in. The students use this aid to follow the lecture and take notes.

New technology is a way to add graphics and visual style to the presentation of the lecture. For example, a computer program called *Power Point* provides a way to include graphics and color into the organization of the presentation. Providing this organization on the overhead will help students stay on task, and this outline will assist students in taking notes and aid their ability to process the information.

Reviewing within guided practice is a way to break up longer lectures. This is accomplished by interspersing in the lecture practice questions on a worksheet or on the overhead. This will help students clear up any misunderstanding and allow them to get a good foundation on one point before building on another. These internal review questions may be used again for the final review. Teachers need to take time every 5 to 10 minutes to conduct a short review. Learners need repetition, review, and time to process information.

SUPERVISE INDEPENDENT PRACTICE

Many teachers do not include independent practice activities during the presentation of a lecture. A teacher who wants to include independent practice for students could choose to let them work in pairs to compare their notes or answers on the note-taking guide. Students could move into groups, check each other's notes and think up more examples. Additionally, learners could list the important points, organize a new structure, evaluate different aspects, or conduct research in the textbook and other source materials for further examples or differing points of view.

For independent practice, a teacher can provide worksheets, problems to be solved, readings, or any other activity that facilitates the learning process. It is important to remember that a lecture need not be presented from beginning to end at one time. There is plenty of time in a block schedule to provide practice and review for the students and then return to the lecture for further illustration or new material.

INDEPENDENT ACTIVITIES

◆ Students generate questions.

◆ Students engage in problem-solving.

◆ Students generate ideas.

◆ Students defend a side of a controversial topic.

Middendorf and Kalish (1994) list several different types of independent activities. Their first category is student generated questions. A possible way to generate student questions is to ask the learners to write down questions on a note card and send these to the teacher to be answered. This can be done individually or in groups. These cards also can be sent to other students or groups to answer, in a process called send-a-problem (Kagan, 1990). Another variation is to have students, alone or in groups, write potential test questions on the presented material and then try to answer each other's questions. Using some of these questions in the actual test will provide incentive for the students to listen and take these questions seriously. A third variation is to have students develop cases or write very short minipapers.

The second category of independent activities is problem solving. This technique involves the teacher posing a question or problem that students attempt to answer individually or in groups. The teacher may pose a discussion question based on the lecture information and again the students in small groups, or the entire class, can discuss the issue. Another variation is to have the students find quotations or facts in texts or other source materials that agree or disagree with the points of the lesson.

Generating ideas is the third category. This process involves the students in brainstorming ideas or facts about the lesson. This technique may be accomplished as a class or in small groups that, in turn, present their ideas on chart paper, to be posted on the wall or put away and retrieved later as a review. Another idea is to have the students make illustrations or a collage of the important facts, events, or people from the lecture.

The final category of independent activities, controversial topics, is a way to explore different sides of the issue. The students pick a side they wish to defend and then plan, research, and prepare their opinions. The teacher may assign sides if desired. A variation is to have students react to the content of the presentation in a silent debate: each student prepares a one-page written response to the lesson and passes it to another student for his opinion. One way to move students and help them to choose a side is to mark an area of the room with a sign representing the different options and ask students to place themselves in the area that represents either a position of agreement or one of disagreement. Role playing, where the teacher or the student develops the skit, is a great way to add student creativity and enthusiasm to the lecture.

REVIEW

What was the three-part structure of a good presentation? What was the last component? "Tell them what you told them." As the lecture is coming to a close, the teacher can return to the organization and say, "The objectives for this lesson were . . . ; let's see how we did."

There are as many ways to conduct the final review as there are teachers. This is the last chance for the teacher to restate the most important aspects of the lesson. Or, if this has been a long lecture, this is a good time for a review game, a Jigsaw II review, or a Teams Games Tournament (Slavin, 1986)

A nonthreatening way to review is the knowledge check sheet (Fig. 9.1). This is not a test but a questionnaire that the students fill out. The teacher writes down the information presented, and the students rank how well they know that information. This is an honest way to get information from the students.

The strategies of sharing the organization with students, using good questions and stories, providing relevant examples, and taking time to review the major points of the talk have stood the test of time. The lecture remains a useful instructional method,

---

FIGURE 9.1. KNOWLEDGE CHECKSHEET

Background Knowledge Probe
(Angelo, 1991)

In response to each item in bold below, circle the number that best represents your current knowledge:

A.   Direct Instruction Steps
   1.   Have never heard of this
   2.   Have heard of it, but don't really know what it means
   3.   Have some idea what this means, but am not too clear
   4.   Have a clear idea what this means and can explain it

B.   Lecture-Recitation Cycle

   1.   Have never heard of this
   2.   Have heard of it, but don't really know what it means
   3.   Have some idea what this means, but am not too clear
   4.   Have a clear idea what this means and can explain it

C.   Scaffolding

   1.   Have never heard of this
   2.   Have heard of it, but don't really know what it means
   3.   Have some idea what this means, but am not too clear
   4.   Have a clear idea what this means and can explain it

D.   Guided Practice

   1.   Have never heard of this
   2.   Have heard of it, but don't really know what it means
   3.   Have some idea what this means, but am not too clear
   4.   Have a clear idea what this means and can explain it

G.   Tell them what you told them...

   1.   Have never heard of this
   2.   Have heard of it, but don't really know what it means
   3.   Have some idea what this means, but am not too clear
   4.   Have a clear idea what this means and can explain it

effective for many topics, if done well. Let us turn our attention to an equally important component of "doing it well"—delivery.

PRESENTING THE TALK

"Speeches are like babies—easier to conceive than to deliver." But teachers can learn to improve the actual presentation of the lecture. In this section, we discuss the proper frame of mind, the use of gestures, the power of voice, and simple techniques to keep the attention of students.

A FRAME OF MIND

Jimmy Valvano, basketball coach of the North Carolina State Wolfpack and an accomplished speaker himself, taught and modeled a formula for success: "You + Enthusiasm = Success." Teachers who demonstrate an enthusiasm for their subject, their students, and their profession usually will be successful.

Being enthusiastic for the subject means that a teacher models, in words and deeds, a genuine interest in the subject; even the quietest teacher can do this. Being enthusiastic for students means taking the time to communicate that they are an important part of the class, that it is important for them to learn the lesson, and that the teacher is glad to be their teacher. Personalizing lessons, continually challenging students, and presenting the lesson in a positive way are effective ways to model this enthusiasm (Good & Brophy, 1991). Enthusiasm for the profession is reflected in the energy put into the lesson itself (Good & Brophy, 1991). The difference between a teacher who is "burnt out" and a teacher who obviously enjoys being a teacher is manifest.

The Greeks called the three elements of a good lecture ethos, pathos, and logos. Ethos, establishing credibility with the audience, and pathos, establishing feelings with your audience, are directly related to the energy of delivery. Logos, the logic of arguments, is directly related to the teacher's knowledge, how well the teacher prepared and organized the lesson, and the energy used in delivery. Enthusiasm is intrinsic to all three aspects of a good speech.

What is the prescription for this enthusiasm? Harvard psychologist Jerome Bruner says, "You're more likely to act yourself into feeling than to feel yourself into action—so act! Whatever it is you know you should do, do it" (Maxwell, 1993).

VOICE

A teacher is like a musician, and his primary instrument is the voice. As a good musician must learn how to manipulate the instrument for effect, the teacher must learn how to use the voice to its best advantage.

The ability to use the full power of voice, which consists of volume, pitch, and tempo, is essential to a successful presentation. Starting the lesson louder than the proceeding announcement will gain attention, but a change in volume also will signal a transition from one point to another. Many students have been startled from a reverie because the classroom suddenly grew quiet. The teacher's skill in lowering the voice forces the students to lean forward to hear. Getting softer at dramatic or important points is also a good way to convey emphasis. Any change in volume will add significance or increase attention.

THE PARTS OF VOICE

- ◆ Volume
- ◆ Pitch
- ◆ Tempo

The human ear is also trained to notice differences in the pitch of the human voice. Teachers can use this built-in sensor; any change in pitch, from high to low or low to high, will be a traffic light to students, signaling an important point or a transition.

Finally, tempo tactics are available to the teacher. Speeding up or slowing down will add emphasis or drama, signal a transition or an important point, and regain wandering minds. Pausing at an important point is one of the most powerful techniques of persuasion. Long pauses add passion to the presentation but also gain the attention of the class, because students think something is wrong and start to pay attention to see what happens next.

All good musicians must practice to gain the full range of their instrument; so must the teacher practice to get the full range of the voice. One week the teacher could experiment with tempo, followed by variations in pitch the next week, and then, sometime later, changes in volume. These skills take practice, but in time the skills become integral parts of the presentation.

EYE CONTACT

Speech instructors teach their students to look around the room while making a presentation. The idea of moving the eyes around the room is sound, but seeing individual students has many advantages.

The teacher needs to look from side-to-side and from back-to-front and make direct eye contact with each student. This will give each student the feeling that the instructor is talking directly to him or her. This tactic is a nonverbal way of giving worth to a student. The rest of the students will notice the teacher looking at individuals, and this will force them to pay closer attention because the teacher might look at them soon. Eye contact should not be maintained with any one student for too long, or the rest of the class will be lost from sight. The eyes should keep moving from student to student. Eye contact also signals a transition; by changing the focus from the individual to the whole class, the teacher indicates that a change in topic is about to take place.

Another advantage of looking at students is that they will provide clues to the teacher if they are confused, lost, or frustrated. This information will cue the teacher to speed up, slow down, or stop and go over that last point again. The advantages of eye contact are enhanced if the teacher moves about the room.

MOVEMENT

Good teachers are always on the move, and this is especially important in longer class periods. Movement not only helps the presentation of the lesson, but also allows for more behavioral management.

Each teacher has a comfort zone, usually near the front of the room. Speakers must force themselves away from that safe space by an act of will. Moving is very difficult for inexperienced teachers because there is a feeling of security by the lectern, but staying there sends a nonverbal signal of discomfort or lack of confidence. A teacher should map out the room and choose three different speaking locations. More than one copy of lesson notes could be left at each speaking location, or the teacher could take note cards from place to place. Better yet, if the teacher has provided a note-taking aid or put the organization of the lecture on the overhead or chalkboard, then the teacher can move around the room because the lesson structure will be visible from anywhere.

Moving also helps in the same way that eye contact helps. A teacher can check to see if students are writing down the information or are following the note aid provided. The teacher can see if the pace should speed up to gain attention or slow down to regain the attention of the students. Moving is an effective indicator of transitions between points or between sections of the lecture.

The teacher's presence in different parts of the room signals the confidence of the teacher, helps increase on task behavior, communicates vital information to the teacher about the pace of the lesson, and signals transitions between points. A teacher on his feet is worth two on his seat!

GESTURES

We communicate at least as much with our nonverbal gestures as with what we say. If facial expression, gestures, and body position are not in tune with the speaker's words, the listener gets a double message that tends to be confusing.

Many speech teachers tell their students that they should have natural gestures and use those that feel comfortable. This is not entirely accurate. Most teachers are comfortable using gestures in small social conversations, but classrooms are not small groups. Gestures must be increased in size in proportion to the size of the class.

In a small group, a gesture such as shrugging the shoulders is enough; but to indicate disbelief to a larger audience the speaker must make a larger gesture, perhaps raising the arms as well. Facial expressions that would make sense to someone nearby would be lost on the person in the back row. The important point here is not to be insincere in exaggerating the motion, but to increase gestures in relationship to the size of the audience. This is not normal for a speaker to do, and is another technique that must be tried and practiced.

OTHER NONVERBAL IDEAS

The face and eyes are a picture into the heart of the speaker. They must show the emotion, surprise, humor, or indicate the importance of what the speaker is trying to say.

Posture is also important. It is very difficult for speakers to make a strong point if they are sitting. Changing body position or making unexpected and quick movements are other useful techniques to gain or regain the attention of listeners. These changes will add emphasis to an important point or to signal another transition.

It is impossible to stop communicating. The smallest item about the teacher communicates—right down to clothing. Speakers who look professional have an easier time achieving credibility with their audience, so teachers should dress up just a bit more on lecture days. Instructors must make sure that nonverbal communication is congruent with what is said; what teachers do speaks louder than what they say.

CLARITY

To ensure clarity of speech, which includes diction, pronunciation, and word habits, a teacher needs to be observed by a peer or be recorded. Each speaker has habits of speech; after a while, these quirks become ingrained and can become a source of distraction to the audience. One way to discover the habits of speech is to ask students if you repeat words too often or say "umh" too much. If a teacher is not observed regularly or if the observations do not address clarity of speech, then the teacher should ask someone to come in to watch or videotape the session. The easiest way for a teacher to hear the clarity of his or her own speech is to put a tape in a cassette recorder, record the class once a week, and then listen to the tape. These tapes will provide the teacher with a way to self-diagnose incorrect speech patterns.

Delivery is the teacher's responsibility and is under the teacher's direct control. Delivery must be flexible, changing in relationship to students and the environment. Effective delivery is supported by an organized and prepared presentation, and enhanced by the teacher's passion for teaching and for students. While ways of relating to others vary with the teacher's personality, lecture techniques employing voice, movement, and gestures can be perfected through practice.

Using the Direct Instruction Steps in Planning

We have seen that the six steps of Direct Instruction are effective in organizing and delivering a lecture in the block. The next objective is to see how powerful these same six steps are in planning for any lesson in longer class periods. The outline given below is generic, for use with any instructional strategy; each step will be reviewed, and a time allotment will be suggested.

Six Steps of Direct Instruction for Planning

1. Review previously learned material.
2. State objectives for the lesson.
3. Present the new material.
4. Guide practice with corrective feedback.
5. Assign independent practice with corrective feedback.
6. Review both during and at the end of the lesson.

Review Previously Learned Material

When planning for any lesson, be it lecture or inquiry, tying information to the last lesson or to information that the students already possess is always the best place to start. Isolating the hierarchy of skills needed to perform the task may provide the starting point of the lesson. This step should take the first 5 to 10 minutes of the class.

State Objectives for the Lesson

While objectives should be listed and are imperative to every lesson, they do not have to be stated at the beginning of class. Sometimes I finish a lesson and ask the students to state what they thought the objectives were. If the lesson is based on an inquiry approach, then waiting until the conclusion of instruction to share the objectives is appropriate. Sharing the objectives at the end of the lesson helps finish the lesson and provides a closing organizer for students. This step is easily accomplished in 3 to 5 minutes.

PRESENT THE NEW MATERIAL

The new material section of any lesson plan allows for many choices. Lecture is one of the styles most used, but many strategies are possible—videos, movies, guest speakers, reading, research, and brainstorming are only a few options. New technologies, like the Internet and the World Wide Web, also are becoming available. Any of these are equally appropriate and successful ways to present new information and are covered in other chapters in this book. The presentation of new material may be broken into several different segments and spread over the course of the longer class, but 15 to 20 minutes per section is best.

PROVIDE GUIDED PRACTICE WITH CORRECTIVE FEEDBACK

Whatever the instructional strategy, be it a demonstration or an inductive approach, every lesson plan must include time to guide students in practicing the skill involved. This section should identify questions or procedures to be done together before the students attempt the skills on their own. Three to 5 minutes per type of problem or task will be needed for this guided practice.

ASSIGN INDEPENDENT PRACTICE WITH CORRECTIVE FEEDBACK

This step can call on any of the other strategies mentioned in this book or included in a teacher's repertoire. Silently working on problems or class discussion are just as viable here as independent research or cooperative learning techniques. Independent practice does not mean students must work the questions by themselves, unless that is what the teacher has intentionally planned. If students are working by themselves, then plan a transition after 10 to 15 minutes; students working in groups can work for longer periods of time.

REVIEW BOTH DURING AND AT THE END OF THE LESSON

Finally, the lesson plan should always have some ending review strategy. The review can be as varied as any other part of the lesson. Students may hand in work, answer questions, or share ideas. The choice is always the teacher's. Plan 5 to 6 minutes for three to five minireviews during the lesson, then plan for at least

10 minutes at the end of class to review the whole period.

PLANNING TIME USE IN THE BLOCK WITH DIRECT INSTRUCTION

Review	5–10 minutes
State objectives	3–5 minutes
Present new material	15–20 minutes
Guide practice	3 sections—5 minutes each
Provide independent practice	15–20 minutes
Review	10–15 for reviews during the lesson
	5–10 minutes at the end

Total Time: 68–95 minutes

The Direct Instruction strategy is a very effective way to teach a lesson, and it is a good way to plan for any instructional strategy. Rarely does a lesson go exactly as planned, but the six steps provide a way to think and plan for any teaching style or method.

HOW TO PLAN THE 90-MINUTE LESSON

One teacher at my high school was not in favor of the block. This teacher had been teaching world history quite well for many years and wanted to be able to continue to lecture. It is a tribute to him that he could adapt and become successful in the new timeframe. This is his schedule:

ONE TEACHER'S SCHEDULE

♦ Use of warmup activities: This will take 3–5 minutes.

♦ Never stay for more than 20–25 minutes with same activity.

♦ Use textbook work for 20–25 minutes.

♦ Lecture for 20–25 minutes.

♦ Use video or other means to present information.

♦ Use a basic "to know" or a "learning check" for 3–5 minutes once or twice each class period.

♦ Include paper and pencil work for some time each day.

♦ Have three different activities or strategies planned each day.

Included in this section are blank lesson plan forms that other teachers and I have used in the block schedule (Fig. 9.2), and an actual lesson plan used by an English teacher (Fig. 9.3).

Many teachers say that moving to a block was like becoming a first-year teacher again, because they had to write more detailed lesson plans and schedule more minute-by-minute activities. Very few of us would like to repeat our first year, yet by the beginning of the second semester many teachers have resumed their accustomed level of planning.

SCAFFOLDING FOR HIGHER ORDER THINKING IN DIRECT INSTRUCTION

Direct Instruction is a very structured format; therefore, it is most appropriate for structured lessons that introduce skills or facts, computations, or procedures. It is also appropriate for students who need structure in their lessons, and for students of lower socioeconomic status (Star & Clark, 1991).

A previous limitation of both the direct approach and the lecture method is that they did not allow for building higher-order thinking skills, otherwise known as cognitive strategies. Rosenshine has described a process, called scaffolding, that makes it possible to build such skills in highly structured lessons (Rosenshine, 1995).

FIGURE 9.2. BLOCK LESSON PLAN

Block
Lesson Plan

Class _____ **Block** _____ **Date** _____

Time	Plan	Materials

Notes:

FIGURE 9.3. AN ENGLISH TEACHER'S ACTUAL PLAN

Block
Lesson Plan

Class ___9th___ Block ___2___ Date _Tues._

Time	Plan	Materials
10 min.	① Warm up 7 apostrophes Write words in journal	overhead
10 min.	I. ② Focus/Review: What is the purpose of introductory paragraphs? What is the format?	overhead
10 min.	③ Objective: Today we are going to write parallel thesis statements. Page 132 - Grammar Book	book
10 min.	Define Thesis Statement (3 parts) p. 134 Find thesis (1) notice how it all balances out	book
10 min.	(2) it is just like balancing an equation (show overhead) ④ Now we will balance these thesis	overhead handouts
10 min.	statements Model 1st one ↓ answers	
10 min.	II. Objective: To understand dramatic foil ⟩ Romeo & Juliet Define dramatic foil, mood, personification	
10 min.	Review: monologue Soliloquy	

Notes:

The first step is to identify and then teach the prompt to help the student get started. These prompts could be guidelines, organizers, keys, or structures that the student uses to complete the task. These must be identified and taught before the actual instruction begins.

An example of this process was used in social studies class. Two important skills that I stressed were writing and the ability to summarize an article that they had read. These two skills were combined in what came to be called the summary assignment. The students were provided step-by-step directions that instructed them to (a) include the date, title and author of the article, (b) write a two-to-three paragraph summary, (c) write a one-to-two paragraph opinion, and (d) compose a one-to-two paragraph impact analysis of the article.

The second step is to provide the framework of the scaffold in small steps. It is best to start with easier material and lay a good strong foundation. The students practice on this easier process before they move on to a more difficult part of the process. The teacher may want to create and use cue cards to help students remember different steps in the process they are learning. Steps of the process should be broken down into the smallest part, and the teacher may complete part of the process for the students. Teachers need to anticipate student errors and plan to provide additional scaffolding for a short time to help students learn.

In the social studies lesson, to break these steps down even further, the whole class read the same short article, then they were taught where to find the title, author, and date. Each section also was broken down. For example, in the two-to-three-paragraph summary section, they were to write using the "Four W's"—who, what, where, and why. Then they were instructed to use an "I think" and an "I feel" statement in the opinion section and tell "who will be affected and why" in the impact section. This framework was visible to students at all times.

The third step has the teacher model the prompt for the students. Demonstration is accomplished by working through the procedure and thinking the steps aloud. This enables the students to see and hear not only the steps in the process, but how they are applied directly to the learning task. To model the process, the class read a second short article, and I worked through the summary assignment completely for that article.

The fourth step is to allow the students time to practice their new skills. This can be done as a teacher-led process or in group settings. It is good at this stage to allow students to verbalize the process to themselves or others, just as the teacher modeled thinking aloud in step two. An evaluation by the teacher or a self-check by the student is important. The teacher also may provide a learning checklist to aid the student. At this point, the student's interest in how to do the problem correctly can be enhanced by providing a model of the whole process. Students and teachers may want to look for new strategies to correct any mistakes made in the process. To complete this step, the students chose one of three articles and used the instructional prompts provided to construct their own summary assignment. These were shared with the class; then they were provided a complete written example of a summary assignment that I had done.

It is now time to begin to remove some scaffolds. A gradual decrease of the cue cards or the checklist of steps accomplishes this goal. If the students are successful with fewer prompts or cues, then the teacher can increase the difficulty or complexity of the examples.

Students now are able to do the whole process on their own, and evaluation of the learning is accomplished by providing new examples and allowing students to use the strategies developed to complete the task. This practice will demonstrate that the process has been internalized. My students were given the task to find an article on their own and carry out the process from start to finish. While this first effort at the scaffolding process took a while to teach, the students turned in progressively better work each week.

The longer classes in block schedules allow for more complicated learning to be broken down into smaller steps and then built back up to the whole concept. Scaffolding is a way to accomplish this, remedying what once was considered a weakness in the direct approach to higher-order thinking.

CONCLUSION

"Whatever will we do for 90 minutes?" is no longer the question most of us who have taught in the block schedule ask. More appropriately we ask, "How did we ever get anything accomplished in those short periods?" Ninety-minute classes allow us to experiment with new teaching techniques and improve those already in our repertoire, to get to know students better, and to teach a subject in greater depth. The six-step process of the Direct Instruction approach can serve as an instructional strategy, provide a way to organize a lecture, or guide planning for any lesson in the longer periods of a block schedule.

REFERENCES

Angelo, T.A. (1991). *Classroom research: Early lessons from success.* New Directions for Teaching and Learning No. 46. San Francisco: Jossey-Bass.

Canady, R.L., & Rettig, M.D. (1995). *Block scheduling: A catalyst for change in high schools.* Princeton, NJ: Eye On Education.

Clark, L.H., & Star, I.S. (1991). *Secondary and middle school teaching methods.* New York: Macmillian.

Clarke, J.H. (1987). Building a lecture that really works. *Education Digest, 53(2),* 52–55.

Cooper, J.M. (Ed.) (1994). *Classroom teaching skills.* Lexington, MA: D.C. Heath and Company.

Dick, W., & Carey, L. (1990). *The systematic design of instruction* (3rd ed). Glenview, IL: Scott, Foresman, Little, Brown Higher Education.

Good, T.L., & Brophy, J.E. (1991). *Looking in classrooms 5th edition.* New York: Harper Collins.

Gunter, M.A., Estes, T., & Schwab, J. (1995). *Instruction: A models approach.* Needham Heights, MA: Simon and Schuster.

Kagan, S. (1990). *Cooperative learning: Resources for teachers.* San Juan Capistrano, CA: Resources for Teachers.

Kauchak, D.P., & Eggen, P.D. (1993). *Learning and teaching.* Needham Heights, MA: Simon and Schuster.

Maxwell, J.C. (1993). *Developing the leader within you.* Nashville: Thomas Nelson.

Middendorf, J., & Kalish, A. (1994). *The "Change-Up" in lectures.* Bloomington, IN: Teaching Resources Center Indiana University.

Ornstein, A.C. (1990). *Strategies for effective teaching.* New York: Harper & Row.

Palmer, S.E. (1983). The art of lecturing: A few simple ideas can help teachers improve their skills. *The Chronicle of Higher Education, 26(7)*, 19–20.

Rosenshine, B. (1995). Advances in research on instruction. *The Journal of Educational Research, 88(5)*, 262–268.

Scriven, M. (1967). The methodology of evaluation. In Tyler, R.W., Gange, R., & Scriven, M. (Eds.) *Perspectives on curriculum evaluation* (pp. 39–83). Chicago: Rand McNally.

Slavin, R.E. (1986). *Using student team learning* (3rd ed.).Baltimore, MD: The Johns Hopkins Team Learning Project, Johns Hopkins University.

Svinicki, M., (1990). How to pace your lectures. In Neff, R.A.,& Weimer, M. (Eds.), *Teaching college: Collected reading for the new instructor* (pp. 71–73). Madison, WI: Magna.

Wallenchinsky, D., & Wallace, A., & Wallace, I. (1977). *The people's almanac presents: The book of lists.* New York: William Morrow and Company.